Two Cultures of Schooling: The Case of Middle Schools

Education Policy Perspectives

General Editor: Professor Ivor Goodson, Faculty of Education, University of Western Ontario, London, Canada N6G 1G7

Education policy analysis has long been a neglected area in the United Kingdom and, to an extent, in the USA and Australia. The result has been a profound gap between the study of education and the formulation of education policy. For practitioners such a lack of analysis of the new policy initiatives has worrying implications particularly at such a time of policy flux and change. Education policy has, in recent years, been a matter for intense political debate — the political and public interest in the working of the system has come at the same time as the consensus on education policy has been broken by the advent of the 'New Right'. As never before the political parties and pressure groups differ in their articulated policies and prescriptions for the education sector. Critical thinking about these developments is clearly necessary.

All those working within the system also need information on policy making, policy implementation and effective day-to-day operation. Pressure on schools from government, education authorities and parents has generated an enormous need for knowledge amongst those on the receiving end of educational policies.

This series aims to fill the academic gap, to reflect the politicalization of education, and to provide the practitioners with the analysis for informed implementation of policies that they will need. It will offer studies in broad areas of policy studies. Beside the general section it will offer a particular focus in the following areas: School organization and improvement (David Reynolds, University College, Cardiff, UK); Critical social analysis (Professor Philip Wexler, University of Rochester, USA); Policy studies and evaluation (Professor Ernest House, University of Colorado-Boulder, USA); and Education and training (Dr Peter Cuttance, University of Edinburgh, UK).

Education Policy Perspectives

Two Cultures of Schooling: The Case of Middle Schools

Andy Hargreaves

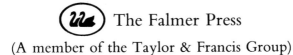 The Falmer Press

(A member of the Taylor & Francis Group)
London, New York and Philadelphia

32611

UK   The Falmer Press, Falmer House, Barcombe, Lewes, East Sussex, BN8 5DL

USA   The Falmer Press, Taylor & Francis Inc., 242 Cherry Street, Philadelphia, PA 19106-1906

© 1986 Andy Hargreaves

First published 1986

Library of Congress Cataloging in Publication Data

Hargreaves, Andy.
  Two cultures of schooling.

  1. Middle schools—Great Britain. 2. Education and state—Great Britain. I. Title.
  LB1623.H34 1986   373.2′36   86-13396
  ISBN 1-85000-108-1
  ISBN 1-85000-109-X (pbk.)

Typeset in 10/12 Bembo by
Imago Publishing Ltd, Thame, Oxon

Printed in Great Britain by Taylor & Francis (Printers) Ltd, Basingstoke

Contents

Contents

For Pauline

List of Figures and Tables

Preface and Acknowledgements

This book is about two things. Firstly, and most directly, it is about the fate and fortunes of the English middle school; a relatively recently established institution that caters for a substantial minority of pupils within the English state education system. This book is, in fact, the first extended published research study of such schools to deal in detail with their internal organization and with their historical development; to examine closely what they are like and how they have come to develop that way.

Secondly, and most broadly, the book sets out to examine some of the implications of educational policy for school practice; the impact that policy initiatives have on school life. Most studies in education tend to focus *either* on the process of policy formation at LEA or national level, *or* on the internal processes of the schools themselves. Few set out to connect the two, to relate policy and practice, past and present. This study explores some of these connections, using middle schools as a particular case.

In other words, the book is designed to contribute to debates about the nature and purpose of education for children in 'the middle years' of schooling as they are often called, and to cast some sociological light on the relationship between educational policy and practice. It does this in particular by looking at the relationship between two dominant traditions or cultures of educational policy and practice on which middle schools have been founded and from which they have grown — the academic-elementary tradition and the developmental tradition. How far, it is asked, in both policy and practice, is the character of middle schools a product of these two cultures of schooling and their interplay in educational life?

The study itself focusses on middle schools in England. But its findings and recommendations have clear implications for middle schools in other countries too. Middle schools, if defined purely in terms of age-range, can be found all across the world: from Germany to China (Blyth and Derricott, 1977) and in many parts of the United States (Eichorn, 1966; Grooms 1967; Kindred *et al*, 1976; Murphy, 1967) for example. Schools termed 'middle' also exist in other countries such as Italy too, although their age range (11–14) is slightly different (Borghi, 1980). Nor are the issues affecting middle schools entirely peculiar to this country either. The problems of establishing a new and distinctive identity for this institution; its origins in administrative and economic necessities; and the tensions it experiences in providing a balance between a specialist and generalist curriculum — these issues have been a central feature of the developing middle school in the United States too (Alexander, 1968; Alexander and George, 1981; Tye, 1985). It is one hope of this book that it may contribute to a greater transatlantic understanding of middle school issues, their problems and potentials.

The book is a shortened and amended version of a doctoral thesis awarded by the University of Leeds in 1985. Despite its undoubted rewards, doing individual research and writing it up is for much of the time not unlike the experience Orwell (1970, p. 29) described of writing a book: 'a horrible, exhausting struggle, like a long bout of some painful illness'. I will always retain a deep gratitude, therefore, to those who have supported me through this experience and who, just as importantly, have shared with me those less frequent but very significant moments of insight and discovery and intellectual breakthrough too.

My wife, Pauline, has provided me with the most enduring support, offering invaluable encouragement when I have been at the most depressive points of my doctoral mood swings. Like most writers, I have at times traded exhaustively on my family's time and patience. For their tolerance of such liberty-taking and for their providing me with a living, daily reminder that there really is more to life than doing a PhD, I will always be deeply grateful. They have both helped me produce the thesis and book and put them into perspective. No-one could reasonably ask for more.

My supervisor, Dennis Warwick, offered friendly criticism and advice throughout, especially in the crucial, early stages. I also received helpful advice from so many colleagues in higher education that there is simply not the space to mention them all by name. Outstanding amongst them all has been my colleague and friend, Martyn Hammersley but I have also received constructive advice and criticism at various points from David Hargreaves, Peter Woods and Andrew Pollard too. John Eggleston and Gerry Bernbaum made valuable suggestions on adapting the thesis for publication.

Whatever assistance I have been given with analysis and writing up, none of the book would have been possible without the fieldwork and historical enquiry on which it was based. I am therefore grateful to Paul Sharp of the University of Leeds School of Education for first drawing to my attention the existence in Leeds Education Museum of the stored memoranda and correspondence of the West Riding of Yorkshire Education Authority. And I am especially grateful to the staff, pupils and headteachers of 'Moorhead' and 'Riverdale' middle schools for first accepting me into their schools to do the fieldwork which now forms the basis for parts 2 and 3 of the book. As a young researcher and one with minimal participant status, I had little that I could directly offer the schools in return for my use of them for research purposes. Their acceptance of me was, in that case, exceedingly generous. Without such unselfish generosity, it is worth remembering, little educational research would ever get done. I have also discussed the contents of the book with many middle school teachers and heads, and the final version owes much to their responses and reactions.

Cynthia Brooks typed the thesis under intense pressures of time and tidied up my messy amendments for publication.

Last, but not least, the research studentship I held while doing the full-time work for the thesis was funded by the Social Science Research Council (now the Economic and Social Research Council), and I wish to extend my thanks to them also.

One final word on the book's format: a detailed empirical study of educational policy and practice such as this which draws on historical studies of official documents, case study work in schools, collection and interpretation of official statistics etc., inevitably consumes a great deal of space — hence the book's length. To keep even that length within the practical bounds of publication, however, some important aspects of the theoretical and methodological background to the study have had to be excised. This information is published elsewhere, though, and if you would like to look further into the theoretical framework and perspectives underlying this study you might care to consult the original thesis (Hargreaves, 1985a), related articles (especially Hargreaves, 1983) or my forthcoming book on *Social Theory and Education* (Hargreaves, (in process)). Similarly, if you wish to read about the methodological underpinning to the study, a detailed biographical account of the research has been published in Hargreaves (1986a).

Some substantive parts of the thesis are, again for reasons of space, not presented in the book either. The focus here is rather more on the properties middle schools hold in common than the differences between them. Readers interested in these differences, in the varying classroom coping strategies that teachers adopt within different sorts of middle school, should again turn to the thesis or to an earlier discussion of classroom coping strategies in Hargreaves (1978). Similarly while very little material here is presented on staffroom cultures and staff decision-making in the middle schools, these issues have been explored in some depth in Hargreaves (1981) and (1984).

Chapter 1

Introduction

In a political and educational climate where most of the emphases, debates and initiatives are very much centred on the 14–19 age range, the group most immediately affected by economic recession and large scale unemployment, it is easy, all too easy, to neglect or overlook the educational needs and requirements of those vast numbers of children who have not yet entered that politically sensitive phase. And it is easiest of all to pass over the needs of those children placed at the very centre of compulsory education, in a political twilight zone beyond the demonstrably vital and much discussed first years of schooling but before the stage when the auspiciously mis-named 'world of work' is encountered for the first time.

These children in the upper primary and lower secondary years of schooling; these children in 'the middle years', as they are sometimes called, have been the target of no wide-ranging government initiatives, no allocations of 'earmarked' funding, no special innovatory attention in recent years. Apart from receiving their due share of reporting by HMI (though in the main, and especially with the 11–13 age group, rather later than other age groups have), they have been an almost invisible, absent feature in recent educational debate.

Yet the needs of these children 'in the middle years' and the character of the educational experience offered to them are surely at least as important as they are for any other group. In fact, before the advent of vocationalism and the growing intrusion of industrial values into the educational system, when educational policy was suffused with a greater spirit of optimism and received more generous financial support, the educational requirements of this group did not suffer from such systematic neglect. On the contrary, many of these children came to be educated in schools which were supposedly expressly designed to meet the special needs of their age group: in middle schools, that is. In recent years, middle schools have drifted from the glare of public attention, but they continue to cater for a fair proportion of the nation's children. Yet our research knowledge of them, their distinctive educational contribution and their special problems remains limited. Let us look, then, at what these middle schools are and what they have set out to achieve.

The Importance of Middle Schools

In England, middle schools are those which cater for pupils between the ages of 8 and 12, 9 and 13, or 10 and 13.[1] At the beginning of 1968, no such schools existed in the United Kingdom. Indeed, until the Education Act of 1964, they were strictly illegal; apart from a small number of discretionary exceptions, transfer from primary to secondary school could not take place at any age other than 11. By January 1982, however, no less than 1413 middle schools had been established; and if the category of first-and-middle schools combined is included, that number is greater still.[2] Taking just one of the middle school age groups, at the beginning of 1983, such schools catered for 143,736 pupils aged 11, some 21.85 per cent of that entire age group within the state education system of England and Wales, and about three times the number of similarly aged pupils within the independent sector.[3] Located in areas as far apart as Northumberland and Northamptonshire, Devon and Derbyshire, Somerset and Suffolk, and situated in eighteen metropolitan authorities and in thirty out of the forty rural shires, these schools provide an education for approaching half a million children throughout the nation.[4]

Clearly, given their large numbers and widespread distribution alone, English middle schools are worthy of careful study in their own right. But there is a further and more urgent justification for their study too. At the time of writing, English middle schools are in a position of severe crisis (Wallace and Tickle, 1983; Wallace, 1985). Their doom has been predicted (National Union of Teachers, 1979); their disappearance prophesied (Fiske, 1979; Razzell, 1978). The impact of falling rolls on the secondary sector, and the resulting pressure to rationalize 16 + provision in many areas on sixth-form college or tertiary college lines has placed some local education authorities with 9–13 middle schools under pressure to lower their ages of transfer, so as to avoid being left with unmanageable 13–16 institutions (Ginsburg *et al*, 1977). At the same time, pressures for more emphasis to be given to specialist subject teaching at all levels (DES, 1983) and for secondary schools to gear themselves more towards producing high levels of conventional examination success (particularly since the 1980 Education Act) have placed middle schools in considerable difficulty, since falling rolls and accompanying staff shortages in specialist subjects have impelled them in just the opposite direction — towards *less* setting and more *generalist* teaching. (Hunter and Heighway, 1980; Hargreaves and Tickle, 1981; Wallace and Tickle, 1983)

Her Majesty's Inspectorate (1983a) noted in a recent survey of forty-eight 9–13 middle schools, that many such schools are finding it hard to produce high standards of pupil attainment in specialist subject areas (in the conventional secondary school sense, that is), because of shortfalls of staff with the appropriate specialist expertise. Add to these things the very substantial problems the harsh climate of cost-effectiveness in education which has accompanied Britain's deep economic recession, along with the difficulties that many middle schools face in meeting subject specialist targets without additional investment in extra staff, and the middle school's particular vulnerability to pressure, the likelihood of the extinction of the species in some areas, is not hard to understand. Nor are such prophecies merely matters of academic conjecture: the winding up of middle school systems has already been announced for Wirral, Stoke-on-Trent and Brighton. Others may follow (Doe, 1981; Hargreaves and Tickle, 1981; Williamson, 1984.)

Thus, having come into being and risen rapidly to prominence during the 'revolutionary' sixties and early 1970s, middle schools, after what in educational policy terms is but a brief span of time, now face full or partial extinction in the recessionary eighties. A clear understanding of the historical emergence of middle schools and of their organizational characteristics, along with an awareness of the wider political, economic and social context in which they have developed and now operate, should help us identify the factors and forces which have precipitated this crisis in middle schooling, and perhaps even generate a greater awareness of possible solutions for dealing with it.

This sort of detailed understanding is particularly important at a time when educational officialdom seems virtually to have washed its hands of middle schools and of the educational ideals for which they once stood. The HMI Report on *9–13 Middle Schools* (1983a) hinted strongly at the desirability or inevitability of their closure in many instances. The *8–12 Report* (1985b), though less robust in its criticism, did not really mark out this kind of school as embodying distinctive models of good practice that other school types might wish to emulate. And most conspicuously of all, perhaps, amid this general climate of disinterest and discouragement, many teacher training institutions have dropped their middle school courses and redesignated them as 'primary' or 'upper-primary' instead. Taking all these things together, it is clear that there has, in recent years, been little to encourage positive senses of purpose and direction for the middle school among serving and intending teachers. Enthusiasm has beem dampened, awareness blunted.

Yet the middle school vision was once a powerful and passionate one, imaginative in design and audacious in its ambitions. That vision, dissipated though it has since become, is worth recalling, to assess how substantial it was, to locate where and why it went astray and to identify elements of it that might now be deserving of resurrection or reconstruction.

The Middle School Vision

When middle schools first emerged in the late 1960s and early 1970s, they were swathed in an optimistic rhetoric of educational justification. While the administrative and economic advantages of middle schools — the fact that they could be conveniently fitted into existing buildings — were commonly acknowledged, a great deal of weight was placed on the *educational reasons* for their development (WRYECR, 1965). In the West Riding of Yorkshire, for instance, where middle schools were first established, the Chief Education Officer, Alec Clegg, argued that he and his Education Committee had considered the educational problem first before deciding what was feasible in terms of existing buildings.

Initially, the educational advantages of middle schools were seen to reside in their capacity to extend the best of primary school practice to older pupils. In this *extension* model of middle schooling (Hargreaves, 1980), middle schools would develop and expand what was already recognized as being educationally worthwhile; they would provide more of a demonstrably good thing.

In those places (now very numerous), which eventually came to adopt 8–12 schemes of reorganization, this extension model of middle schools continues to be the dominant one even now (Campbell, 1982). But the 9–13 middle school is and was less easily justified as an extension of primary school practice than its 8–12 counterpart. The proximity of subject option choice less than one year after children enter the upper school placed 9–13 middle schools under very great pressure to ensure and demonstrate adequate coverage of the traditionally defined high-status areas of the upper school curriculum. Furthermore, the recruitment into middle schools of teachers who were, in the main, either primary or secondary in experience and training, and who often had no specific commitment to the idea of middle schools as such, presented middle school heads and LEA administrators with the problem of how to cement together teachers with two very different kinds of background and experience into a single, coherent and agreed educational philosophy that would secure their loyalty and commitment. In time then, a new *invention* model of the middle school emerged; a set of claims for the distinctive character and contribution of middle school education. What was at the heart of this educational case?

One of the main arguments on which the middle school case hinged, concerned what was called its *unique identity*. As middle schools developed, people quickly became aware that they would be vulnerable to inner tensions and conflicts; not least because of their often involuntary inheritance of teachers whose professional roots were in the divergent and, at points, opposed systems of primary and secondary education. As a result, one of the distinguishing features of the invention model of the middle school emphasized the institution's *uniqueness* which would transcend pre-existent educational categories, and its common *identity* which would unite a fragmented teaching body around a set of agreed-upon ends. Middle schools, it was hoped, would be more than a mere 'half-way house', not just a simple hybrid of previous traditions (for example, Culling, 1973). Rather, in the words of a pamphlet on middle schools published by the West Riding Education Committee in 1967, they would be

> a *new* departure, a *new* kind of educational and social grouping, and not a *half-way house* between primary and secondary as we have come to use these words ... These schools must find their own *identity* and must develop their own form of organization and way of working in response to the needs of their children. (p. 1, my emphasis)

During this period, phrases like 'a new departure', 'fresh thinking', 'their own ethos', 'an entirely new concept' were distributed liberally throughout writings on the middle school (for example, Schools Council, 1972; Gannon and Whalley, 1975). There was an excitement about something that was new and innovative. And what was new was good. It was progress. In this view, middle schools were to stand apart from previous educational identities and traditions. The use of such phrases as 'the primary school tradition' or 'the secondary school approach' it was said, 'can get in the way of clear thinking' (Schools Council, 1972, p. 7).

But while middle schools would be distinctive and have their own identity, they would not be oblivious to all else around them. They would not stand entirely aside from the hitherto separate primary and secondary sectors, but provide a bridge, afford a smooth transition between them. As the Schools Council (*ibid*, p. 8) put it:

> It is to be hoped that the attention now being given to the middle years will result not in the further introduction of unnecessary breaks in the child's education, but in the creation of a *transition* period that will smooth rather than interrupt the change from what is distinctively 'primary' to work that is distinctively 'secondary'.

In this way, the special character of middle schools was to be found in their status as a *zone of transition* between primary and secondary education. They would gradually move children from the class-teacher, generalist environment of the primary school, to the subject specialist curriculum of the secondary school. They would bring about a 'marriage' between primary and secondary approaches, achieving 'a nice balance' between these two viewpoints' (*ibid*, p. 70). This was a vision of 'middle schools for the middle way' (MacLure, 1975), bringing together and easing the movement between two very different traditions.

Middle schools would therefore be institutions with their own unique identity, providing a balance, a zone of transition between primary and secondary approaches. In doing so, it was argued that they would cater for the special needs of children in a particular and important phase of their development; the middle years of childhood. (Schools Council, 1972, pp21 and 77). Fortunately, no writers on the English middle school indulged in the conceptual excesses of their American counterparts who coined a motley assortment of quasi-psychological terms to refer to the American 'middle years' child such as the 'inbetweenager' and the 'transescent' (Eichorn, 1966). Supporters of the English middle school characterized the middle years rather more subtly than this as a *zone of transition* where children move from the concrete stage of operations to the formal (abstract) stage, and begin to develop powers of judgment and discernment, along with a quest for self-discovery. A little ironically, perhaps, to the extent that the middle years was a distinctive stage, it was a stage of transition. But this transitional phase was regarded not just as one fleeting moment in a developmental progression, no better or worse than any other in its implications but, like the chrysalis stage in the growth of a butterfly, more as a crucial formative period upon which the quality of all further life would depend. Hence:

> The middle years are the decision years when children not only discover themselves as people but invariably develop attitudes towards studies in general and certain subjects in particular. (Gannon and Whalley, 1975, p. 15)

The brave and bold vision of the middle school for many people then was of a school that would serve educational, rather than political ends, a school with its own unique identity, providing a balance and point of smooth transition between primary and secondary approaches, and catering specifically for the needs of children at an identifiable stage of their development — the middle years.

Yet, brave as this vision was of middle schools for the future, it was also flawed. Indeed, in many respects, that view of the middle school gave it not purpose, direction and destiny, but created confusion, uncertainty and ambiguity. And instead of meeting square on many of the problems and difficulties the middle school would inevitably have to face, the vision simply sidestepped them, albeit with considerable verbal sophistication.

This vision of middle schools — and its elements of unique identity, zone of transition and the developmental needs of the middle years — I want to propose, was actually an *ideology*. It presented a distorted picture of middle school actuality; refracting rather than reflecting middle school history and practice.[5] Optimistic and unifying in tone, and advanced with passionate sincerity and commitment, this ideology nevertheless disguised, underestimated or drew attention from some of the major difficulties the middle school would have to face.

For one thing, the ideology of the middle school contained within it certain tensions or contradictions which were rarely made explicit or resolved. Most centrally of all, there was an unresolved tension between the middle school having a *unique identity* quite distinct from other sectors and traditions, and being a *zone of transition* which would simply smooth the path between these other things. How separate they should be from other parts of the system; how closely they should be integrated with these other parts; whether middle schools should 'fit in' with the existing system and make it operate more smoothly, or whether their own distinctive contribution should challenge and redefine some of the central and most sacred assumptions of that system — these questions were never really settled, solutions never really agreed. These tensions and all the ambiguities of purpose they generated have been allowed to persist, making middle schools vulnerable to challenge and attack.

This leads to a second point about the ideology — the level at which it has been pitched. The appeals to sentiments of unity and balance while having a consensual tone and arousing a sense of common purpose, were also unhelpfully vague, abstract and generalized. They lacked clear reference points, distinct indications of the shape that middle schools might take. And where the particularities of practice and organization were raised, these were seen as needing to be dealt with in the light of the special circumstances faced by individual schools and the professional judgments of their headteachers. Here, middle schools, like other schools, were seen to serve local needs, even at the expense of a coordinated national system. (Schools Council, 1972, p. 18)

In this respect the ideology of the middle school shares much in common with the ideology of comprehensive schooling more generally. It creates social and educational sentiments which, however persuasive and emotive, contain no necessary implications for the kind of educational practice that ought to follow. These more specific matters are simply devolved to the realm of individual professional judgment. Yet, as David Hargreaves (1982) and others have pointed out, the absence of any such guidance within the comprehensive movement in general led not to a diversity of comprehensive practice but, by and large, to heads and staffs in individual schools in individual localities solving their experienced problems in exactly *the same* way. For whatever the peculiarities of their own institutions, many of their problems to do with the recruitment of ex-grammar and ex-secondary modern teachers, to do with continuing strong parental pressure for conventional examination success and so on, were absolutely common. The result of this contradiction of a rather vacuous ideology of comprehensivism on the one hand, and an accumulated muddle of individual practice within common but unrecognized constraints on the other, was the now widely recognized failure of secondary reorganization to produce a distinctive form of comprehensive educational practice, and the persistence, indeed the expansion of the conventional grammar school curriculum as a result. Whether intended or unintended, the principle of divide and rule appeared to win the day.

As the study reported in this book will show, the consequences for middle school practice have been similarly ironic. The vagueness of middle school ideology, together with the devolution of educational problem-solving to the local level has allowed the persistence of a primary/secondary split at 11 +, and, if anything, has strengthened the more dominant of those two influences (the secondary ones) within the new middle school environment.

This raises a third point, that the broad appeal to notions of uniqueness and transition tended to draw attention away from the question of what to do with staff drawn, in the main, from two very different backgrounds and traditions, of how to resolve the deep-rooted division between middle school staff on primary/secondary lines which would seriously threaten the creation of a shared identity and the achievement of smooth transition. Specific guidance on these matters — on organizational solutions, staff deployment policies and in-service initiatives was disappointingly sketchy or absent.

Fourth, the ideology of the middle school, by stressing educational justifications in general and by emphasizing the generational needs of the *middle years*, also tended to play down the political and administrative origins of middle schools; historical influences which would come to have far-reaching implications for middle school practice. While it was acknowledged early on that middle schools offered a cheap, expedient option of going comprehensive in many localities, once the decision to establish middle schools had been taken and the audience to be convinced had switched from a political to a professional one, the argument was presented less and less (see Hargreaves, 1980.) What mattered now was purpose, direction and unity.

All this search for unity is entirely understandable. But one cannot help wondering that if policy-makers and practitioners had grasped the political and administrative nettle rather more firmly at the outset, if they had faced up more to the middle school's historical inheritance and all its practical implications, if more direct guidance had been offered, then the middle school may have taken a rather different shape from the one it assumes today, and the threats to its existence of the kind that the middle school is currently experiencing may not have been quite so easy to pose.

These last two issues — the middle school's vulnerability to internal division, and the political and administrative context of its development — point to educational implications of this particular study which stretch far beyond the middle school itself. Middle schools, that is, have a wider educational and political significance which their own problems and difficulties bring into particularly sharp focus.

This wider significance of middle schooling is not immediately obvious. They are sponsored by no political parties. They serve no clear cut set of political interests. Nor, unlike private education or comprehensive school reform, for instance, do they seem to have any direct implications for social reform or the class struggle. Yet middle schools do serve as a *critical case* for the analysis of broader educational and political issues in two important respects: first in highlighting the conflict between, and relative priority accorded to, different educational traditions in British society; second in pinpointing key features of the relationship between educational policy and practice. Before the report of the study itself commences, I want to say a little about these broader educational questions.

Traditions of Schooling

Middle schools occupy a central place in the educational system; not just chronologically but sociologically and politically too. They are situated at the point where pressures from the upper and lower ends of the educational system meet; where tensions and contradictions which beset the system as a whole are subject to conflict and debate at the level of both policy and practice, and where different educational ideologies rooted in the primary and secondary sectors of schooling clash and compete.

On the one hand, middle schools emerged in the context of comprehensive school reform which first received firm government support through Circular 10/65 that strongly 'requested' LEAs to reorganize on comprehensive lines. On the other hand, their development ran alongside that of educational progressivism in the primary sector, which received the national seal of approval in the *Plowden Report* on primary education, commissioned in 1963 and published in 1967. Thus, the degree to which issues concerned with secondary school reorganization and primary school progressivism respectively have affected the growth of middle schools are a useful indicator of the relative importance of primary-based as against secondary-based influences in the educational policy process as a whole. Middle schools, in this sense, act as a marker of educational and political priorities throughout the system.

In addition to this, once they were established, the fact that middle schools (particularly those of the 9–13 variety) cut across the traditional dividing line between primary and secondary education often meant that they tended to serve as sites for conflict and struggle between the proponents of some of the dominant traditions associated with those two sectors. Yet these associations between sectors and traditions are not absolutely direct: the two do not correspond identically. A little explanation is needed here to indicate the sorts of traditions that are at work and the part they play in the two sectors — primary and secondary — in each case.

In primary education, Blyth (1965) has pointed out that at least three dominant traditions have exerted a powerful influence on that sector. The child-centred *developmental* (or 'progressive') tradition — strongly represented in the classic writings of Rousseau, Froebel, Pestalozzi and Montessori, and a growing feature of official reports on primary education from the 1930s onwards — is perhaps the best known and has been established for a long time in 'infants' departments which were well cushioned from the restrictive effects of the nineteenth-century system of 'payment by results' and of the 11 + scholarship. And it showed signs at the time Blyth was writing in the mid- to late-1960s of consolidating its ground with older age groups too, not least in the *Plowden Report* (1967).

However, this developmental tradition, although it is perhaps the one most readily associated with the primary sector, is far from unchallenged (Blyth, 1965, p. 43). The challenge arises from the two other major components of English primary schooling. The first is the long-standing *elementary school tradition*. This tradition, with its emphasis on basic skills of literacy and numeracy along with strict pupil discipline, has origins which stretch back as far as the song schools of the sixteenth century. But as Blyth (*ibid*, p. 23) tells us, 'it was during the age of early industrialism that the elementary tradition attained its most characteristic development. For now, instead of being confined to haphazard local initiative ... elementary education began to affect the majority of children.' Elementary schools kept children off the streets while their parents were at work and prepared them with the skills and discipline that would equip them for factory life. With the introduction of the system of payment by results in the middle of the nineteenth century, rote learning methods became firmly embedded in the elementary schools. Nor did the extension of the scholarship system in 1907 do anything to alleviate this. Instead of teaching for the inspection, teachers now taught for the 11 + ; the effect was much the same.

As Blyth (*ibid*, p. 28) concludes, given 'the circumstances in which the elementary tradition developed, and the inflexibility induced in its principal exponents, it is not suprising that its influence has persisted long after its institutional framework has been abolished.' These influences may have lost favour in the 1960s and early 1970s at the level of public policy, but research on primary teachers showed that they were never far from the surface (Bennett, 1976). While these elementary concerns were overshadowed for a time in post-war years by the Plowden-like emphasis on individualistic, creative learning, they began to be asserted with some force from the mid-1970s onwards in a politically and media-led campaign of neo-elementary rhetoric, strongly urging the restoration and promotion of 'basic skills' within the primary curriculum.

A second source of challenge to the developmental view came from what Blyth called the independent *preparatory school tradition*. This tradition, curiously neglected in a number of accounts of the history of primary education (for example, Pollard, 1985), again has its strongest roots in the nineteenth century. Here preparatory (prep) schools were designed to prepare their pupils for the public school education for which it was assumed they would be destined, and for the liberal, academic curriculum which that kind of education essentially comprised. Nor was this tradition entirely confined to the socially favoured private sector either, for as Blyth (1965, p. 34) notes, 'some day grammar schools began eventually to look for part of their recruitment to the cream of the elementary tradition itself, a practice which became systematized after 1907' (with the introduction of regulations allocating 25 per cent of grammar school places to open competition from children in state elementary schools). Coupled with the basic skills of the elementary tradition, key features of this preparatory tradition with its emphasis on conventional academic knowledge, firm subject boundaries and exam or test-relevant skills, continued to exert a substantial influence on primary 'scholarship' teaching over the years. Recent calls for primary schools to concentrate more on subject specialist teaching, and for the training of primary teachers to devote more time to 'subject studies' indicate that elements of this preparatory tradition continue to prosper in primary schooling, even today (for example, DES, 1983; Bolton, 1984).

In the secondary sector, similar traditions are at work, though to different degrees and in rather different forms than in primary education. Foremost and best known among them, perhaps, is the *academic tradition* (Ball, 1981). This tradition, grounded in the public schools and the grammar schools which aped them, placed, and still places, a premium on knowledge which is academic, literate, abstract and propositional. Through the guardianship of the universities and the influence they have exerted on systems of public examining at 16 and 18 +, the kind of knowledge and the subjects which epitomize it, reorientated the curriculum of the once exclusively vocational secondary modern schools in the 1960s — turning them over more and more to academic, examination work (Taylor, 1963) — and it continues to maintain a powerful grip on the secondary school curriculum even now (Young, 1971), ensuring that the academic or grammar school tradition continues to thrive even inside the new comprehensives (Hargreaves, D., 1982). It was for this, in fact, that preparatory schools prepared.

Running alongside and interpenetrating with this academic tradition in the secondary sector is the equally influential *elementary tradition* too. What is interesting about this tradition is that not only did it continue to be influential in the primary sector, but it strengthened its hand even further through its development in the inter-war all-age schools and the early post-war secondary modern schools too which, until they began to enter their pupils for 'O' level and 'CSE' examinations, laid almost exclusive emphasis on vocational education and the inculcation of basic skills for their intake of non-academic pupils (Taylor, 1963). In the 1980s, with the rise of the new vocationalism, the advent of work experience programmes, and the development of the Technical and Vocational Education Initiative (TVEI) for certain pupils, it is clear that this elementary tradition with all its old secondary-modern associations is still very much with us. (Simon, 1984)

Least well-developed of all in the secondary sector, perhaps, is the *developmental* or progressive *tradition*. Given the strength of its other two competitors, the persisting pressures of the universities on examinations and the curriculum, and the imminence of work or non-work for secondary school leavers, this tradition's difficulty in gaining a firm secondary foothold is understandable. Nevertheless, the developmental tradition has made a substantial impact in particular parts of the secondary system. There are, for instance, a small number of influential and distinctive independent secondary schools such as Abbotsholme and Dartington Hall[6] which are ·self-avowedly 'progressive' in nature. (Skidelsky, 1969). Moreover, 'progressive' methods have also made a mark, if only a small one, in a few comprehensive secondary schools, some of which, like Countesthorpe College in Leicestershire, Stantonbury Campus in Milton Keynes and the Sutton Centre in the East Midlands, now have national reputations (Moon, 1983). And even in ordinary secondary schools there are still enclaves where developmental principles are often especially visible — in certain subjects such as English, for instance (Ball, 1981; St John Brooks, 1983), in programmes of tutorial work (Baldwin and Wells, 1979), and in pupil profiling or records of personal achievement. (Hargreaves, 1986b)

The British educational system, then, shows different emphases between sectors — primary and secondary — and between traditions — academic (preparatory), elementary and developmental (progressive) — that in part relate to and in part cross cut those sectors. As a new institution attempting to establish its own distinctive identity and tradition while having to draw on staff whose roots are in others, and as an institution that exactly cross cuts the conventional boundary between primary and secondary education, the middle school provides us with a unique opportunity to gauge the relative strength and importance of these different sectors and traditions in English education, to examine the impact that each has made on educational policy and practice.

This poses important questions for the historical study of middle schools — which sector's interests, which educational principles most influenced decisions to establish them? And it sets important tasks for the investigation of middle school practice too — have middle schools succeeded in uniting and blending two sectors and a range of educational traditions, or is their identity, like their cultural inheritance, a divided one with practices like ability grouping, subject organization, discipline policies and so on taking a very different shape in the top and bottom ends of the middle school respectively? It is these broader questions to do with the relative influence of different sectors and traditions within the British educational system as a whole that this book in part seeks to address by examining the middle school case.

Educational Policy and Practice

This focus on the different priorities embedded in educational policy and practice does, of course, raise further questions about the relationship between these two spheres. This relationship between educational policy and practice, the consequences of policy initiatives and priorities — past and present — for school life, is clearly an important issue with which teachers and other educators ought to be and often are concerned. Yet the explanation of this relationship has been a curiously neglected feature of educational research. Despite occasional overviews attempting to relate policy and practice at the level of theory (for example, Hargreaves, D., 1982), empirical studies have focussed *either* on LEA and/or national policy, *or* on school processes. The two areas have tended to be kept very much apart. As a result, the implications of educational policy for schools, or the consequences of school processes for policy have been left to rather general speculation.

Where the sphere of policy has been virtually neglected altogether, explanation of the relationship between schooling and the world outside, between schooling and 'society', has been subject to even greater speculation than this. What has commonly happened in this kind of work is that detailed observations and interpretations of what goes on in schools have been supplemented by overarching and rather speculative assertions about the nature of the surrounding society. All too often, evidence at school level has been used to provide loose and rather unsystematic illustrations of preferred theories about the requirements of capitalist society and such like (for example, Sharp and Green, 1975, Anyon, 1981). This 'society', moreover, has, in many respects, been treated as an undifferentiated unit. This single, vast unit, a whole bundle of economic, social and political characteristics, has then been placed alongside the closely chronicled work of the school. Empirical energies, it seems, have been focussed on the microcosmic world of the school or the classroom, and everything else beyond those walls has been bracketed off by default as belonging to 'society', a society whose properties are asserted through theoretical speculation. What happens as a result, is that school processes are said to serve or threaten the needs or requirements of this society but by mechanisms to which we do not have access and which we therefore cannot understand. As long as school and society are counterposed so bluntly, it is unlikely that such understanding will be taken much further.

The difficulty is not an intractable one, though. For what is usually overlooked, is that many so-called societal constraints that teachers and pupils face actually originate in interactions *outside* the classroom — in County Hall, the Department of Education and Science examination boards, and so on — the world conventionally known as educational policy. And this is in principle just as open to empirical study as is the world of the classroom — even though problems of access to the powerful may mean that we have to rely rather more on documentary sources than we usually have to in schools. Of course, this does not solve all our problems at a stroke, for policy processes need to be linked with theoretical understandings of the major social, economic and political characteristics of our society too. Theory is not ducked that easily. Nor should it be. But our understanding of the relationship between school and society can certainly be enhanced through detailed empirical study of the relationship between policy and practice. It can help clarify theories of the social context of schooling and give us a better basis of evidence for testing them.

Of course, this distinction between educational policy and practice can be a little misleading — for classroom teachers clearly have their own policies on ability grouping and other matters (Pollard, 1984), and LEA policy-making is evidently a practice too. But despite its difficulties, the distinction between policy (concerning matters outside the school) and practice (concerning matters within it) is such a widespread feature of conventional understanding that its retention for the sake of conceptual shorthand is worthwhile (providing the preceding caveats are borne in mind).

The study of middle schools, I want to argue, offers an important opportunity to study and clarify this link between policy and practice. Because of their relative recency, the contentious circumstances surrounding their establishment, and their tight and specific institutional focus (as compared with, say, the comprehensive debate in general), the study of middle schools highlights particularly well broader aspects of the policy process and its links to school practice. The issue is sufficiently recent to be open to retrieval. It was, initially, sufficiently controversial to generate explicit and open discussion of principles and priorities that otherwise tend to remain tacit and assumed within the policy system. And it is sufficiently tightly focussed to allow the patterns and consequences of educational policy in one key area, at the centre of the system, to be traced clearly.

More than this, the legacy of policy decisions, in terms of the kinds of buildings allocated to middle schooling, the sorts of staff who elected to join or who were deployed to this new sector, and the purposes that policy-makers expected these schools to serve, makes it possible, with the benefit of hindsight, to trace through the links between the goals and constraints of educational policy and the character of middle school practice. Thus, the internal organization of middle schools, the occupational cultures of their staff, and the constraints and pressures they have had to meet, can all be traced to changes in educational policy which are not too distant to grasp or retrieve. The emergence, development and more recent decline of middle schools, therefore, provides us with a rare and valuable opportunity to enrich our understanding of the relationship between policy and practice in education.

The Organization of the Book

With these broader purposes in mind, this book sets out to establish the links between and the social context of the policy and practice of English middle schools, particularly those of the 9–13/10–13 variety, in an empirically grounded and theoretically informed way. Part I of the book is concerned with the analysis of educational policy, with the origin and development of middle schools and the factors which determined their establishment. This is based in the main, on an empirical study of the development of middle schools in the area where they first emerged — the West Riding of Yorkshire.

Three chapters are devoted to the historical case study. Chapter 2 considers the extent to which middle schools in the West Riding and elsewhere were a product of administrative convenience, of implementing comprehensive reorganization in a way which made cheap and efficient use of existing buildings. In chapters 3 and 4, however, it is argued that while the economically induced limits of administrative convenience explain much of the reason for the emergence of middle schools, they do not explain why middle schools were widely adopted in preference to other patterns which were equally or similarly convenient, such as 11–14 junior high schools. The discriminating factor in these cases, it is suggested, is the nature of and priority given to different educational and social goals which were being pursued at the time middle schools emerged. Chapter 3 evaluates the goals pursued in relation to matters of *secondary* reorganization; goals of meritocracy, egalitarianism and social unity. Chapter 4 evaluates the status of primary arguments and justifications for the establishment of middle schools as a way of extending the best Plowden-like primary practice to older age groups. It is argued that although such arguments provided an important additional rationale for middle schools in an educational climate where primary progressivism had a good deal of currency, not least in the West Riding, nevertheless it was secondary arguments, particularly ones of a meritocratic kind, that were most decisive at the level of policy implementation.

The stage is thus set for Part 2 of the book which is devoted to an analysis of the internal organization and practice of middle schooling. This is predominantly based on case studies of two neighbouring middle schools, one 9–13, one 10–13, situated somewhere within the old West Riding Education Authority, though other published case studies and available national survey data are also drawn on where appropriate. This part of the book is concerned with establishing how far the reality of middle school practice matches up to ideological claims about that practice, and with identifying the consequences its pattern of policy development has had for the forms of practical organization, for the patterns of curriculum and pupil grouping, which middle schools have subsequently adopted.

Chapters 5–7 concentrate on three organisational indicators of whether middle schools are unified or divided institutions; whether they offer pupils a smooth transition or an abrupt break between primary and secondary forms of educational experience: the year system, setting and subject specialism. Middle schools, these three chapters indicate, are fragmented not unified institutions. They tend to be characterized by a strong split at the age of 11 instead of providing a smooth transition, and in many respects, in their top two years, they appear to be even more 'secondary orientated' than secondary schools themselves.

Part 3 of the book explores why this is the case, looking at the training and experience of middle school teachers in particular. The form of this experience, of teacher biographies, it is found, arises not from its roots in specific sectors (primary or secondary), but from distinctive occupational cultures of teaching which are linked with but in some respects also cross cut those sectors. Middle schools, that is, tend to deploy their teachers according to a principle of culture match, not phase match. Two cultures are focussed on here: the *academic-elementary* traditon (chapter 8) with its roots in secondary modern schools and/or the scholarship classes of primary schools; and the *developmental* tradition (chapter 9) with its base in progressive primary teaching. In chapter 10, however, attention is also paid to the middle school's attempt to create its own distinctive culture and to the teachers whose training or experience in middle schools themselves seems to fit them best for it. What hope, it asks, can be lodged in teachers who have been specifically prepared to teach in 'the middle years'?

The conclusion is reached that these patterns of cultural inheritance, their links with educational policy and with social and economic policy beyond that, and their rootedness in the middle school's particular historical development, make the middle school what it is today.

After a summary of the book's main findings, the conclusion examines their implications for the future of middle schools in a climate of tightening economic stringency and of mounting demands for more attention to be given to subject specialism within the school curriculum. It also suggests some possible directions that middle schools and their staffs might consider taking in years to come, not least if they wish their institutions to survive.

Notes

1 There are also a very small number of 10–14 schools also designated as 'middle'.
2 These figures are taken from table A3/83, Schools by size and type, *Statistics of Education: Schools*, Department of Education and Science, London, HMSO (1983).
3 These figures are taken from table A4/83, *Statistics of Education: Schools*, Department of Education and Science, London, HMSO (1983).
4 Compiled from DES (1981) *Maintained Primary, Middle and Secondary Schools: Statistics for each Local Education Authority, Statistics Return No. 62*, London, HMSO, January.
5 My use of ideology here is a traditionally Marxist one as employed by MARX and ENGELS (1976) in *The German Ideology*. A more extensive discussion of ideology, as it underpins the analysis presented here is available in HARGREAVES (1985).
6 Auspiciously, perhaps, the closure of Dartington Hall has been announced since this book went to press.

Part I
Educational Policy

'Men make history, but not in circumstances of their own choosing'

(Karl Marx)

Introduction

This first part of the book focusses on the nature and dynamics of educational policy as it has affected the development of middle schools in Britain. First, taking middle schools as a critical case, it examines whether, within British educational policy, issues connected with secondary education, its reorganisation and improvement and with the pupils of that phase, take priority over those connected with the education of younger age groups in the primary sector. Second, through analyzing the specific development of middle schools, it deals with much broader policy issues too — the economic conditions and assumptions of administrative convenience that underpin educational reorganization (chapter 2) and the multiple arguments and conflicts that surround new policy developments (chapters 3 and 4).

The Data

The analysis of these issues concerning middle schools in particular, and the dynamics of educational policy in general, is based on a detailed historical study of the emergence of middle schools within one local education authority — the West Riding of Yorkshire — though references are made to developments elsewhere too where appropriate. The data consist mainly of the memoranda and correspondence of that LEA prior to and during its consideration and implementation of the middle school system. It is not known whether the West Riding is typical of other LEAs in its conduct of educational policy and its attitudes to middle schools. On the other hand, three things can be said in defence of its selection for special study. First, a number of findings in relation to educational policy in the West Riding have parallels with those which have emerged from historical studies of the development of middle schools elsewhere. As Howell and Brown (1983) argue in their own case studies of educational policy making, 'it is unlikely that any one study will by itself convince the sceptic that a sufficient basis for generalization has now been established'. But, they go on, 'the cumulative knowledge that can be gained from a collection of case studies on a common topic, is extremely valuable in enhancing our general understanding of aspects of educational policy' (p. 14). The study of middle school policy in the West Riding, when taken with similar studies in other localities, therefore adds to our cumulative understanding of educational policy as a whole.

While this appeal to the cumulative nature of educational research could be made in defence of the selection of almost any case, two further features of the West Riding recommend it particularly strongly for selection. The first is the LEA's immense internal diversity. The West Riding was subdivided into no less than twenty-eight regional divisions and a number of 'excepted districts'. In effect, then, the study of the West Riding amounts to an examination of not just one case but many, making it possible to study differences; to concentrate on divisions in which policy outcomes were dissimilar. The task of explaining such variations presents a formidable challenge to theory and is a useful safeguard against the inclination to back up theoretical assertions with easy illustrations from single cases. In addition to this, the West Riding was the first LEA to open middle schools, in 1968. In this sense, it had a crucial and perhaps decisive influence on national policy in relation to middle schools.

This, then, is the nature of the *evidence* on which claims about the development of middle schools will be based. But these claims are also located within a *theoretical framework* too — a set of orientations and guiding interpretations about the determinants and dynamics of educational policy. While it is not really appropriate in a book of this kind to fill in the theoretical background in great detail (readers who are interested in that should consult the thesis from which the book arises or my more extensive accounts of *Social Theory and Education* in Hargreaves (forthcoming)), a brief indication of the general theoretical position in which the study is set might assist readers who would like to scrutinize its findings particularly closely. Just one cautionary note before this is done: the adopted theoretical stance did not precede, nor was it assumed before the commencement of the study, or before the available evidence was analyzed. The study *did* begin from certain theoretical starting points, but these were very different from those that had emerged and developed by the end, after close examination of the evidence and after comparing, then synthesizing different, and until that point, discrete and competing theoretical positions in order to explain that evidence.[1] The theoretical stance I shall outline, then, is an outcome of the research; not its starting point. Readers not immediately interested in these kinds of concerns should now turn to page 27.

Some Notes on Theory

The details of the adopted theory will become clear as the report of the historical study itself unfolds. In broad terms though, the stance taken is essentially a synthesis of two dominant and very different traditions of educational policy analysis that have to date remained rather separate — pluralism and Marxism.

Until very recently, it was the pluralist tradition that dominated the study of educational policy. This work has been rich in empirical detail. It has pointed to the presence and influence in educational policy of a *plurality* of interest groups of political, professional, administrative and lay kinds. (for example, Peschek and

Brand, 1966; Batley, O'Brien and Parris, 1970; Saran, 1973; James, 1980). And it has highlighted the ways in which different groups pursue different kinds of interests or goals through education — those to do with *economic* improvement, the enhancement of social *status*, or the strengthening of *party* political interests. (Weber, 1968; King, 1980)

At the same time, however, in emphasizing such diversity and in seeking to rebuff Marxism and its allegedly crude doctrines of economic determinism, contemporary pluralism has tended to prejudge the relative unimportance of economic factors among these diverse influences, instead of letting empirical study decide the matter. In addition, it has tended to minimize the importance of economic interests by defining these too narrowly. It has, for instance, not counted the pursuit of economic growth and technological development as economic goals, even though these have had a major impact on the comprehensive movement and the expansion of higher education in the 1960s.[2] And it has also tended to ignore the *limits* to diversity and variation in educational policy that are fixed by the nature of a nation's economy and by the taken-for-granted assumptions of those who operate and work within its political system.[3]

Contemporary Marxism has, by contrast, tried to take account of these limits to educational policy *and* of the variations and complications within them. But it has tended to do this in a rather obscure and mystifying way, through the concept of *relative autonomy*. *Relative autonomy* is not just a synonym for the partial independence of the educational system or the state more generally from external pressures and influences. It is not just a more tentative, less strident brand of educational theorizing than its more vulgar Marxist predecessors which tended to see education and the state as directly serving the needs of the capitalist economy. Its central and distinguishing characteristic, rather, is its claim that the economic mode of production (capitalist, socialist etc.) is the determinant of education and the state *in the last instance*, despite any degree of independence that education admittedly otherwise has.

Thus, while it is said that education and the state must meet (or, at least not be threatening to) the fundamental needs of capitalism for a skilled workforce, for a harmonious society in which production can take place, and for widespread acceptance that capitalism is the only legitimate pattern of economic organization, relative autonomy theorists also recognize that educational systems and states more generally vary in how they meet these central requirements, that they often do so in a rather messy and uncoordinated way, and that this may be further complicated by all kinds of political conflicts and struggles (Dale, 1982). Clearly, the complications are very great. Yet it is still asserted that somehow, these economic requirements determine the broad shape and orientation of the state and of educational provision and practice within it, *in the last instance*.

This seems rather like trying to have one's cake and eat it — to admit some degree of independence for educational and political factors, while distancing oneself from the pluralism such an admission might imply, by emphasizing the ultimate importance of economic determinants *in the last instance*. Relative autonomy theory, that is, embraces complexity (educational events are determined by other factors as well as economic ones), while excluding pluralism (economic factors are not *necessarily* more important than any other determinants). This reluctance to admit any element of *genuine* pluralism, while still wanting to account for complexity and variation in educational and state policy has led relative autonomy theory only into circumlocution and incoherence. (Crouch, 1977)

There are, then, serious weaknesses in each of these traditions. But each also has important contributions to make to our understanding of educational policy. Yet, because of the ideological thrust in each approach to provide a total explanation of educational policy entirely from within its own preferred framework, and because of the emphasis on negating or discrediting the claims of its main theoretical competitor, important areas of compatibility and complementarity between the two traditions have been overlooked. The stance adopted in this part of the book tries to identify and build upon such points of compatibility.

The Marxist tradition, it seems to me, is at its strongest when it is dealing with questions of the limits to educational change and variation; when it is examining the things that do not happen, the educational changes that do not take place, the radical social transformations that fail to come to fruition (Dale, 1982). What Marxism importantly recognizes here is that economic structures limit what is possible and heavily influence what is probable within education and the state as a whole (Wright 1979). Of course — and this is a point that Marxists tend to overlook — there are other *structural limits* to what is politically and socially possible and probable too, as well as economic ones — race in South Africa, religion in Northern Ireland and patriarchy almost everywhere, for instance. Nevertheless, as we shall see, economic factors do play an important, if not exclusive role in determining the limits of educational policy. And in explaining such economic limits, Marxism has undoubtedly made a more powerful contribution than any other tradition to date.

Two kinds of limits appear to be important here: conditions and assumptions. In the first case, Marxism has drawn our attention to the limiting economic conditions to educational policy-making in Western capitalist democracies that arise from the contradictory role played by the state within such societies (Adams, 1978; Dale, 1981; Gough, 1980). On the one hand, in order to guarantee the survival of the capitalist economy, to maximize profits and fend off decline, the state is faced with the task of tailoring human fortunes and ambitions to that economic system's needs.[4] The effect of this in the 1960s and early 1970s — the period that will immediately concern us in this first section — was to encourage growing state involvement in a number of areas, not least in educational expansion, to produce a technically equipped, socially compliant workforce; and to 'buy' public loyalty to the system by accommodating educational and broader welfare demands. On the other hand, though, the financing of this expansion entailed deduction from the very thing the state was meant to enhance; from revenue or profits.

Educational expenditure, like state expenditure more generally is, in this sense, as much a drain on society's scarce resources as a crucial investment in its supposed well-being. In consequence, despite rhetorics of expansion and investment in 'human capital', actual educational expenditure, even at times of relative prosperity, has been consistently limited. The pattern of comprehensive reorganization by administrative convenience, using existing buildings wherever possible, has been one effect of these limiting conditions.

To these economic conditions circumscribing the options for educational policy can be added a second set of limits — those which are embedded in dominant assumptions, especially among policy-makers — about the workings and purpose of education, state, economy and society. These assumptions have a *hegemonic* character (Gramsci, 1971). That is to say, they amount to taken for granted, unquestioned views of what is true, proper, sane, reasonable, normal and natural; views whose breach would be regarded not as an occasion for legitimate disagreement and debate, but as an unwarranted, outrageous or subversive threat to the essential and worthwhile order of things. By 'normalizing' and 'naturalizing' existing beliefs, practices and procedures in this way, such ingrained assumptions routinely, undramatically, but very effectively serve the preservation of existing dominant interests in society.

In education, the dominant hegemony is in large part consolidated through innumerable public and semi-public statements by policy-makers about the purposes of education and schooling, especially in relation to the economy. From the 1870 Education Act right up to the interventions of the Manpower Services Commission, education and schooling have been consistently presented as important contributors to industrial prosperity, technological development, wealth creation etc. But in all this, while the best ways of harnessing education to economic ends has been much discussed, the character of the economic system which education is supposed to enhance has never really been placed in question. Indeed to raise such questions would have been seen not as support for an alternative model of economic growth, but as being simply *against* growth and prosperity Tapper and Salter, 1978). Whatever particular changes they have favoured, therefore, educational policy-makers have invariably assumed, in public at least, that schooling would contribute to, or at least, in Dale's (1982) words, *not be inimical to* capital accumulation, and the schemes and proposals they have presented — for meritocratic rather than egalitarian kinds of comprehensive schooling, for instance — have tended to reflect those hegemonic assumptions.

Within these economic and hegemonic limits to educational policy options, it has been the pluralist tradition that has been most effective in identifying and explaining the diversity, the variation in educational policy and practice. There are, it seems to me, at least three kinds of variation that are important here.

First, educational policy is subject to competing pressures among a wide range of groups pursuing different goals and realizing different interests. The struggle for and implementation of comprehensive schooling provides an excellent illustration of such many-sided conflicts and alliances in the process of educational change. Invested in that one reform were many of the hopes and aspirations of a wide range of social groups (Marsden, 1971); radical and egalitarian social reform for certain sections of the working class and the Labour Party (Parkinson, 1970); greater all-round educational opportunities within a truly meritocratic educational system for the Labour mainstream (Crosland, 1964); and promotion of economic growth and prosperity among many politicians and their advisors. It is not uncommon for the ends that different groups pursue to be opposed to one another, this leading to intense and protracted political conflicts. But equally, they may at times be rendered compatible, presented as all things to everyone, within a single educational proposal — as in many of the specific schemes of comprehensive schooling that were adopted in different LEAs (Reynolds and Sullivan, 1981). It is at this point that the workings of the system of educational administration and politics, along with the actions of key figures within it, becomes crucial. This points to a second form of variation; that which arises from the complexities of the administrative system.

Educational change is complicated not only by interest group pressure, but also by variations in outlook and interpretation between different localities, and between different levels of the educational decision-making process. There are sometimes substantial differences between the DES and particular LEAs over educational policy (in relation to comprehensive reorganization, for instance), or even between an LEA and some of its sub-divisions. Where disagreements occur, central government can draw on its financial powers to withhold money for capital projects, or resort to Parliamentary powers to ensure that LEAs comply with its wishes; but in return, LEAs can also have recourse to the law in resisting central government direction, and can use their greater local knowledge about building provision, transport arrangements, consultation procedures etc. to delay compliance with policy directives. (Pattison, 1983)

The outcome of these bureaucratic complexities is commonly one of difficulty in coordinating different parts of the system. Equally, though, as Gouldner (1973) points out, the autonomy of parts of a system, either from one another, or from the system as a whole, may well be functional, allowing flexibility of response to tensions within the system. In the case of education, as Bidwell (1965) notes, a certain degree of what he calls *structural looseness* may actually be necessary for the school system, allowing policy directives to be adjusted to the circumstances of each locality. It was on these lines, for instance, that Government Circular 10/65 outlined six different possible ways of going comprehensive from which LEAs could choose according to local needs and circumstances.

This is the point where the role played by key educational politicians and administrators becomes crucial. For in responding to economic, social and political constraints and competing educational demands, such politicians and administrators also realize social and educational goals that are distinctively their own. They do not just cobble together administrative compromises, but take the educational themes of their time and move them forward giving them their own personal stamp and securing for them broad social support. These people are not mere conciliators but active 'educators' (David, 1977), people who intervene creatively in the policy process, not only resolving but also exploiting the administrative complexities of a structurally loose system to secure and gain support for their own preferred patterns of educational innovation. It is this process which has brought to prominence the 'great' education officers of the English educational system — the likes of Alec Clegg in the West Riding of Yorkshire, and of Stewart Mason in Leicestershire, along with their policies of middle schooling in the first place, the Leicestershire plan pattern of secondary reorganization in the second, and progressive primary education in both.

As well as competing pressures and the administrative complexity of structurally loose systems, variation in educational policy and its shortcomings in meeting economic and political requirements can also be explained by the strange and often unwanted inheritances of history. Educational change can, in this sense, be impeded or distorted by problems of historical lag. These problems may be cultural — as in the difficulties faced by comprehensive schools when they had to meet bold new challenges with staff drawn from and attached to the grammar and secondary modern traditions respectively. But they may also be material; for past policy commitments make themselves felt not just in teachers' attitudes and habits but in harsh and intractable material realities too — in the very bricks and mortar of schooling (Williamson, B., 1979). The difficulties of establishing team teaching in old Victorian elementary school premises; of providing equal opportunities in practical subjects for girls in single sex schools when such schools were originally designed and equipped with more narrowly domestic interpretations of practicality in mind; and of bringing about comprehensive reform within a stock of small grammar and secondary modern school buildings — these are just some of the material handicaps to educational reform that have been left by the inheritances of history.

To sum up: the theoretical approach adopted within this part of the book examines both the limits to educational change and policy options (be these economic or hegemonic in nature), and the complicated and varied processes — multisided pressure, structural looseness and historical lag — that occur within those limits. It is difficult, and perhaps futile, to argue that the limits to change are more important than the different possibilities contained within them (or *vice versa*); to argue, in effect, that either pluralism or Marxism is theoretically or politically superior. Choosing between the two is a matter of value preference, not one of theoretical correctness. What I have tried to show in this brief theoretical review, is that when it comes to analyzing educational policy, studying the limits or what goes on within them are complementary, not competing ventures. Acknowledging that complementarity has implications for what we understand by the notion of policy itself.

What is Policy?

For pluralists, policy operates as 'a guide for taking actions and for making appropriate choices or decisions towards the accomplishment of some intended or desired end' (Jennings, 1977, p. 30). It is a broad stance or framework within which decisions and non-decisions are made (Hill, 1980, pp. 71–2). In addition to this concern with 'means', some pluralists also regard policy as involving the consideration or taken-for-granted acceptance of social and educational 'ends' too, since political considerations are often built into the very procedures and assumptions within which administrators work (Hill, 1972, chapter 10). However, as two Marxist writers argue, the problem with many pluralist studies in this respect, is that in them,

> Social policy is analyzed as if it were an autonomous set of social institutions unconnected with the normal processes of the social and political system in which it is set and which it serves. This lack of theorizing is not a politically neutral approach to social policy but an implicit conservative stand, for it accepts social and economic relationships unquestioningly. (George and Wilding, 1976, p. 1)

Both these aspects of the policy process, it is worth emphasizing, are important. They are complementary, not competing definitions. This first part of the book will, accordingly, deal with *both* of them in its explanation of educational policy. It will deal with social ends as well as technical means, with political and economic assumptions as well as administrative procedures. Through all this, it will attempt to show how, together, these different aspects of educational policy — means and ends, assumptions and procedures, limits and variations — have determined the origin and shaped the course of the development of English middle schools. It is to the nature of that development that we now turn.

Notes

1 A full account of just how the theory developed and changed during the course of the study is presented elsewhere in a biographical account of the process of researching this book (HARGREAVES, 1986a).
2 See, for instance, COLLINS (1979) who defines economic goals in terms of economically productive practical skills only.
3 Pluralists do deal to some extent with the limits to educational change, but they do so in a rather restricted way — referring vaguely to 'inherited assumptions and attitudes' (BYRNE, 1974, p. 304), 'ideological and structural factors' (DAVID, 1977, p. 202) and the 'limitations that social structures impose on interaction' (ARCHER, 1979, p. 5) without locating them in the particular dynamics of the British economic and political system.
4 This necessity arises from inner tendencies within the long-term development of the capitalist economy, for the tendency of the rate of profit to fall (TRPF). DALE (1981, p. 30) provides one of the most succinct summaries of what is involved here:

> this ... law is based on the fact that surplus value can only be realized from labour power and not from machines; and that there is a continuing tendency for the relationships between these two components (respectively 'variable' and 'constant') to change, with the latter growing faster than the former (a process known as the rising organic composition of captial). Unless there is an increase in the rate of exploitation of labour, the rising organic composition of capital will cause the rate of profit to fall. Associated with this tendency, then, is an increasing concentration of industry ... and even greater pressures to raise the productivity of labour.

Chapter 2

Middle Schools and Administrative Convenience

Background

Middle schools were made legally possible by the Education Act of 1964. This allowed, for the first time, transfer between primary and secondary education at ages other than 11. But it was an Act of more mature vintage — Butler's Education Act of 1944 — which created the problem to which middle schools would eventually provide an answer. From the point of view of post-war education reorganization, this Act left two important legacies. The first was what might be called the tripartite inheritance. In formal terms, the 1944 Act provided secondary education for all. Access to a grammar school education was no longer something which could be bought by economically advantaged parents but now was contingent on a seemingly open and fair system of competition based on the criterion of merit.[2] All children up to 14, and later 15, years of age were to receive a genuinely secondary education in schools which were to have 'parity of esteem'. In practice, however, most LEAs reorganized on tripartite lines as recommended in the Spens (1938) and Norwood (1943) reports. The Act, and the reports which preceded it, were thus crucial in establishing the framework for secondary school reorganization in post-war years — a framework which was consolidated through the building of many new and rather small secondary modern schools.

In retrospect, we now know that the differences between grammar and secondary modern schools meant that 'parity of esteem' was never achieved (Banks, 1955). Subsequent concern about these institutional differences in the education of the nation's children, along with worries about the mechanisms by which children were allocated to these different types of school (by examination at age 11) ultimately led to various proposals to reorganize secondary education again — this time on comprehensive lines during the 1950s and 1960s. The difficulty the architects of this second reorganization then faced was having to take account of the existing framework of small secondary modern and grammar schools in formulating their plans for the new comprehensives.

This difficulty was compounded by the second legacy of the 1944 Act: its establishment in law of what was later to become a crucial distinction between 'primary' and 'secondary' education. Under the terms of the Act, LEAs were required to provide full-time primary education for junior pupils and full-time secondary education for senior ones. In section 8, the Act was quite clear about the age categories which applied to junior and senior pupils, the former being those pupils who had not yet reached the age of 12. In this sense, the 1944 Act placed the stamp of legal authority on an arrangement of transfer at 11 + which had previously been recommended in the Hadow Report of 1926 and which had been the accepted age at which 'scholarship' children moved from elementary to grammar school since the 'free place' regulations of 1907.

When several LEAs did eventually begin to push hard for comprehensive schooling in the late 1950s, these two legacies — the tripartite inheritance and the legally fixed age of transfer — placed policy makers in a difficult dilemma. The reason for this was the Ministry of Education's insistence that unless new school building was warranted by population expansion or urban renewal, LEAs who wished to reorganize their secondary education should do so within the existing stock of school buildings. The effect of these constraints of administative convenience was to prevent the establishment of inevitably large 11–18 comprehensive schools in many areas since they would far outstrip the accommodation then available. Those LEAs who retained a strong commitment to comprehensive schooling therefore had to divide up the secondary school sector in some way or other. But one of the most manageable ways of doing this — a three-tier system of 5–9, 9–13 and 13–18 schools — was then illegal and therefore either ruled out by most LEAs after the briefest of enquiries (Marsh, 1980) or not really seriously considered by them at all.

Let us now examine how just one LEA — the West Riding of Yorkshire — attempted in some of its regional divisions to resolve this legal and administrative dilemma; to formulate a comprehensive solution which was acceptable within the bounds of administrative convenience.

The Rise and Demise of the Junior Highs

In 1958, after Labour had regained political control at the local authority level, Alec Clegg, the West Riding's Chief Education Officer, informed his Education Committee that

> In the last few months, the Committee has received a number of requests
> from governors of schools and divisional executives in the South of the
> Riding that either comprehensive schools or a comprehensive system of
> education should be established in their areas.[2]

From 1949, each of these divisons had been granted the autonomy to choose its own desired pattern of secondary reorganization. In a county with vast social and economic variations (and therefore political ones too) between localities,[3] such flexibility was important, not least because political control at Country Council level was very finely balanced, shifting regularly from one election to the next. (Sharp, 1980; Gosden and Sharp, 1978)

As divisional requests for secondary reorganization flowed in to county offices during the late 1950s, Clegg and his Education Committee set up a framework for considering and implementing these proposals. It was decided that when requests for comprehensive reorganization were received from any division, they would be taken through committee for the Education Officer (i.e. Clegg) to devize a set of alternative plans from which the division could make a choice. The matter would then be referred back to the Divisional Education Officer concerned who, in consultation with county staff, would draw up a scheme for reorganization, which would in turn be resubmitted to the Education Committee at county level for further ratification. Such a procedure was undoubtedly very complicated and it led to severe problems of coordination between different parts of the system in some places; to sharp and protracted disagreements over policy between the CEO and some of his divisions. But the procedure also allowed for, in fact it necessitated, a variety of schemes tailored to local circumstances — the great merit of 'structurally loose' systems of educational administration. However, the range of such diversity and autonomy was clearly contained within, as the autonomy itself was in part occasioned by more centrally defined limits which Clegg and his Committee specified at county level. Paramount among these was the necessity to use existing buildings within each division. Mindful of the ministerial restrictions on school building expenditure and of the constraints of administrative convenience which this imposed, Clegg himself pointed out that

> In areas where no new building can be justified (and they are now many) any proposal to establish a comprehensive scheme of education must be made to fit existing buildings, and this is far more difficult than building a new school.[4]

Clearly, this meant that any scheme involving major building programmes would be ruled out unless significant population expansion warranted the creation of new schools. As a result, for many divisions, the development of comprehensive reorganization based on all-through 11–18 schools was not a viable proposition; a restriction which was tightened still further by Clegg's unwillingness to approve plans for split-site schools where he considered the distance between such schools to be excessive. These were the circumstances in which Clegg and some of his area education officers turned to a scheme which appeared to offer the possibility of dividing schooling between 11 and 18 into two stages, and thus of making good use of existing accommodation. This scheme, originally called the Leicestershire Plan, came to be known within the West Riding as the junior high school system.

The Leicestershire Plan first emerged in the county of that name in September 1957. It involved, first of all, the transfer of all children at age 11 to a junior high school. Then, at age 14, if their parents so wished, pupils could transfer to the senior high school, but in so doing had to undertake to remain there beyond the minimum school leaving age which was then 15. The remaining pupils ended their school careers at the junior highs, where they left at that minimum age. As Clegg himself remarked, the scheme had distinctly innovative features: it avoided premature selection at age 11 and even at 14 still allowed children to be educated according to their parents' wishes. At the time, it was a radical scheme indeed. As Leicestershire's Director of Education, Stewart Mason, remarked in 1965, 'it is important to remember that the climate of opinion was by no means as favourable in 1956 as it is today, nearly ten years later'. (Mason, 1965, p. 8)

In Clegg's view, there were good reasons for adopting a straight or modified Leicestershire Plan scheme in certain areas of the West Riding. In a memorandum to his Committee in 1959, he wrote:

> This arrangement of division by age has certain obvious points to commend it. It avoids the problem of sheer size which is often levelled against the school to which all 11-year olds are admitted. It yields a more workable group of abler pupils in relation to total size. It avoids selection and it separates the adolescent from the child.[5]

Moreover, Clegg went on, 'One of the most powerful advantages it has over the truly comprehensive school with an age-range of 11–18 is that it can be fitted more easily into existing buildings', clear recognition, it would seem, that a system of junior and senior high schools had not only 'educational' advantages, but practical ones too. No wonder, then, that Clegg should write to Mason in 1959 saying 'what you yourself have started in your own county is certainly going to inspire a number of us to follow suit'.[6]

In a number of divisions the junior high school idea was promptly floated as one possible means of going comprehensive. So unsuited was the building accommodation in many of these divisions for conversion to large 11–18 campuses; so great, that is, were the constraints of administrative convenience, that novel ways of breaking up the pupil body into smaller units could not afford to be ignored. Three localities — Ecclesfield (part of the Wharncliffe division), Mexborough and Hemsworth — which sent in requests to reorganize their secondary education, will serve as useful examples here. These localities are of particular interest because while they all considered junior high schools as a possible way of going comprehensive, the final schemes that emerged were very different in each case.[7]

In *Ecclesfield*, the West Riding Education Committee noted that school buildings were generally of high quality. The one existing grammar school contained some excellent post-war extensions, three of the secondary moderns had been built since the 1944 Act, and of the remaining three, one was an attractive pre-war school, another required some improvements which had already been in-corporated into the school building programme, and only one required much larger scale alterations. In these circumstances, the Committee felt it most unlikely that any proposed scheme for 11–18 schools would be accepted by the Ministry, given the amount of rebuilding involved.

> The Committee must . . . realize that the accommodation does completely limit what can be done. It is inconceivable that when children are so excellently accommodated, this or any future Ministry would allow any bids for comprehensive adaptations until the more squalid old buildings elsewhere have been replaced or improved.[8]

The story was much the same in *Mexborough* where 'the amount of building involved would be so considerable that it would be unlikely that the scheme would be brought into operation for a very long time indeed'.[9] Suggesting a similar solution as that proposed for Ecclesfield, Clegg continued, 'It seems to me, therefore, that if the Division wishes to avoid this, it will be necessary to think in terms of some sort of a junior and senior high school organization'.[10]

In the third division, *Hemsworth*, the conditions of administrative convenience were more restrictive still. 'The difficulty about the Hemsworth division', Clegg wrote, 'is the existence in it of a large number of small secondary schools, which means that there is no easy or obvious solution to the problem'.[11] He later stressed that, given the buildings available, a programme based upon 11–18 comprehensive schools would be utterly impractical.[12] His solution, yet again, was a junior high school system — in this case one where all and not just some of the pupils would be transferred from one school to the other at age 14.

In November, 1959, Clegg paid a visit to the Hemsworth Divisional Executive Committee to outline the nature of such a junior high school scheme and in the following February was requested by that Committee to construct a plan for reorganization on junior high school lines.[13] But the proposal, practical though it seemed, became caught between two competing forces. While the existence of many small secondary modern schools meant that any new scheme would have to make use of at least some of the buildings in which those schools were housed, at the same time a considerable proportion of those schools were regarded as inadequate and needing replacement. Indeed, Hemsworth's Divisional Education Officer, in a letter to the West Riding Education Committee complained that, 'the facilities in the division are appalling when compared with other divisions'.[14] And Clegg himself had commented earlier that 'Quite apart from the question of the organization of secondary education ... new building is urgently required in this division'.[15]

In view of the 'very considerable capital expenditure' which would be involved in any scheme, the Committee decided to press in the first instance for reorganization in the southern part of the division only. In northern Hemsworth, the expenditure involved in reorganizing on junior high school lines would have been very great indeed. In addition to extending Hemsworth Grammar School from a four-form to the equivalent of a ten-form-entry school (so that it could function as a senior high), considerable sums needed to be spent on the junior high school sector, since many existing schools which might be converted into junior highs were regarded as being 'in very bad buildings'. Only one existing secondary school, it was felt, could be brought up to standard. The remaining six would have to be replaced by two brand new junior highs. In the north, then, only one new school was submitted to the Ministry of Education for inclusion in the 1962/63 Major Building Programme — for a secondary modern which, it was hoped, might eventually function as a junior high. Attention, meanwhile, was redirected to the more modest, yet still sizeable requirements of southern Hemsworth. Here, a proposal was submitted to the Ministry for a new senior high school. The division had already submitted a claim for a ten-form-entry comprehensive in the previous year (which had been rejected). It was now hoped that since the newly proposed senior high was equivalent only to an eight-form comprehensive in size, this would now leave a small surplus in the building programme for improving and adapting its feeder junior highs.[16]

Even this rather more modest plan was not sufficiently persuasive, though. The Ministry withheld its approval and, despite repeated pressure from the West Riding, had still not granted it by late 1963. This saga had now been in progress for four years. A number of local councillors became impatient, suspecting delaying tactics on the matter of comprehensivization. But as Clegg wrote to one to them in May, 1962:

> Unfortunately, the Minister of Education has so far not been prepared to include either of these schools in a Major Building Programme ... It is the failure of the Minister to include the projects in a building programme which is causing delay and not any question of secondary reorganization.[17]

In September, 1963, when the stalemate had still not been broken, the Divisional Education Officer accused the County Authority of leading his local Executive 'up the garden path' by leading them to believe 'that if the Leicestershire scheme were decided upon it could be implemented in a comparatively short period of time'.[18] But as Clegg explained in reply,

> The recent delay in the development of secondary education in the Hemsworth Division is due to one thing and one thing alone and that is the failure of the Ministry of Education, despite all the efforts of the County Education Committee, to sanction the building of the necessary new schools ... The Authority is only too anxious to build these schools but ... despite the most vigorous protests by the Education Committee the Ministry has simply not sanctioned the schools which are so badly needed.[19]

The difficulties were becoming almost insuperable. Clegg was being pressed by his Divisional Executive to force through a scheme of comprehensive schooling, yet the building limitations restricted the feasible proposals to a junior high school scheme only. Furthermore, while the scattered provision of small secondary schools certainly prevented 11–18 schools being established, the poor physical condition of many school buildings meant that virtually *any* scheme, including one involving junior high schools, would entail considerable expenditure which the Ministry would not be prepared to sanction.

In large part, it was this highly restrictive set of conditions which first pushed Clegg into raising the middle school idea with the Ministry in May 1963, naming Hemsworth as one of two possible areas where such a plan might be implemented. For as Clegg later confided to Councillor Palmer in March 1964, 'It is more likely that we shall be able to use and adapt existing premises if we can have 9–13 schools than if we have to make the transfer at 14'.[20] Certainly, figures for Hemsworth's new middle school scheme presented to the Ministry in October 1964 did not appear to exceed those already agreed for its junior high school predecessor.[21] Moreover, the middle school alternative would allow reorganization throughout a larger area of Hemsworth than would have been the case had the junior high school scheme been adopted.[22] Though Clegg would later question the fact,[23] it appears that in this area at least — one of the very first in which middle schools were established — such schools offered an even more expedient solution to going comprehensive than did junior highs.

To sum up: it was the 'roofs over heads' problem which was very much responsible for both the creation and the baulking of the junior high school proposal in the West Riding; a process which eventually left the space in which the middle school alternative could emerge. The rise and demise of junior highs was in this sense affected by two sets of pressures and conditions — the growing demand in certain areas for reorganization of education at the *secondary* level and the restrictive conditions of limited state expenditure, of administrative convenience, in which this was to be achieved. We shall see in the next chapter that this is not the whole story; that other factors accounted for the shifting fortunes of the junior high school idea also. But the priority attached to educational reform at the *secondary* level, and the limiting conditions of administrative convenience certainly exerted a powerful influence on this forerunner of the middle school.

Middle Schools First Emerge

Middle schools emerged as a second line of attack upon the problem of implementing schemes of comprehensive reorganization in administratively and economically difficult circumstances. The first thrust had been made by the junior high school movement but this had been well parried by the Ministry. That the Ministry was reluctant to accept schemes of this type was indicated not only by their repeated refusal to include the submissions of the Hemsworth Division for new school buildings in their annual building programme but also by some comments that Clegg made in a letter to L. R. Fletcher, Under Secretary at the Schools Branch of the Ministry. The letter was concerned with the question of reorganization in the Castleford district of the West Riding which like Hemsworth, had proposed a system based on junior high schools. Clegg wrote

> The Castleford scheme that is before you assumes that the children will go to the Junior High School at the normal age and will stay there for three years, which is similar to what happens in Leicestershire, with the exception that we don't like the accelerated stream being written into our arrangements, and, furthermore, we would hope that everybody would spend some time in the Senior High School. *I am aware, of course, from what you and Morrell said on Monday that you don't think much of this* . . .[24] (my emphasis)

With the baulking of the junior high school scheme, itself a hard-fought pragmatic compromise, the existing framework of possible solutions now seemed exhausted. By May 1963 the difficulties encountered by the West Riding in devizing particular schemes of reorganization and getting them accepted were becoming so acute that some new initiative was obviously required. As the writer of a retrospective tribute to Sir Alec Clegg put it: 'It was at this point that the Clegg genius most clearly manifested itself ,[25] in the form of a proposal that transfer should occur at 9 and 13, rather than 11. Clegg's originality in 'inventing' this proposal has almost certainly been exaggerated.[26] But it *was* he who first raised the matter explicitly with the Ministry. In a letter to Fletcher, dated 3 May 1963, Clegg advanced various reasons as to why a change in the age of transfer might be a good idea. His suggestions, he appreciated, were somewhat tentative, and he stressed that he was 'merely flying a kite'. Yet this was more than idle speculation on his part. It amounted, rather, to a delicate sounding out of Ministerial opinion about schemes involving a change in the age of transfer to see 'if there is even a remote chance of getting it accepted if we put it forward officially'.[27]

One of the most crucial decisions Clegg then took was to publish and publicize a document in May 1963, presenting the arguments for middle schools. This document was not only circulated within the county but also sent to officials at the Ministry, to other CEOs and to the national press. It was a highly influential piece of writing. Interestingly, in its very first paragraph, this document advocated middle schools on the grounds of administrative expediency:

> This report has been written to meet the demands of a number of Divisions in the Riding which have asked for Comprehensive education but cannot have it in large schools for children of 11–18 because there already exists in these areas a number of smaller schools which cannot be easily extended, which are unsuitable as Primary Schools, and which are so sound that they will have to continue in use for the foreseeable future. (WRYECR, 1963, p. 1)

The proclaimed purpose of this report was to place pressure on the Government and bring about a change in the law regarding the age of transfer, so as to allow schemes of reorganization based on 5–9, 9–13, 13–18 principles. In the report's own rather blunt words, 'This law is obviously so peculiar that the scheme is put forward in defiance of it in order that the Minister may be pressed to consider the issues involved'. (*ibid*, p. 2)

During 1963, even as he was preparing this report, pressures were increasingly being placed on Clegg from all sides to devize a speedy and satisfactory solution to the problem of secondary reorganization in some West Riding divisions. In Hemsworth, it will be recalled, there was mounting frustration about the delay in getting a junior high school scheme accepted. Meanwhile, in Castleford, where reorganization plans had first been approved at divisional level in 1962, public criticism was growing into a simmering pot of local discontent. The negotiations that took place between Clegg, the Ministry and the Castleford Divisional Executive were of such significance here, that much of the history of the 1964 Education Act (which legalized a change in the age of transfer) can be accounted for in terms of them.

The time between the late months of 1963 and the passing of the 1964 Act was one where Clegg attempted to broaden the base of support for the middle school idea among civil servants at the Ministry and to persuade them to get the Minister to make the necessary political moves. Castleford was his most pressing concern here. Like Hemsworth, its proposal for reorganization on junior high school lines was long-standing. And like Hemsworth, that proposal met with repeated rejection by the Ministry. Clegg wrote a letter to one of Her Majesty's Inspectorate at the Ministry proclaiming that he was at his 'wits end about Castleford'.[28] Local reaction was building up to an uncomfortable level, yet Clegg could only report to them that there was 'complete lack of progress of any kind'. 'The local folk', Clegg pointed out, were 'getting restive and critical'. A postscript to this letter reveals that Clegg's complaints did not entirely fall on deaf ears and that already there was some sympathy for his middle school proposal at the Ministry. Clegg wrote, 'I realize, of course, that *it was your hope* that we might do something on the 9–13 lines here and we have a resolution from Normanton asking for this. But where do we go from here?' (my emphasis).

A few weeks later, these rhetorical cries of desperation were translated into specific proposals for change, when Clegg wrote to Fletcher detailing how a middle school scheme might be implemented in Castleford. Once again, he stressed the urgency of a solution because he was 'subject to very severe pressure' and he emphasized the fact that reorganization on these lines could be achieved 'in the existing buildings'. [29] Fletcher then passed the letter on to Miss Small at the Schools Branch of the Ministry who gave Clegg the opportunity to document the economic and administrative advantages of the 9–13 scheme over its junior high school predecessor in Castleford, when she asked him how the junior high school places would be distributed if 9–13 schools eventually became possible on the one hand, and if they did not on the other.[30] Clegg replied:

> May I emphasize that, if approval were to be given to our present suggestions, all these developments could take place without the provision of major new building, whereas the solution described in the Public Notices (of junior high schools) referred to the future and depended on new buildings being provided.[31]

In a further letter, Clegg went on to ask Miss Small if she 'could indicate whether, in the view of the Ministry, the Authority's proposal would be strengthened by substituting the age of 13 for that of 14'.[32] While awaiting her reply he continued to press his case on other fronts. Just before the New Year, for example, he wrote an important letter to Fletcher enclosing details of the new middle school scheme for Castleford.[33] He stressed the importance of reorganization in that division and pleaded for a 'divine Dispensation' so that reorganization could occur 'according to the attached schedule'. He then implored Fletcher 'Could you not wrestle with your conscience and persuade the Minister to wrestle with his?'

A month later, a reply from the Ministry must have given some encouragement. Miss Small was now able to say that 'The revised proposal which you have under consideration, with transfer at 13 instead of 14 . . . seems to us in some respects an improvement on previous proposals',[34] though she also appended a dampening reminder that 'so far as the proposal for a 9–13 school is concerned, you are aware of our views that such a proposal is illegal at present'.

Clegg was undeterred. His representations to the Ministry had met with some success, however limited, and they had also secured for him some allies at the national level. Even if the middle school proposal was against the law, Miss Small's reply hinted that this situation might only be temporary. It was, as she put it, illegal *at present*.

The debate was now being switched to the national level. And while other LEAs such as Worcestershire (Droitwich Working Party, 1969; Marsh, 1980), Hull (Gorwood, 1978), Wallasey (Davies, 1973; Bryan, 1980), Bradford and Kent (David, 1977) were making similar, if less persistent, representations to the Ministry during this period too, the influence of the West Riding, and in particular of Clegg's emphasis on the economic and administrative advantages of 9–13 schemes even over their 11–14 Leicestershire-like competitors, appears to have been crucial. Such arguments, as we have seen, were dominant in his presentation of the Castleford case, and the Hemsworth case too. Moreover, they figured prominently in the West Riding document, *The Organisation of Education in Certain Areas of the West Riding* which was given such a wide circulation.

These points about the economic and administrative advantages of 9–13 schools as against their junior high school counterparts cannot be stressed firmly enough for they run directly counter to claims and protestations which Clegg has frequently made elsewhere that 9–13 schools were actually *less* expedient than junior highs and were therefore selected on purely educational grounds. For instance, in a retort to an argument made by Young and Armstrong (1964) that the break at 13+ had been falsely presented by the West Riding as a natural rather than an administratively expedient one, Clegg asserted that

> 14 is the obviously convenient date administratively for the transfer. If you change at 14, it works; your modern schools become high schools. But I know how in 1926 we chose 11 because we had to have senior schools of 3 years' duration and 14 minus 3 equals 11. So I determined I would go for the educational issue and not the administrative one.[35]

And in a letter to Tyrell Burgess, then Assistant Editor of *New Society*, Clegg, after outlining some of the educational arguments for middle schools, went on

> But, and it is a very big but — if you break at 14, those above fit into the grammar schools and those below into the modern. So once again, what is administratively convenient is not educationally sound . . . . I'll bet we all fall for 14 — it's so much easier. But I am not prepared to delude myself that it is right.[36]

These claims are not supported by the evidence available in Clegg's correspondence to the Ministry and to members of his own Authority. One reason that might be offered to explain this discrepancy might be that Castleford and Hemsworth were somehow exceptions — that junior highs were indeed more expedient than middle schools elsewhere but not in these two particular divisions. However, if these two divisions are exceptions, they are extremely important ones, being instrumental in raising the middle school debate from the local to the national level.

A second explanation for the discrepancy is that the economic advantages of the middle schools might have been purported, not real. Desperate to push through schemes of secondary reorganization in divisions like Castleford and Hemsworth and frustrated by the Ministry's reluctance to approve junior high school schemes, Clegg may have felt justified in playing up and perhaps even exaggerating the economic advantages of middle schools to cost-conscious political and administrative audiences he knew would be sympathetic. On the evidence available, it is impossible to judge whether he was indeed as Machiavellian as this.[37] But whether he was or not, the arguments do appear to have swayed policy makers at the national level towards a guarded acceptance of the middle school idea.

The result of all this pressure and influence was that during the summer of 1964, the Minister of Education, Sir Edward Boyle, when on a visit to the Don Valley, informed the Chairman of the West Riding Education Committee, C.T. Broughton, that an Act of Parliament would be passed to allow schemes of the kind that the West Riding and a small number of other LEAs were then proposing (Sharp, 1980). In Boyle's own words:

> It became perfectly clear that we would have to have some changes in the law and allow middle schools . . . In fact, as soon as the 1964 election was announced, I got on to the Prime Minister and asked if we could please have that Bill which would legalize middle schools. (quoted in Kogan and Van der Eycken, 1974, p. 78)

Shortly afterwards, the 1964 Education Act — what Boyle called his 'parting gift' to the Ministry — was passed.[38] This raised restrictions on the age of transfer and allowed a small number of middle schools to be established as a 'limited experiment' (Edwards, 1972). In the words of one commentator, although middle schools had not been *strongly* advocated at the national level, they had at least now 'received an amber, if not yet a green light'. (Burrows, 1978, p. 38)

Middle schools had now been elevated to national importance. They were no longer the mere parochial concern of one or two isolated LEAs. Yet it was the negotiations conducted by the Chief Education Officer of one of those LEAs — the West Riding — on behalf of one or two of his divisions which led to such an elevation. In these negotiations, the matter of *secondary* school reorganization was the most pressing and urgent concern. And here, a vital consideration was the weight given to *economic and administrative factors* in evaluating middle schools against other schemes of secondary reorganization. Thus, the 1964 Education Act which marks the beginning of national policy on middle schools can be seen as the result of more localized pressures and processes to do with secondary reorganization where administrative and economic considerations played a very great part.[39]

Acceptance to Promotion — Advances Through Circulars

Although, with the passing of the 1964 Education Act, middle schools had now been legalized, no specific schemes of reorganization involving such schools had yet been approved. With the advent of a Labour Government in 1964, along with its manifesto commitment to comprehensive schooling and its recognition embodied in a House of Commons motion in January 1965, that 'the method and timing of such reorganization should vary to meet local needs', there was good reason for pro-middle school LEAs to press the Ministry for an extension of this 'experiment'. With such an end in view, Alec Clegg sought permission from the newly-created Department of Education and Science to send a deputation to see the new Minister, Mr Reg Prentice.[40] Clegg was anxious to discover 'what is meant by experiment in the context of the 1964 Education Act' and therefore asked his deputation to 'sound the Minister as to what he is prepared to permit in other areas' where only three-tier schemes were feasible.[41] Before the meeting took place, Clegg laid some of the groundwork for the discussion by pointing out the main advantages of middle schools in a letter to the Assistant Under-Secretary of State, D.H. Leadbetter. Among these once more was the pragmatic argument about the use of existing buildings. 'If we transfer at 11', Clegg noted, 'we have to make such massive additions to the grammar schools in order to make them accommodate the older children that the cost would be prohibitive'.[42]

Having outlined the by now familiar arguments for a three-tier system of reorganization in some areas, Clegg then proceeded to arm his deputation to Prentice with a set of relevant points on the specific divisions and Excepted Districts where a 9–13 system had been asked for or seemed likely. The Hemsworth case was documented in most detail, though consideration was also given to reorganization in areas such as Shipley, Normanton, Craven, Keighley, the Don Valley, and even Castleford where the Divisional Executive was still holding tenaciously to the 11–14 scheme, but where Clegg still hoped ultimately to bring about his desired changes on middle school lines.[43]

Following the meeting with Prentice on 11 February, Miss Small of the Schools Branch wrote to Clegg informing him that 'we can in principle encourage you to proceed with your proposal for a 5–9, 9–13, 13–18 type of organization in the Hemsworth area'.[44] No decision on reorganization in the other areas mentioned was immediately forthcoming but the promise was made that 'further consideration will be given . . . to the authority's desire to extend the proposed type of organization to other divisions in their areas'. The first specific proposal for a system of middle schools had now been approved, if only in principle.

Creation of space in which further schemes of middle school reorganization could be established was then cautiously sanctioned by the subsequent issue of Circular 10/65 (DES, 1965). In response to the House of Commons' call for a declaration of national policy on secondary education, this Circular requested local authorities to submit plans 'for the reorganization of secondary education in their areas on comprehensive lines' (paragraph 1). The general spirit of the Circular was one of enlightenment and encouragement, but it was also permeated by a sense of administrative constraint and of the local flexibility that would be needed to deal with this. As it stated in paragraph 2, 'the views of individual authorities, the distribution of population and the nature of existing schools will inevitably dictate different solutions in different areas'. In this spirit, the Circular listed middle schools with transfer at either 12 or 13 as one of six possible modes of reorganization which had 'emerged from experience and discussion'. But while it conceded that they had 'an immediate attraction in the context of secondary reorganization' insofar as 'they seem(ed) to lead naturally to the elimination of selection' and to allow 'smaller all-through comprehensive schools' (paragraph 21), it also warned that 'the Secretary of State does not intend to given his statutory approval to more than a very small number of such proposals in the near future' (paragraph 22). Further approval, the Circular stated, would have to await the deliberations of the Advisory Council for Education which was looking into primary education and the advisability of different ages of transfer and which would not produce its final report, the *Plowden Report*, until 1967. Until that time, it stressed, 'the normal age of transfer should be regarded as 14'. (paragraph 30)

Before publication of the Plowden findings, however, the Secretary of State for Education, Anthony Crosland, reported to the House of Commons in April 1966, that 'Our thinking has shifted in the light of experience ... We would be more willing than we were to consider possible 9–13 schemes'.[45] Some advocates of 'grassroots' educational democracy viewed this move as a victory for the power of the LEA periphery against the DES centre (Marsh, 1973; Benn and Simon, 1970). Benn (1973a, p. 294), for instance, argued that 'within a year ... it was so obvious that many authorities wanted to try (middle schools that) ... Anthony Crosland was forced to retreat'. However, as two critics remark, it is difficult to establish what kind of 'experience' the Secretary of State had in mind (Bryan and Hardcastle, 1978), for given the short period of time between Circular 10/65 and the Secretary of State's pronouncement, the opportunities to accumulate such 'experience' then evaluate it could not have been great. Why, then, should there have been such a sudden U-turn in educational policy only one year in advance of the publication of those findings and recommendations of the *Plowden Report* which Crosland had been awaiting so eagerly?

The reason soon became apparent. Shortly after Crosland's statement to the Commons, the raising of the school-leaving age (ROSLA) — planned for 1970 (though not implemented until 1972) — was announced. Crucially, Circular 13/66 which heralded ROSLA also stated that no additional new building projects would be available for this purpose (DES, 1966b). While Circular 10/65 had made it clear that no extra resources were to be made available for the *reorganization* of secondary education, Circular 13/66 now applied such limitations to its *extension*. Because of these tight restrictions, LEAs were therefore given the freedom to change the age of transfer 'if justified by reference to some clear practical advantages in the context of reorganization on comprehensive lines or the raising of the school leaving age, or both' (Circular 13/66, paragraph 4). Emphasizing the twin factors of administrative constraint and local flexibility, the Circular went on,

in some areas, the operation of the raising of the school leaving age can be carried through more easily if it is accompanied by a change in the age of transfer, and a consequent reduction in the age range of the secondary schools which will have to accommodate the extra pupils ... there are urgent practical reasons why a greater degree of flexibility should be allowed now to Authorities. He (the Secretary of State) will therefore regard a change in the age of transfer for the time being as a matter for *local* option, and he is prepared to consider proposals from Authorities on this basis.

As Edwards (1972) has observed, the Government had, for reasons of economic expediency, now put aside its interest in placing a limit on the number of middle school schemes it was prepared to approve. This was confirmed by the subsequent and timely publication of *Building Bulletin 35* (DES, 1966a) very shortly after the issuing of Circular 13/66, which laid down guidelines for the architectural design of middle schools and for the conversion of existing premises to middle school purposes. This Bulletin effectively translated an agreement in principle into the first expression of practical guidance at the national level.

Evidently, then, the impact of economic and administrative considerations in the context of reorganizing *secondary* education was great. The effect of the changed state of affairs wrought by the growth of comprehensivization and in particular of ROSLA was dramatic. It not only allowed existing middle school proposals through the administrative pipeline but also generated new ones. Before the announcement of ROSLA, some LEAs had actually found it *un*economic to reorganize their secondary education on middle school lines. But with the tacking of an extra year group of pupils on to the secondary sector and the need this would generate for even larger 11–18 schools with more and bigger building extensions, some LEAs quickly discovered that the middle school solution might now be economic after all.

In Leeds, for instance, an Education Sub-committee of the Authority published a report in May 1966 (before the announcement of ROSLA), which *rejected* the idea of 9–13 middle schools because 'only a scheme which *made full use of existing and proposed buildings* would be workable educationally and financially' (Leeds City Council Education Committee Reports, 1966 — my emphasis). But by 1967, after Circular 13/66, the Council had revised its position and decided that 'all county schools should be reorganized as first, middle and upper schools' with transfer ages at either 8 and 12 or 9 and 13 (Leeds City Council Education Committee Reports, 1969). Similar switches occurred elsewhere such as in Oxford (Pritchard, 1977). Thus, the raising of the school leaving age and the administrative problems it created for secondary reorganization was a critical element in precipitating broad national endorsement of middle schools.

Overall, then, there is some justification for concurring with Sharp (1980) when he argues that comprehensive education might never have emerged in the late 1960s and early 1970s had it not been for the administrative advantages of middle schools. In other words, not only was the movement for comprehensive schooling a necessary condition for the emergence of middle schools, but, given their administrative advantages, middle schools in turn acted as important facilitators of comprehensive reorganization too.

Conclusion: The Scope of Convenience

Middle schools were, to a large extent, a direct result of comprehensive reorganization at the secondary level under conditions of severe economic stringency. They were an administrative convenience, 'created for the best of all educational reasons — because they were cheap' (Doe, 1976, p. 22) Middle schools enabled many LEA's to squeeze comprehensive reorganization into their existing stock of rather small school buildings, unwillingly inherited from the tripartite era.

Elsewhere, Marsh (1980) has recorded how middle schools were established in rural Worcestershire to avoid the problems of very large comprehensive schools (with the high costs of building and transportation these would involve) and very small ones too (given their inevitably restricted range of curricular choice). And other local studies of middle school reorganization, such as those of West Suffolk (Bornett, 1976), Hull (Gorwood, 1978), Wallasey and Chester (Bryan, 1980), have highlighted similar effects of administrative expediency elsewhere. More generally, Edwards (1972, pp. 64–5) has asserted that the middle school was surreptitiously sponsored by the Department of Education around the time of the Education Act in 1964

> since it was seen as a useful experiment which would be an economic method of going comprehensive and which would also relieve considerably the pressures on secondary school accommodation which would follow the projected raising of the school leaving age.

Other critics have also concluded that the middle school was determined *primarily* by the forces of pragmatism and expediency (for example, Holness, 1973; Bryan and Hardcastle, 1977). Nor have these observations and criticisms been confined to academic commentary. The teacher unions have complained about the influence of administrative convenience on the middle school's development too. (National Union of Teachers, 1969; Assistant Masters' Association, 1976)

Important though all these findings and criticisms are, it is not really sufficient merely to dismiss middle schools as an administrative convenience and let the matter rest there. For one thing it is unjust to single out middle schools for special criticism since economic expediency has been a dominant and widespread feature of educational reform in British society as a whole. Each phase of educational change has, under conditions of limited state expenditure, been restricted by the one which preceded it. Thus, after the 1944 Education Act, secondary reorganization consolidated a pattern of educational provision that had already been emerging during the 1930s. The tripartite system merely built upon processes that had already been accruing at local level (Fenwick, 1976). So firmly established had this tripartite system become through the piecemeal initiatives of individual LEAs in the inter-war period, that it was sufficient to deter the post-war Labour Education Minister, Ellen Wilkinson, from seriously entertaining any notions of comprehensive schooling. (Bellaby, 1977)

Once the Labour Government had chosen or been constrained not to attack tripartism, it then left itself a further legacy which made future reform of secondary education even more problematic (Marsden, 1971, p. 113).[48] The investment in a post-war school building programme that effectively consolidated the tripartite system meant that the eventual introduction of comprehensive schooling was delayed and that when it did come to be considered, the existing material resources proved a major obstacle to its implementation. A few new comprehensive schools *were* established in early post-war years, but these were either in areas of expanding population such as large new council estates, where new school building would be required anyway and where no existing grammar schools would be threatened with replacement (Benn and Simon, 1970); or in sparsely populated rural districts like Windermere, Anglesey and the Isle of Man where selective grammar schools would have entailed the drawing of very wide boundaries for the school catchment area, and therefore, a good deal of expense in transporting pupils from home to school and back (Rubinstein and Simon, 1963). The first comprehensive schools were, in this sense, almost entirely pragmatic in origin.

When comprehensive educational reform did get underway on a relatively large scale, the considerations of administrative convenience continued to dominate the patterns of reorganization that were produced in different localities. We have already seen how this was the case with middle schools in many LEAs. But the same principle applied also to the adoption of the Leicestershire Plan (Mason, 1964; Halsall, 1973). And in some areas, like Gateshead, middle schools were actually *rejected* on the grounds of administrative expediency. As the authors of a study of educational policy-making in that borough remark, 'ultimately, the age of transfer was settled on the grounds that only 14+ was possible, given the existing school buildings' (Batley, O'Brien and Parris, 1970, p. 68). Thus, the claim advanced by Clegg and others (for example, Halsall, 1973, p. 193) that 14+ was a more convenient age of transfer than 13+ as far as school buildings were concerned does indeed appear to hold for some LEAs. But clearly, by 1970, the range of comprehensive school provision was not only extensive but also complicated (MacLure, 1984); a result of the practical limitations imposed by existing buildings. (Seaborne and Lowe, 1977, p. 157)

Administrative convenience, then, is not a peculiar characteristic of middle school reform, but a dominant feature of educational policy-making in Britain. This leads to a second point: that even if administrative convenience *is* the main determinant of the establishment of middle schools, this begs further questions about the origins of that convenience in British society.

A central consideration here is a tension in Britain and other Western capitalist democracies between state expenditure having to enhance the process of capital accumulation (economic growth) by creating the social conditions in which it can continue (supplying it with a skilled workforce, an acquiescent citizenry and so on) while having to deduct this very expenditure from capitalist revenue, from the very thing it is supposed to enhance. It is this that leads to social and educational reform on a shoestring, to the administrative convenience of which middle schools are a product. To criticize administrative convenience in this sense, therefore, is not to criticize the foolishness or deviousness of educational administrators and politicians, but to pass judgment on a deep-seated, structurally generated form of administrative irrationality (Habermas, 1976) within British society as a whole.

However — and this is the third point — the limiting conditions of administrative convenience do not give a complete explanation of the determinants of educational reform in general or of the establishment of English middle schools in particular. It may be that the structural looseness of the English educational system accords LEAs a helpful degree of flexibility and autonomy in devizing administratively expedient ways of going comprehensive which suit the idiosyncratic inheritance of school buildings in each locality. And that combination of structural looseness, administrative convenience and the historical inheritance of the tripartite system does indeed help explain why middle schools were adopted as the solution to secondary school reform in some areas (for example, certain parts of the West Riding) and rejected in others (for example, Gateshead).

But not all the variation can be explained in these terms. Some West Riding divisions actually rejected the middle school solution even though it appeared the most expedient one for them. Nor can the ditching of the junior high school scheme by that LEA be explained entirely in economic terms either. The economic differences between junior high school schemes and middle school ones do not appear to have been all that great, and often, where junior high schools *were* rejected, other influences appear to have been at least as important.

It is by considering these discrepancies, the cases that do *not* conveniently fit the administrative expediency argument that another aspect of structurally loose educational systems is highlighted — the difficulty, as Bidwell (1965) pointed out, of coordinating policy between the different parts. Within such systems there is certainly room for flexibility, but there is also space for conflicts and differences of opinion over policy and for the pursuit of different goals, as well as a host of other problems that bedevil administratively complex systems, such as problems of timing, misunderstanding, breakdowns in communication and so on. The next chapter examines some of these differences and variations. It analyzes the different goals which people pursued in relation to middle schools and to the junior high schools which preceded them. It examines the different perspectives of comprehensive schooling in general that people held in different localities, and assesses the impact of these perspectives on their attitudes to middle schools and junior highs in particular. Thus, having studied the *direct* effects of secondary reorganization on the development of middle schools in this chapter, the next chapter looks at some of the more indirect effects of that powerful educational movement.

Notes

1   The exceptions to this rule were, of course, the direct grant schools.
2   Memorandum: 'The request for comprehensive schools or a comprehensive scheme of education: Ecclesfield area', presented to the Policy and Finance Sub-committee, 9 December 1958.

3 The West Riding encompassed districts as different as rural Settle on the one hand and the mining town of Mexborough on the other.

4 'The request for comprehensive schools or a comprehensive scheme of education: Ecclesfield area', *op. cit.*

5 Memorandum: 'The organization of secondary education in the West Riding', presented to the Policy and Finance Sub-committee, 9 December 1959.

6 Letter to MASON, 24 June 1959.

7 In that sense, by illustrating a diversity of outcomes in relation to a single policy initiative, these three cases have been specifically selected as a challenge to and aid to developing theories of educational policy formation.

8 'The request for comprehensive schools or a comprehensive scheme of education: Ecclesfield area', *op. cit.*

9 Letter from CLEGG to Mr STOCKDALE, Divisional Education Officer for Mexborough, 21 September 1959.

10 *Ibid.*

11 Letter to Mr COCKELL, Divisional Education Officer for Hemsworth, 19 June 1959.

12 Further letter to Mr COCKELL, 22 September 1959.

13 Internal memorandum to CLEGG, 'Organization of secondary education: Hemsworth division', 11 February 1960.

14 Letter from Mr THORPE, Divisional Education Officer for Hemsworth, to West Riding Education Committee, 10 April 1963.

15 Memorandum: 'Hemsworth Division — organization of secondary education' presented to the Policy and Finance Sub-committee, 8 March 1960.

16 All these details of this policy proposal for Hemsworth are contained in 'Hemsworth Division — organization of secondary education', *ibid.*

17 Letter to Councillor KENNINGHAM, 16 May 1962.

18 Letter from Mr THORPE, Hemsworth Divisional Education Officer, to CLEGG, 13 September 1963.

19 Letter to Mr THORPE, 16 September 1963.

20 Letter to Councillor PALMER, 4 March 1964.

21 As CLEGG recorded in a memorandum to the Policy and Finance Sub-committee, 13 October 1964:

> The future organization of the Hemsworth division was under discussion at the time the Department of Education and Science was compiling the 1966/67 (Building) Programme and for this reason a specific project could not be included for Hemsworth ...
>
> Some new secondary provision for Hemsworth was however included on the understanding that whatever projects the Authority did put forward (for example for middle schools) ... would be financially comparable to the proposals for (junior high) schools already made.

22 *Ibid.*

23 As in the second West Riding published document presenting the case for middle schools (WRYECR, 1965).

24 Letter to FLETCHER, 15 May 1963.

25 In the last issue of the West Riding *Schools' Bulletin*, March 1974.

26 While CLEGG was clearly pressing the middle school idea very hard with the Ministry, some correspondence of his with a CEO in Southend-on-Sea, D.B. BARTLETT, suggests that the idea of middle schools as such was not entirely his own. It read:

> Some time ago you made some bright suggestions to me about change of dates (of transfer — A.H.); I cannot think what they were, but I am pretty sure they were something to do with this report. I told you that once I got a good idea I churned it over and turned it out as my own, and you will probably find that this is it. (Letter to Bartlett, 1 October 1963)

27 Letter to FLETCHER, 3 May 1963.
28 Letter to Mr HAYTER, 12 September 1963.
29 Letter to FLETCHER, 31 October 1963.
30 Letter from Miss SMALL to CLEGG, 11 November 1963.
31 Letter to Miss SMALL, 26 November 1963.
32 Letter to Miss SMALL, 16 December 1963.
33 Letter to FLETCHER, 30 December 1963.
34 Letter from Miss SMALL to CLEGG, 29 January 1964.
35 Letter to YOUNG, 25 November 1963.
36 Letter to BURGESS, 11 December 1963.
37 What would be needed here would be a detailed analysis of submissions made to the Ministry for capital expenditure under the School Building Programme which compared those made for junior high and middle school systems respectively, and which did this in relation to detailed local knowledge of the actual buildings available and their condition at the time. No such data were available to me.
38 Quoted in KOGAN and VAN DER EYCKEN (1974, p. 78).
39 It is ironic, perhaps, that the division which was probably more influential than any other in precipitating the 1964 Act — Castleford — should later choose to *reject* the middle school solution which had been proposed for it and, to the West Riding's and CLEGG's embarrassment, cling stubbornly for some time to the earlier solution of junior and senior high schools.
40 This permission was granted in January 1965.
41 Memorandum: 'Comprehensive schools', presented to the Policy and Finance Sub-committee, 21 January 1965.
42 Letter to LEADBETTER, 12 January 1965.
43 The cases were outlined in notes distributed under the title of 'Reorganization of Education' to members of the deputation on 9 February 1965.
44 Letter from Miss SMALL to CLEGG, 25 February 1965.
45 *Hansard*, Vol. 727, 25 April 1966, p. 494.

Chapter 3

Egalitarianism, Meritocracy and Social Unity

To the extent that the English middle school was chiefly a product of comprehensive reorganization, many of its main difficulties and uncertainties about identity and direction have arisen from the fact that there was, at the time, no clear definition of or agreement about the comprehensive principle or the comprehensive ideal. Though many advocates and critics of comprehensive schooling have written as if there were such a thing, in practice, their statements of principle were so broad, so general, as to be virtually meaningless. Claims of the kind made by Daunt (1975, p. 16), that a comprehensive education should be one where 'the education of all children is held to be intrinsically of equal value' bore all the hallmarks of uncontentious missionary work, of people seeking to secure the largest possible number of converts to their cause by enunciating high-minded principles devoid of any detail that might occasion unhelpful disagreement.

Such vagueness and vacuity was perhaps unavoidable, for in practice, the nature and purpose of comprehensive schooling has been widely, strongly and sometimes bitterly disputed. Historically, people have argued and fought for comprehensive schooling for very different reasons. Sometimes these arguments have been opposed to one another and given rise to substantial conflicts over the direction of educational policy. On other occasions, the various justifications have been blended together by professional teachers, administrators and politicians into powerful statements of policy which have offered most pressure groups some part or purpose of comprehensive schooling to suit their interests. The very diversity of justifications here has often given comprehensive reorganization the appearance of being virtually all things to everyone. As Reynolds and Sullivan (1981, p. 122) put it, by 1964

> there was what can only be labelled as coincidental support for comprehensive reorganization from many groups. For the working class, reorganization offered the prospects of upward social mobility. For the 'new' middle class, caught vulnerably between the capitalist class and the working class, the expansion of education was a kind of insurance policy that could preserve them and their children as employed in the burgeoning empire of Welfare State provision ... For the traditional middle class denied

grammar school places by the population bulge, for the capitalist class seeking to maximise profit potential by utilization of the new technologies — for all these groups, comprehensive education had much to offer and much to promise.

Although Reynolds and Sullivan's account is a little too exclusively class-bound — for there were surely professional, administrative and political interests at stake in comprehensive reform, as well as class ones — their historical interpretation does give a good sense of the diversity of groups who supported comprehensive reorganization and of the range of arguments on which they drew to promote their cause. But more than this, whether the different definitions of comprehensive schooling were competitive or complementary — these very differences tell us that one cannot properly speak of one comprehensive principle or ideal but only of many.

Disentangling these various principles from one another is not an easy task. As Ball (1981, p. 10) remarks, 'most comprehensive schools would undoubtedly demonstrate a mixture of these philosophies, if only at the ideological level'. And the same applies in the grand arena of policy debate at local and national levels too. The arguments about comprehensive schooling here are not always locked into tightly insulated and immediately recognizable compartments. They interweave and overlap in quite complicated ways and in the writings of the shrewdest educational reformers, they are not simply added together but carefully synthesized with persuasive skill. Nonetheless, particular strands of justification for the comprehensive school, along with the groups who tend to support them or at which those justifications are directed, can be identified. Marsden (1971) identifies three types of justification, those concerned with meritocratic, social engineering and community aims for the school. Bellaby (1977) speaks of educational, egalitarian and communitarian arguments. Ball (1981) picks out meritocratic (equality of opportunity), integrative (social engineering) and egalitarian models as being the dominant ones. And Shaw (1983), again working with the magic number *three*, identifies comprehensive principles organized around the ideas of equality of opportunity, equal value and social unity.

These typologies are remarkably similar. The egalitarian model recurs a lot and is strongly represented in Shaw's category (derived from Daunt) of equal value. Similarly Bellaby's 'educational' category conforms very closely to the meritocratic model with its emphasis on equality of opportunity. And there are strong overlaps too between the communitarian, integrative and social unity models as identified by Bellaby, Ball and Shaw respectively. So strong are the similarities between these definitions, in fact, that in this case I am inclined to the view that a rose by any other name is just as sweet. For that reason, I shall adopt two of the most commonly used definitions of comprehensive schooling — the egalitarian and meritocratic ones — and add to these Shaw's model of social unity, since this captures more completely than the integrative and communitarian models both the radical (i.e. community-centred) and conservative (i.e. order-directed) aspects of the arguments that are contained therein.

This chapter assesses which sets of arguments for comprehensive schooling — those based on egalitarianism, meritocracy or social unity — were most prominent in discussions which surrounded the establishment of middle schools, and the promotion and subsequent rejection of the junior high school proposal which preceded them. With which model or models of comprehensive schooling, that is, were middle schools regarded as being compatible? And to what extent were the ultimately unfavoured junior high schools felt to be unsuited to closely cherished comprehensive ideals?

Egalitarianism

It has often been said that comprehensive schools were politically inspired by the Labour Party, which sought to improve and even equalize opportunities for the children of its working class supporters. Indeed, whether viewed critically from the right (Szamuely, 1971; and, arguably, Shaw, 1983) or admiringly from the left (Parkinson, 1970; Finch, 1984), comprehensive schooling has often been seen as inextricably connected to the pursuit of egalitarianism and the fulfilment of the educational needs and demands of the working class. Thus, Shaw (1983, p. 23) states that 'it is . . . not surprising to find comprehensive reformers to be Marxists and socialists'. While, from the other side, as it were, Parkinson (1970, p. 70) claims that 'the original dynamic force in the demand for these schools was a concern for social justice and the problems of the socially and educationally deprived child' and that the Labour Party 'has primarily been interested in comprehensive education for its impact on the social class structure'.

This conception of the 'popular' character of comprehensive education has not gone uncontested. A number of Marxist writers have put forward the contrary view that the movement towards comprehensive schooling was largely *unpopular* in its orientation and implications. At the time Anthony Crosland — one of Labour's most influential promoters of comprehensive schooling — was writing in the early 1960s, they say, 'there were . . . few signs of distinctively working class claims upon education' (CCCS, 1981, p. 111). The Labour Party's failure to go for comprehensive reorganization in the immediate post-war period (Barker, 1972; Marsden, 1971, p. 112); the fact that some of the first comprehensive schools were not established to further broad political ends at all, but merely for reasons of convenience in rural districts with large catchment areas (Rubinstein and Simon, 1963); the increasing anxiety among some middle class parents that their children might be eternally condemned to educational and occupational failure if they failed the 11 + (Ford, 1969; Griffiths, 1971); and the astuteness of the Labour Party in responding to these concerns among this new section of potential supporters (Bellaby, 1977) — these were all indicators of the way in which comprehensive schooling ironically marked the Labour Party's betrayal of working class interests and its defection to middle class concerns. In fact, Marxist writers have claimed, the distinguishing features of Labour Party policy concerning comprehensive reorganization were 'its middle class character, the absence of a real popular and especially working class connection, the failure to speak directly to women and the limits of a politics of access' (CCCS, 1981, p. 165).

While there is something in these counter claims about the middle class appeal of comprehensive schooling, they are almost certainly overstated. The evidence for any intensification of lower middle class support for comprehensive schooling is rather thin. We do know from Bryan's (1980) analysis of reorganization in Wallasey that the first moves there were made by the local Ratepayers Association in New Brighton — a solidly middle class organization if ever there was one. But we are not told from what section of the middle class these ratepayers were drawn. This is important, for Pedley (1969, p. 61ff) contends that those pressure groups most closely associated with the cause of comprehensive education, like the Confederation for the Advancement of State Education (CASE) and also the Comprehensive Schools' Committee, had their roots not in the lower levels of the new middle class, but in its professional and academic layers.

More than this, what evidence there is suggests that, if anything, middle class pressure was more vociferously slanted in favour of the grammar schools (Batley, O'Brien and Parris, 1970; Fenwick, 1976; Marsden, 1971). As the Chief Education Officer of one borough in the 1960s expressed it, 'There were parents' pressure groups at the time the Council was going forward with a more rapid scheme for comprehensive reorganization'. But, she continued, 'The pressure from that group was to retain grammar schools'.[1] And in the West Riding, one of the most notable pressure groups was the parents and friends of the selective girl's high school in Bately who convinced the Minister that reorganization of the girls high school while Bately Grammar School for Boys — a direct grant school — remained in existence, amounted to a flagrant breach of equal opportunities between the sexes.

Whether or not there were any substantial changes in middle class attitudes towards state education during the 1950s and 1960s is therefore a moot point, but the more important issue is that the Parliamentary Labour Party clearly felt that such shifts *were* underway, and therefore began to gravitate more towards middle class concerns, a movement that was reflected in the overall cast of its educational policies. Grassroots feeling on comprehensive education among local Labour Party members was sometimes of a rather different kind — a point that is easily missed if attention is focussed exclusively on national policy. Writers like Simon (1974), for instance, have pointed to the existence of a long if intermittent tradition of radical support for comprehensive or 'common' schooling among trade unions, local Labour groups and so on, which stretches back before the war right through to the nineteenth century. In the Mexborough division of the West Riding, for instance, councillors rejected a junior high school scheme with transfer at 14 because it was not 'full-blooded' comprehensivism.[2]

This antipathy to the non-egalitarian, selective slant of Leicestershire Plan-type schemes was also a feature of Clegg's initial reactions to such proposals. In a memorandum to the Education Committee in 1959, he expressed disapproval of the practice in the Leicestershire scheme of selecting out the top 10 per cent of each age group and giving them express progress into the senior secondary school.[3] A 'more leisurely pace' of education, he indicated, might be appropriate for *all* children.

Moreover, he worried about those children who did not transfer from the junior high school at age 14 and who would therefore be left behind as a 'truncated group'. When middle schools were first aired publicly by the West Riding in its document, *The Organisation of Education in Certain Areas in the West Riding*, Clegg, in the second paragraph, compared the proposed middle schools with their nearest competitor, the Leicestershire Plan, thus:

> The proposals put forward are similar to those adopted by Leicestershire, but the Leicestershire scheme did not arise from a demand for comprehensive education, and its accelerated course for the brighter and younger children and its division of pupils by the same age between grammar and high schools at the age of 14 would not be accepted in the Riding as consistent with the comprehensive idea. (WRYECR, 1963, p. 1)

These are sound egalitarian objections. But, it should be pointed out, they apply only to the Leicestershire Plan in its 'pure' form. It is therefore rather curious that Clegg should still be advancing them as late as 1963, for as the previous chapter indicated, the junior high school schemes that had been proposed for divisions like Hemsworth and Castleford assumed that *all* children would transfer at 14 and that *no* express arrangements would operate. In other words, all the egalitarian objections to the original Leicestershire Plan could be and had been accommodated *without* rejecting the idea of transfer at 11 and 14. If we are looking for reasons why middle schools came to be preferred to junior highs, then, they cannot be found here. Egalitarian objections to the junior high school idea may have assisted the task of public persuasion but they do not explain why policy preferences should have shifted from 14 to 13 as the desired age of transfer.

At the national level, egalitarian arguments were largely absent from discussions of the advantages and disadvantages of three-tier schemes. Only Circular 10/65 gave the faintest hint of egalitarian sentiments when it argued that middle schools 'seem to lead naturally to the elimination of selection' (DES, 1965, paragraph 21). But even this was mistaken, as a number of LEAs — most notably Norwich and Buckinghamshire — went on to establish 8–12 middle schools within selective systems.

While the egalitarian model of comprehensive schooling was prominent in certain mining districts of the West Riding, and therefore possibly also in other particularly solid working class communities like them, it did not usually figure largely in general statements about middle schools (or comprehensive schools in general) at county level and above. Indeed, some parts of the West Riding's first public document promoting middle schools were distinctly anti-egalitarian in tone. In two paragraphs, for instance, it assumed very different destinies for boys and girls respectively on leaving school, objecting to 11–18 schools where it was possible 'to teach men liable to national service and women likely to marry, with children of 10 +' (paragraph 9.4; also paragraph 5). Moreover, support for transfer at 13 was also gained by associating that practice with the distinctly non-egalitarian private school sector where transfer at that age was commonplace. This was no idle comparison. The government in power at the time was not only a Conservative one, but 87 per cent of its Cabinet had received a public school education (Glennester and Pryke, 1973). Although this unexpected act of flattery was never directly reciprocated by the independent sector — indeed, the Incorporated Association of Preparatory Schools published strong criticisms of their middle school competitors in the state system (Mould, Wickham and Woodcock, 1973) — transfer at 13 in the state system did hold out *one* important attraction for those who subscribed to the independent sector. This was neatly put by the Labour group on an evenly balanced Oxford City Council in 1966 at the time that middle school reorganization was being proposed by the Conservatives there as the most desirable way of going comprehensive. They accused the Conservatives of preferring a system with transfer at 13 mainly on the grounds that it would allow Oxford's more affluent parents to get another two years' respectably free education out of the state system before moving their offspring into the private sector. (Pritchard, 1977, p. 262)[4]

In the West Riding and elsewhere, then, it appears that egalitarian arguments played little part in the establishment of English middle schools, even if their role in the politics of educational decision-making in some localities was more significant than this.

Meritocracy

More crucial for the development of middle schools and for the rejection of some other possible modes of comprehensive reorganization were arguments which stressed the role of the comprehensive school in advancing the cause of meritocracy. The meritocratic model of comprehensive schooling offered 'grammar schools for all' as Harold Wilson once put it.[5] According to this model, comprehensive schools would not abolish educational selection but improve it; they would provide not equality as such but equality of opportunity. In Ball's words, according to the meritocratic model 'the comprehensive school must be evaluated in terms of its ability to maximise its pupils' qualifications' (Ball, 1981, p. 6). In part, this is a matter of achieving social justice for each individual pupil, by realizing his or her potential to the full. But the maximization of talent was also linked to the need to draw on hidden reserves of ability that had thus far remained untapped, in order to fuel economic growth (Newsom, 1963; Robbins, 1963). In this view, comprehensive schooling did not offer a way of substantially modifying the nature of capitalist society (as in the egalitarian model), but promised only to make that system work more efficiently. (Bellaby, 1977)

This justification of comprehensive schools serving not the sectarian interests of any particular class but the general 'national interest' of economic growth was central to Labour's appeal to what it took to be its new, increasingly middle class constituency (CCCS, 1981). And in the West Riding, Alec Clegg was certainly very much aware that such meritocratic arguments provided persuasive support for comprehensive schooling. Perhaps because of his membership of the Crowther Committee who highlighted these issues concerning the national wastage of ability in their report in 1959, Clegg commissioned a survey of the educational opportunities and achievements of secondary school pupils in the North and South of the Riding. Summarizing the findings of the survey, he complained that gifted children in the South Yorkshire Coalfield were achieving well below their potential compared to those in the North and were therefore being placed at a serious educational disadvantage. While this was a clear breach of social justice, Clegg argued that it also represented a wastage of 'good material' (one of Crowther's most celebrated phrases), the consequences of which could be highly damaging to the economy. 'In the last forty years', he argued,

> vast new industries have arisen dealing with plastics, non-ferrous metals, aeronautics, radio, television, not to mention the nationalised industries and the welfare state all of which have to be manned and serviced by people who are much more highly trained than those who manned the nineteenth century economy. In these circumstances, it appears to be the height of national folly to waste ability as we are wasting it in South Yorkshire.[6]

While Clegg's recommendations for policy here involved proposals for changing the nature of the sixth form, his comments which prefaced the report clearly set it in the context of comprehensive reorganization in the South of the Riding. 'In the next few months', he wrote,

> the Committee will be considering the applications from certain areas that comprehensive schools should be established in those areas. It is the purpose of this memorandum to draw attention to certain difficulties which beset the education particularly of gifted children in the coalfield.[7]

These meritocratic aspects of the comprehensive school model — the concern with able pupils, efficient selection and economic growth — played a vital role in the public arguments for middle schools. In particular, the importance of success in secondary school examinations was central to Clegg's thinking. It was one of the main criteria, in fact, according to which he consistently ranked the Leicestershire Plan scheme below the middle school one as a viable mode of secondary reorganization. As Clegg put it in a 1965 reprint of the West Riding's influential document on middle schools, now titled '*The Organization of Comprehensive Schools in Certain Areas of the West Riding*', 'a two-year course to the 'O' level examination, or indeed to any leaving examination, is too short; therefore the break cannot be made at 14' (WRYECR, 1965, p. 4). Earlier, in the 1963 document, Clegg had recommended that 'the Ministry should be approached with a view to establishing secondary schools with a clear run of three years to 'O' level and middle schools . . .' (WRYECR, 1963, p. 15), and indeed, when a county deputation was sent to see Mr Prentice in 1965, this was one of the three main arguments in favour of middle schools which Clegg instructed them to stress.[8]

To be fair, one of the reasons why Clegg wanted the upper school to give children three and not two years' run up to 'O' level was to insulate the middle school from the direct effects of examination pressures; to protect it from having to put on exam-orientated courses in the final year; to enable it, in other words, to maintain more features of the primary school ethos. This justification will be examined more closely in the next chapter. The important thing to note here is that with a Labour government in 1964 whose dominant idea of comprehensiveness was not one of the egalitarian common school but of schools where everyone would be given access to a grammar school education, schemes which maximized the chances of examination success and promoted opportunities for able pupils were very attractive propositions indeed. And for a preceding Conservative government whose support for the idea of comprehensive schooling in general was at best only lukewarm, such schemes — if there had to be any schemes at all — were, if anything, more attractive still. For Alec Clegg, these meritocratic considerations may or may not have been close to his heart but, not least because of his involvement with the Crowther Committee, they were never very far from his head.

Meritocratic arguments were therefore highly influential in shaping preferences for transfer at 13 rather than 14. But such arguments and their effects in leading to the rejection of junior high schemes with transfer at 14 were probably most clear cut, if not exaggerated, in the Ecclesfield sub-division of the West Riding. Here, while junior high schools offered definite administrative advantages in going comprehens-ive, Clegg worried that such schemes did not allow pupils to be prepared sufficiently for external examinations at 16 plus.[9] Moreover, in a letter to the Divisonal Education Officer, Clegg argued that the junior high school proposals for Ecclesfield ignored what he rather misleadingly called the 'purely educational problem'.[10] By this, Clegg meant access to Oxbridge. In the 1950s and 1960s, this was dependent upon an examination qualification in Latin. Continued access to Oxbridge therefore required that

> it will have to be possible for every child of appropriate ability in . . . the Junior High Schools to take Latin, and for that matter a modern foreign language, and science and mathematics from the first year.[11]

To get around this problem, a solution was tentatively advanced for itinerant teachers based in the senior high schools to devote four or five periods a week to teaching in the junior highs. Although Clegg was less than happy about this, he felt constrained into putting it forward because 'We have to face the fact that Oxford and Cambridge demand it (Latin) for all students, and almost every Arts Faculty in every red-brick University also demands it'.[12]

In the event, this arrangement for peripatetic Latin teachers proved too difficult and the junior high school proposal was dropped. Nevertheless, the very reason the scheme was rejected and comprehensive reorganization in Ecclesfield subsequently delayed was because the Divisional Education Committee along with Clegg himself, only wanted a system of comprehensive schooling if it was compatible with efficient grooming of the tiniest proportion of pupils for a privileged Oxbridge education. In Clegg's own words:

> the able child in the South of the Riding is obviously at the present time labouring under a severe handicap. It is important that this handicap should be reduced and not increased by the introduction of a comprehensive scheme.[13]

These sorts of deep reservations about the education of a small secondary school elite helped lay the foundations for the creation of the idea of middle schools — though not, so it turned out, in Ecclesfield itself. Thus, in the case of the Ecclesfield sub-division in particular, and of the arguments that were mounted against the Leicestershire Plan in general, the meritocratic model of comprehensive schooling and its continuing emphasis on external examinations at sixteen plus provided powerful arguments for middle school as against junior high school modes of secondary reorganization.

Social Unity

The movement behind comprehensive schooling was not only concerned from a meritocratic point of view with the creation of equal opportunities in education, but also nurtured the hope, so central to the socialist vision, that such schools, as mixed social communities, would increase tolerance and trust among pupils and break down the barriers of class distinction. Comprehensive schools would in this sense be embryonic versions of the socialist 'good society'. In this society, as Anthony Crosland, one of the most committed advocates of this view, put it: 'the socialist . . . seeks to weaken the existing deep-seated class stratification, with its concomitant feelings of envy and inferiority, and its barriers to uninhibited mingling between the classes'. (Crosland, 1964, p. 77)

In the West Riding, Clegg was certainly opposed to modes of secondary reorganization which prejudiced the maintenance of a viable, stable school community. For this reason he refused to establish split-site schools where the distance between these schools was excessive. Similar concerns were expressed in his opposition to 11–13 schools where all pupils would be either entrants or leavers. And he also held reservations about conventional 11–18 comprehensives because of problems incurred by their 'sheer size' and the fact that they awkwardly juxtaposed children not yet in their teens alongside young adults. (WRYECR, 1963)

In part, these arguments had a genuine community-centred emphasis, encouraging the creation of stable, cooperative and enduring social relationships among secondary school pupils (Daunt, 1975; Hargreaves, D., 1982). But there was also a more pragmatic side to them which would appeal to those who saw the control of pupils as a major problem, and who would want to head off any pattern of school organization which would place that control in jeopardy. The attractions here were connected much less to the ideals of the socialist community than to conservative conceptions of social order.

These more pragmatic, control-centred concerns are evident in the worries which Clegg extracted from the Crowther Report that 'the presence of quite young boys and girls (in 11–18 schools) involves a paternalism in discipline which often spreads upwards to those who do not need it' (WRYECR, 1963, paragraph 9.4). 'Moreover', he continued, betraying an intuitive awareness, perhaps, that many teachers' allegiance to an educational reform can be won if they can be convinced it will ease their problems of classroom discipline,

It is an accepted fact amongst teachers that in any secondary school the first and second year are easy to teach and the 'playing up' does not really start until the third year. Much of the energy that they then display might be turned to good account if children could be moved to a new school at that age. (ibid, paragraph, 9.12)

The Crowther Report's talk of children having 'a second wind at a time when personality changes rapidly and boredom often sets in' was also cited in support of dividing the 11–18 span of schooling into two parts (paragraph 9.4). Crowther had, of course, first used this argument to support the idea of transfer at 14, as indeed had Clegg when he promoted the junior high school option of going comprehensive in the late 1950s. But the argument applied equally well to the middle school case too and Clegg did not fail to see it.

Perhaps one of the most important community concerns in the West Riding's struggle to find administratively expedient yet educationally desirable means of going comprehensive was that which arose in the context of discussions surrounding the adoption of the Leicestershire Plan. In Leicestershire, pupils transferred to the senior high school at 14 only if their parents so wished. The serious drawback of this, Clegg remarked, was the creation in the junior highs of a 'truncated group' of less able, poorly motivated pupils who might well, by virtue of being the oldest, dominate the ethos of the school. In Clegg's judgment, 'the school community must suffer something from this annual decapitation'.[14] Nor was Clegg alone here, for Lord Boyle, Conservative Education Minister at just the time that many junior high school schemes were being submitted to the Ministry for approval, himself commented that the Leicestershire Plan never received the credit it deserved because of the acknowledged deficiency of leaving a one-year educational cul-de-sac in the junior highs, with all the problems of order that this then created.[15]

To sum up, arguments concerned with social unity, whether community-centred or order-directed were somewhat influential in the development of three-tier schemes of secondary reorganization. They were a source of objections to large and impersonal 11–18 schools and to forms of organization which produced divided or unstable school communities (split-site and 11–13 schools respectively). Also, along with egalitarian objections, they seriously undercut the case for an unmodified Leicestershire Plan system where pupils were in practice selected by parental choice at 14. But again, like egalitarian arguments, they offered no ground for adjudicating on the respective merits of a modified Leicestershire Plan where everyone transferred at 14, and a middle school system; between transfer at 13 and at 14, that is. On this question, the meritocratic argument was the decisive one.

Conclusion

Chapter 2 argued that middle school systems offered an administratively expedient way of bringing about the reorganization of secondary education. Economic expediency and the administrative irrationalities of the capitalist state which gave rise to it presented powerfully limiting restrictions to educational reform which the proponents of comprehensive education had to meet. Often, these conditions ruled out the construction of all-through 11–18 schools. But there were many other ways in which the conditions could be met. Middle schools were by no means the only option.

Within these broad limits, a multisided process of conflict and debate came into play through which different preferred schemes of comprehensive reorganiz-ation were promoted and resisted. The restrictions of administrative convenience still exerted some influence even over the selection of schemes of reorganization which did not propose particularly lavish expenditure and which were not suggesting the construction of large, all-through 11–18 comprehensives. They had some impact, for instance, on the West Riding's choice of 13 rather than 14 as its preferred age of transfer for many of its divisions. But other arguments were important too in the choice of expediential arrangements for reorganization.

Among these arguments, the egalitarian model of comprehensive schooling had little significance for the establishment of middle schools. It carried some weight among Labour councillors in one or two isolated localities and it offered some strong objections to a 'pure' Leicestershire Plan system of junior and senior high schools which retained selection by parental choice at 14, but it provided no grounds for evaluating the merits of 13 as against 14 as an across-the-board age of transfer.

The model of social unity provided ammunition against 11–18 schools, 11–13 schools and split-site arrangements. And it provided another set of persuasive objections to the ill-fated Leicestershire Plan. But it too offered no basis for distinguishing whether middle schools with transfer at 13 or junior high schools with transfer at 14 should be the preferred pattern of reorganization.

The model that was dominant and decisive for the middle school's develop-ment was the meritocratic one as indeed it was within the comprehensive debate in general. Transfer at 14 rather than 13, it was argued, would pose threats to examination success at 16, with all the consequences this would have for Oxbridge entry, economic growth and so on. By a complicated process of elimination, then, if these meritocratic goals of comprehensive schooling were to hold sway, middle schools seemed to provide the only answer for parts of the West Riding — where middle schools were first established — and other LEAs like it. In this sense, middle schools came into being not only as a result of secondary interests and pressures in general, but as part of one dominant model of comprehensive schooling whose major aims were not to abolish selection but to improve it; not to transform the economy of British society and the relations on which it was founded, but to make it work more efficiently (Bellaby, 1977); not, in other words, to do away with grammar school education with its emphasis on competitive examinations, able pupils and university entrance, but to make this available to (or impose it upon) everyone. (Hargreaves D. 1982)

Middle schools, then, were convincingly and persuasively presented as the allies of meritocracy in particular and as one of the few feasible ways of bringing about secondary reorganization in general. They were, it would seem, firmly 'secondary' in their genesis. However, before a conclusive judgment can be made about this, it needs to be pointed out that middle schools have, to the contrary, often been associated with the development and expansion of *primary* schooling and its methods. If the judgment on the 'secondariness' of middle schools is to be sustained, therefore, the relationship of primary-based arguments and influences to the middle school's emergence must be examined very carefully.

Notes

1 CLAIRE PRATT, CEO for Hillingdon Borough, quoted in KOGAN and VAN DER EYCKEN (1974) p. 119.
2 This view persisted even though the scheme proposed that *all* pupils transfer at 14 and not just a selected group, as in Leicestershire. The overall association with the Leicestershire Plan, it seemed, overrode any particular differences from it.
3 Memorandum: 'The organization of secondary education in the West Riding' presented to the Policy and Finance Sub-committee, 9 June 1959.
4 Though an influential member of the Conservative Group in the Education Committee — JANET (later Lady) YOUNG, who was advancing the three-tier idea — dismissed this suggestion as without foundation, it is an accusation that remains difficult to refute in its entirety.
5 The phrase was originally HUGH GAITSKILL's (see CCCS, 1981).
6 Memorandum: 'The education of the gifted child in the comprehensive schools of the Yorkshire coalfield', presented to the Policy and Finance Sub-committee, 9 December 1958.
7 *Ibid.*
8 'Reorganization of education': notes distributed to the members of the deputation seeing Mr PRENTICE, 9 February 1965.
9 Memorandum: 'The request for comprehensive schools or a comprehensive scheme of education, Ecclesfield area', presented to the Policy and Finance Sub-committee, 9 December 1958.
10 Letter to Mr WRIGHT, Wharncliffe Division Education Officer, 20 August 1958.
11 *Ibid.*
12 *Ibid.*
13 'The request for comprehensive schools . . .' *op. cit.*
14 Memorandum: 'The organization of secondary education in the West Riding', presented to the Policy and Finance Sub-committee, 9 June 1959.
15 BRYAN (1980).

Chapter 4

Primary Factors

The Primary Case Stated

Though middle schools were an administratively expedient way of realizing the meritocratic ideal of comprehensive schooling at the level of secondary education, their emergence was also harmonious with and could be justified in terms of the child-centred, progressive ethos of the primary school which was gaining in popularity and influence in the 1960s. In the words of an ex-West Riding adviser I interviewed, middle schools were 'based on attitudes held about the age of transfer and child development'.[1] As far as this man was concerned, 'the educational argument was always uppermost'. In the 1965 redraft of the West Riding's first middle school document, Clegg himself argued that 'When the Committee first considered the possibility of this kind of organization they sought the answer to the educational problem before considering what was feasible by using existing buildings' (WRYECR, 1965, p. 3). In part, this 'educational problem' consisted of 'secondary' issues to do with such issues as the fate of highly selected able pupils and the orderliness and coherence of school communities. But primary matters also ranked highly amongst what Clegg designated as educational arguments. Thus, in his crucial letter to the Ministry on 3 May 1963, which first raised with them the very idea of middle schools, Clegg argued that 'one of the big attractions of the whole idea from my point of view is that we could introduce the best primary school methods into the schools which took children from 9–13'.[2] And in the West Riding middle school document published in October of that year, Clegg outlined his first educational justification for middle schools as follows:

> The advances made in the last ten years by children of all ability groups in those primary schools which have come to rely more on the exploitation of the pupils' individual experience and less on the inculcation of subject knowledge have been so outstanding that they must be regarded as of major significance. Standards in this County have risen considerably and many who have observed this approach to education are convinced that it is wrong to cut it short at 11. (WRYECR, 1963, paragraph, 9.1)

Moreover, he went on, citing an anonymous grammar school headmaster in his support, 'there has been a growing concern in the grammar schools about the extent to which examination pressures are forcing too much specialization on children who are too young for it'. (paragraph 9.2)[3]

These sentiments were echoed in other LEAs proposing middle schools, in some cases in words which repeated Clegg's almost exactly.[4] Clegg was also prepared to hazard a guess that his views on the 'primary' benefits of middle schooling would be endorsed at the level of national policy too, in the findings of the Plowden Committee which was about to deliberate on the age of transfer. Writing to Fletcher at the Ministry on 15 May 1963, Clegg predicted that if the Committee were to 'examine these transfer dates in the light of the *purely educational issues involved*' then they would 'come down in favour of a 13 year-old transfer'.[5] Notwithstanding his own submission of evidence to the Plowden Committee when he stressed as his very first point in favour of transfer at 13 that 'The primary school approach to education which has proved so successful should continue until the child is 13' and that accordingly 'examination pressures should be kept away from children below the age of 13', this prediction was not fulfilled.[6] The Plowden Report ultimately identified 12 rather than 13 as its preferred age of transfer (though only just). Nevertheless, like Clegg, it did pronounce in favour of deferring the age of transfer beyond 11. In this it may have been helped by evidence submitted by the National Union of Teachers (1964, p. 15) who reached the conclusion that 'there is a balance of educational advantage in extending a primary-type regime for pupils to a later age than is now generally the case'. But it is the Report itself which best captures the middle school mood of the mid-sixties in a passage which proposed that

> If the middle school is to be a new and progressive force it must develop further the curriculum, methods and attitudes which exist at present in junior schools. It must move forward into what is now regarded as secondary school work, but it must not move so far away that it loses the best of primary education as we know it now. (paragraphs 383–384)

At both local and national levels, then, the mid 1960s saw the emergence of powerful arguments in support of middle schools which stressed their potential to protect pupils up to 13 from unwanted secondary school influences such as examination pressures and subject specialization, influences associated with the meritocratic model of comprehensive schooling. Middle schools, that is, would extend the benefits of primary school practice, an increasingly valued educational tradition in Britain and one in which the West Riding had established an enviable reputation. If middle schools would hasten into existence some of the new meritocratic comprehensive schools and their promotion of equal educational opportunities, they would also protect young pupils from the hard nosed if more open process of competition for educational credentials which that meritocratic model of comprehensive schooling necessarily entailed. Middle schools would in this sense not only further the cause of meritocracy at the secondary level, but in the best spirit of romantic individualism, with its emphasis on the worth of childhood in its own right, would protect pre-adolescent children from these worldly concerns and foster their personal growth and development through processes of exploration, collaboration and discovery.

These, at least, were the implications of the primary arguments underlying the middle school case. But although the arguments were widespread, just how influential were they in relation to their secondary counterparts? What role did they play in influencing policy-makers? Were they crucial determinants of the English middle school without which such schools might never have come into being, or just so much ornate icing on the administrative cake?

It is perhaps worth stressing at the outset that at least as far as the West Riding is concerned, there is little reason to doubt that primary-based arguments in support of middle schools were embraced and advanced with the utmost sincerity. At the time that the middle school debate commenced, the West Riding was already in the forefront of developments in primary education. By 1957, for instance, it had introduced a novel scheme of educational selection at 11 into the Thorne area of the county which was based not on formal written tests but on rather more subjective procedures of assessment by panels of headteachers. Though the greater class bias of such informal judgments might well give rise to legitimate concern, the scheme's first declared aim 'to free the primary schools from the externally imposed examination' had, according to a team of HMIs who visited the area seven years later, 'obviously been achieved'.[7] Moreover, they went on, once this immediate constraint had been removed, styles of teaching and learning appropriate to the 'open' primary school were allowed to flourish.

The idea of liberating younger pupils from the strictures of external examinations was not peculiar to the middle school innovation, then, but an extension to older pupils of a principle which had already met with proven and widely recognized success in the primary sector. But whatever the educational worth, whatever the sincerity of this proposal as it was advanced in association with the middle school case, this says nothing of its causal influence vis-à-vis other arguments and justifications. To make *this* kind of assessment we need to look not at the intrinsic educational merits of the primary case itself, however great they may be, but at the placing and timing of that case within educational documents concerned with the establishment of middle schools.

The Primary Case Assessed

One of the most striking features of the debate about patterns of secondary reorganization during the period immediately preceding the middle school initiative, is the almost total absence within it of any reference to possible benefits that might accrue to the primary sector or to the dissemination of 'good' primary practice in general. During this period of intense discussions about the possibility of establishing junior high school schemes of reorganization, arguments about the extension of primary school practice were notable only by their absence. A characteristic example is an extensive item which Clegg submitted to the Policy and Finance Sub-committee in June 1959, which outlined the different possible patterns of secondary organization that might be or were already established within the County.[8] One of these alternatives, the junior high school system, offered the option of what he called 'division by age'. Many advantages of this option were listed — the fact that it used existing buildings efficiently (the administrative convenience argument), that it 'avoids selection' (the egalitarian argument), that it 'yields a more workable group of abler pupils in relation to total size' (the meritocratic argument), and that it avoids the problems of 'sheer size' (the case of social unity). All of these arguments were exclusively secondary in emphasis. No mention was made of the benefits that junior high schools might bring to the extension of primary practice. The context in which junior high schools were considered and, for a time promoted at County level was firmly secondary.

The same is broadly true at divisional level also. In Hemsworth, for instance, which wrestled with the problem of junior high schools longer than almost any of its fellow divisions, discussion proceeded without any reference to primary-like innovations: the pressing concern throughout was the achievement of secondary reorganization within existing buildings. In Castleford, some mention *was* made of the primary case which might favour the setting up of junior high schools. In a memorandum to his Committee, for example, Clegg argued that in junior high schools, 'it might well prove much easier to introduce many of the approaches to education which are now being so successfully applied in the primary schools'.[9] Nevertheless, this justification came *after* an opening remark which referred to matters of much greater urgency — the fact that some areas, like Castleford, 'which desire a comprehensive type of secondary school organization can only have this if approval is given to a system of senior and junior high schools'. And again, in the details of deliberations about reorganization in Castleford, it was the need to establish an administratively convenient pattern of comprehensive schooling which dominated the debate, not any question of extending primary practice.

It seems fair to conclude that primary-based arguments had very little to do with the promotion of junior high schools in the West Riding. But if these observations are accurate, they add to rather than detract from the argument that middle schools were established on primary grounds, precisely because such schools had a *greater* potential to extend the best of primary practice than their junior high school predecessors. Spanning the traditional divide at 11 +, placing within their walls many pupils of primary age and teachers of primary experience alongside their secondary counterparts, and setting a transfer–out age early enough to keep external examinations at a sufficient distance to remove their most direct and constraining effects, what institutions other than the middle schools could be better placed to fulfil such a mission? In the context of the middle school debate, then, the primary case had not only the weight of an emerging tradition of educationally valued practice behind it, along with a strong note of professional sincerity, but also that necessary degree of plausibility which the junior high school model, with its transfer-in age at the conventional point of 11 and its transfer-out age perilously close to external examinations, clearly lacked. If it turned out that primary arguments were not especially influential for the middle school's development then this would be despite, rather than because of their educational plausibility.

The first point at which middle schools became a public issue, it will be recalled, was when Clegg corresponded with the Ministry on this matter in May 1963. What status did primary justifications have in this important correspondence, designed as it was to sway ministerial opinion in favour of changing the legal age of transfer? In the letter to Fletcher of 3 May when Clegg first flew his middle school kite, he did indeed emphasize one of the attractions of middle schools as allowing the best primary school methods to be extended to children up to 13 years of age.[10] But, it should be added, this point was made towards the end of the letter, long after Clegg had drawn the Under-Secretary's attention to such other matters as the arbitrariness of the existing arrangements for transferring at 11, the precedent for transferring at 13 that was to be found in the independent sector, and the social advantages of having secondary school communities with their 'centre of gravity' at 15 or 16.

These priorities were reflected in the records of the deputation which the West Riding sent to meet Mr Prentice, in February 1965. The purpose of that meeting from the County's point of view was, amongst other things, to get the go-ahead for implementing one or more specific three-tier schemes within the West Riding. Not surprisingly, perhaps, the immediate briefing for the discussion and the documented summary of it contained little reference to educational justifications for the middle school case — either primary or secondary.[11] Once more, it was the question of fitting comprehensive reorganization into existing buildings which dominated proceedings. However, the background papers sent one month earlier to those officials at the Ministry who would presumably have been briefing Mr Prentice on this matter, did make more extensive references to educational justifications. In one paragraph, the case was persuasively put that

> It is educationally important that good primary school methods should move up through the secondary schools rather than that examination-dominated teaching should move down. For this reason a lower school should work out its own solution for all its pupils and in doing so should not be controlled by what the upper school requires its examinees to do.[12]

But again, this primary justification came *after* the old administrative chestnut of using existing buildings, and *after* the meritocratic argument that middle schools would, in contrast with their Leicestershire Plan counterparts, give senior pupils an adequate three-year run up to 'O' levels. Moreover, as if to confirm the rule that the lower the age of the pupils, the less status they have as justification for far-reaching educational change, the point about extending primary methods upwards, low in the batting order as it was, did at least precede the tail-end argument that transferring at 9 would lengthen infant school life and thus help improve reading standards.

In documents of a more public character, the primary argument assumed somewhat greater significance than it did in correspondence involving the Ministry. The purpose of these documents was rather different, though. Thus, the West Riding's influential paper on patterns of secondary reorganization published in October 1963 and reprinted, with some important changes, two years later, was sent not only to people at the Ministry but also to other LEAs, national and local newspapers, and to a number of leading educationists in higher education. The prime and clearly stated purpose of this document was to press the Minister into action on changing the law regarding the age of transfer; but a further and closely related intention, it would seem, was to generate interest in and support for the middle school idea amongst the broadest possible constituency and thus increase that pressure on the Minister. In this kind of persuasive exercise, when interests are cultivated and educational passions roused on a wide front, educational justifications become very important indeed.

The opening gambit in the West Riding's 1963 report was the standard and, for that time, almost obligatory point about administrative convenience. The justifications which then followed were not fundamentally different from those offered by Clegg in his direct correspondence with the Ministry earlier that year. But there was an important alteration in their ranking. The justification which was given far greater force than in any previous statements on 9–13 *or* junior high school systems was that connected with the extension of primary education to older age groups. This now appeared first on the list of 'educational' arguments in support of middle schools. And by the time of the report's redraft in 1965, the primary argument had become more pivotal still to the middle school case. Having gained some degree of acceptance for middle schools at the national level, and having secured the all-important change in the law regarding the age of transfer, the administrative convenience argument was not so crucial now. Not only did it have diminished importance within the 1965 report overall, but at one point, when middle schools were being compared with systems which transferred at 14, Clegg, as we have already seen, asserted that when his Committee first considered the idea of middle schools, they sought the answer to the educational problem first before studying the availability and suitability of existing buildings. (WRYECR, 1965, pp. 3–4)[13]

By highlighting the importance of educational justifications overall, this more general claim conferred even greater status on the primary argument. But as the previous chapter indicated, plausible, worthwhile and sincerely held as they were, primary arguments came to prominence only once the administrative convenience argument had been won. In the vital discussions with the Ministry concerning the age of transfer in general and the acceptance of specific middle school schemes in particular, middle schools were presented first and foremost as an administratively convenient way of bringing about the reorganization of *secondary* education, and secondly as a method of doing this which would also preserve the meritocratic ideal of comprehensive schooling with its minimum three-year run up to examinations. In the period surrounding the initial establishment of middle schools then, while 'primary' arguments became increasingly prominent, it was 'secondary' ones that remained persistently influential.

8–12 or 9–13: Plowden v. ROSLA

In examining the determinants of the English middle school, it is important to consider not only their initial establishment, but also the changing patterns of middle schooling that came to be preferred during the early years of their development. In this sense, one of the most powerful arguments in support of the primary-base thesis of middle school development is that once middle schools emerged, the 'primary' argument gained strength to such an extent that the preferred age of transfer dropped from 13 to 12, with the 8–12 pattern of middle schooling now becoming the dominant one. This argument deserves very close scrutiny.

By the middle of the 1960s, despite the elaborate consultative machinery of teachers' working parties which many LEAs set up at the behest of Circular 10/65, it was becoming clear that in many areas, the middle school solution to the problem of secondary reorganization was the only administratively feasible one; so much so, in fact, that LEA administrators often presented it to their Education Committee as a virtual *fait accompli*. Constrained by such administrative necessities, many LEAs were already committed to middle school schemes by this point. This perhaps explains why from about 1967 onwards, middle schools were increasingly justified in 'educational' terms and why the weight given to administrative factors was considerably reduced. Now that many LEAs had made their choice — even if this was, for them, only Hobson's choice — finer distinctions were able to be drawn. Discussion was devoted to such matters as the kinds of middle schools that would be most desirable and the sort of identity they should be allowed to develop. Part of that discussion involved questions about what would be the most appropriate age range for middle schools — 8–12 or 9–13.

Until 1973, the majority of middle schools fell into the category known as 'middle schools deemed secondary'. Apart from a very small number of exceptions, in practice, this meant 9–13 or 10–13 schools. Although, in 1970, more 'deemed primary' than 'deemed secondary' middle schools were established, the original pattern was restored once more during the following year. By 1973, Benn (1973b) was writing that 'the middle deemed secondary of 9–13 ... is still the most numerous'. Indeed, so well entrenched did the 9–13 option appear to be by this point that Benn went on to say that future plans showed no indications of any reversal in the trend. She could hardly have been more inaccurate. In that very year of 1973 — a year when more middle schools were established than at any time before or since — the number of new middle schools deemed primary which were established far exceeded (by some two-and-a-half times) those deemed secondary (figure 1). Since that point, the numerical advantage held by 8–12 schools has been maintained and the deemed primary category is now the dominant one within English middle school education.

One popular argument is that the growing preference for the 8–12 school was a gradually emerging, evolutionary one, coming from a developing appreciation of the merits of the primary case. This imputation of a 'steady move' (Bryan and Hardcastle, 1978) is not really supported by the evidence available however, for most of the numerical advantage which the 8–12 school has held over its 9–13 counterpart is rooted in a single year — 1973. After that, the annual rates of establishment for 8–12 and 9–13 schools respectively have fluctuated considerably, giving few signs of any consistent trend. Before different explanations of the apparent increase in preference for 8–12 schools are evaluated, some features of the relevant statistics require clarification. Take the figures for January, 1978. Here, in terms of schools

Figure 1: Number of Middle Schools coming into existence yearly in England 1968-77.

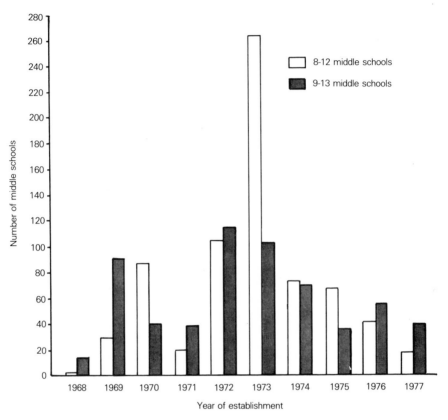

Source: Times Educational Supplement, 13 November 1981, p.9.

alone, the 8–12 type outnumbers the 9–13 type by a little over 6 per cent of the total.[14] And if the 5–12 first-and-middle schools combined are included in the 8–12 category, the schools transferring out at 12 have as much as a 27.8 per cent lead over their 9–13 counterparts.

By this measure, the preference for 8–12 schools seems overwhelming (table 1).[15] However, comparing the two types of middle school provision in terms of schools alone can be misleading for 8–12 middle schools are, on average, considerably smaller than 9–13 ones. In January 1978, for instance, the mean number of pupils on roll for the two types was 327 as against 423 respectively.[16] Once the comparison is made in terms of pupils, not buildings, the 8–12 middle school loses its apparent popularity. Indeed the trend becomes reversed: the 9–13 type middles catering for 7.1 per cent more pupils than their 8–12 type competitors (table 1).[17] And although when middle school age-range pupils from 5–12 schools are included

Table 1: Numbers of middle schools and pupils on roll in different types of middle schools at January 1978.

Type of middle school	Number of schools	Total number of pupils	Mean number on roll (NOR)	Weighted total for four year groups	Weighted Average
5–12	387	120937	312	69107	179
8–12	686	224542	327	224542	327
9–12	7	1737	248	2316	331
TOTAL	1080	347216	321	295965	274
9–13	565	238925	423	238925	423
10–13	43	21057	490	28076	653
10–14	2	843	422	843	422
TOTAL	610	260825	428	267844	439
GRAND TOTAL	1690	608041	360	563809	334

Source: Compiled from Department of Education and Science lists of schools as shown by the returns made on Form 7 (1978)

in the figures, and when the numbers from 9–12 and 10–13 schools are similarly weighted to give them four rather than three year groups of pupils (a measure which ensures strict comparability), this restores the advantage enjoyed by the 8–12 type of middle,[18] this is achieved only by including pupils in schools with a centre of gravity as low as 8+ — schools which are scarcely worth the designation 'middle' at all (table 1). The apparent clear administrative preference after 1973 for the 8–12 as against the 9–13 middle is therefore not nearly so great as is often claimed.

And yet, important though all these statistical qualifications are, none of them wipe away the remarkable surge in the number of 8–12 (and indeed 5–12 schools) which were established in 1973. The reasons for this sharp rise have often been attributed to the influence of the Plowden Report on primary education, published some six years earlier. The Report was emphatic in its suggestion that the age of transfer ought to be shifted from what until three years previously had been the legally fixed point of 11. But it was much less decisive about whether the preferred alternative should be 12 or 13. The Committee were not helped by the contradictory nature of the evidence they received. Her Majesty's Inspectorate, for instance, came down in favour of 13 as the age of transfer (Bryan and Hardcastle, 1977), as did Sir Alec Clegg. Permanent DES officials and many LEA advisers, meanwhile, re-commended 12+ instead (*ibid*). For its part, the National Union of Teachers, the body which represented most primary teachers, felt unable to make a definite decision either way, and preferred to await the Report's findings on the matter. (NUT, 1964)

Eventually, after long and careful deliberation, the Committee produced a measured but nevertheless unequivocal conclusion. 'The arguments in favour of 12 or 13 as the age of transfer', the Report stated, 'are fairly evenly balanced and there is ... no one age which is right for every child. But on nearly every count it seems to us that the balance of advantage is just with 12 year old transfer' (paragraph 385). It is not absolutely clear what swung the Committee behind 12 + transfer in the end, but the fact that the Chairman of the 'ages and stages' working party — Harold Tunn — was an ex-Chief Education Officer of one of the first LEAs to introduce 8–12 middle schools (Sheffield), may not have been irrelevant. (Bryan, 1980, p. 64)

Most of the numerous schemes implemented in 1973 were devized in the immediate post-Plowden era and it might therefore seem that in contrast to their 9–13 counterparts, they were indeed heavily influenced by Plowden's primary-based recommendations. Freeland (1973, p. 73), for instance, argues that 'the Middle Schools of Southampton can be seen as a direct implementation of the Plowden proposals'. The argument is a persuasive one. Although the Plowden Report had little direct effect on national policy — it did not, for instance, lead to the inauguration of a single nationwide age of transfer, as it hoped — it *was* influential and well received in much more diffuse ways within LEAs and individual schools. It is quite possible, then, that such influence might have extended to LEA decisions about what age of transfer should be incorporated into their schemes of secondary school reorganization.

However, against the claims of such 'educational rhetoric' in the middle school debate, Bryan and Hardcastle (1977 and 1978) have mounted a powerful argument that 8–12 middle schools were actually preferred by many LEAs because they were cheaper to run. They were chosen, they say, simply on the grounds of economic expediency. Middle schools, they point out, are, under Section 2 of the 1964 Education Act, not treated as a separate administrative category, but, for purposes of financing are officially 'deemed' to be either primary or secondary. In practice, this means that all of the 8–12 and 5–12 schools are deemed primary, while virtually all of the schools which transfer out at 13 or beyond are deemed secondary. As the DES document *Statistics in Education* puts it, middle schools

> for pupils aged 8 to 12 are deemed primary by Order of the Secretary of State for Education and Science, those for ages 10 to 13 are deemed secondary, while those for ages 9 to 13 may be deemed either primary or secondary according to the choice of the local education authorities.[19]

This deeming of middle schools as either primary or secondary is more than just an administrative exercise in tidy classification: it has important and far-reaching consequences for resources of staffing and equipment which are allocated to each type of school. Middle schools deemed primary and middle schools deemed secondary, that is, do not enjoy parity of resourcing. At one level, this has not helped attempts to develop a coherent policy for middle school education as a whole — a problem shrewdly anticipated in 1968 by J.E.B. Hill, Conservative M.P. for Norfolk South, when in a House of Commons debate he urged the then Secretary of State for Education and Science, Mr Patrick Gordon Walker, to get 'away from the concept of a rigid distinction between primary and secondary education'. (quoted in Gillespie, 1968, p. 3)

But more important than the threats of this distinction to the middle school's identity, are its implications for the long-term running costs of each type of school.

In terms of teacher-pupil ratios and therefore staffing levels, and in terms of capitation allowances and space allocations per pupil, 8–12 middle schools are, as officially designated 'primary' schools, treated much less generously than their 'deemed secondary' counterparts (Bryan, 1980, p. 67). This makes them an economically attractive proposition to those LEAs committed to three-tier patterns of reorganization. This, argue Bryan and Hardcasle (1977 an 1978), is what explains the growing preference for 8–12 middle schools, and not any influence of the Plowden Report.

Bryan and Hardcastle are accurate in identifying the long-term financial benefits which accrue to those LEAs opting for 8–12 patterns of middle school reorganization. But what remains at issue is whether these considerations of long-term cost-consciousness played any practical part in the decisions taken by those LEAs on secondary reorganization. If indeed there was a 'steady move' towards adoption of the 8–12 pattern among LEAs, then such an argument might be tenable. But the sudden upsurge of interest in 8–12 schools in 1973 raises problems for this interpretation. If the long-term economic advantages of 8–12 middle schools were so demonstrably strong, why was their rise to popularity delayed until five years after the first middle schools had been established? If they were economically expedient *after* 1973, why were they not so expedient *before* that date also? Either LEAs took an inexplicably long time to wake up to the long-term economic benefits of 8–12 middle schools — which seems unlikely. Or it must be assumed that such long-term considerations, politically fortuitous as they might have been, did not have a decisive influence on educational policy, in which case some other explanation for the sudden expansion of 8–12 schools in 1973 must be sought.

The temptation is to be drawn back once more to the argument that the Plowden Report influenced educational policy makers in their decisions regarding the age of transfer. But there was another major initiative in educational policy around the same time as Plowden which may also have influenced such decisions: the announcement of the raising of the school leaving age (DES, 1966b). Chapter 2 has already documented how ROSLA acted as a catalyst in the expansion of middle schools as a whole. My argument here is that it exerted a further catalytic effect with respect to the *type* of middle school provision that was favoured too.

Before the decision to raise the school leaving age had been announced, or the Plowen Committee had produced its Report, most LEAs who had opted for a middle school system had already decided upon the 9–13 version. The availability of buildings made this solution the 'obvious' one for many administrators (O'Connor, 1968). In West Riding divisions such as Hemsworth, for example, a 9–13 system of reorganization most effectively utilized existing buildings by housing middle schools in what had previously been secondary modern accommodation (Gosden and Sharp, 1978). Gorwood (1978) has produced similar findings for Hull which was also one of the first LEAs to submit plans for reorganization on 9–13 lines. He notes that 65 per cent of Hull's 9–13 middle schools were located in converted secondary modern premises, with only a minority being housed in adapted primary accommodation. Thus, before ROSLA, the 9–13 solution was frequently the most expedient one in terms of existing resources.

With the announcement and implementation of ROSLA and the necessity to cater for an additional number of pupils who would previously have left school at 15, recalculations needed to be done. For many LEAs this now meant that not only were middle schools the most expedient way of going comprehensive, but with the need to redistribute a larger number of pupils among existing buildings, the 8–12 pattern was particularly convenient (Blyth and Derricott, 1977; Bryan and Hardcastle 1977). In Brighton, for instance, a working party of teachers noted that one of the three reasons why 'the 8–12 span is particularly apposite for Brighton' was that

> The deferrment of transfer by one year (beyond 11) will provide relief to the secondary school and facilitate the retention of the remainder of the 15–16 age group not already remaining at school without entailing a large-scale disruption of the secondary system. (Brighton Education Committee, 1973, p. 1)[20]

In Chester, despite his own initial preference for a 9–13 system, the Chief Education Officer stated that if secondary reorganization was to be implemented in conjunction with ROSLA, an 8–12 scheme would be cheaper than a 9–13 alternative by some £586,000 (Bryan, 1980, p. 131). And in Hampshire LEA, its Chief Education Officer admitted that 'the real justification for the introduction of particular patterns of non-selective schools owes as much to historical accident and to the oft-resented but inescapable realities of the size and distribution of existing schools, as it does to the predilictions of educational theory'. (Aldam, 1978, p. 82–3)[21]

Further support for the administrative convenience argument is provided by the extremely speedy publication of *Building Bulletin 35* (DES, 1966b) shortly after the announcement of ROSLA. This bulletin offered guidance on the design of middle schools. What is significant about it is that whereas most LEAs which had by then reorganized on three-tier lines had mainly adapted secondary modern school buildings for 9–13 middle school use, the bulletin deliberately excluded any examples of how such conversions might be achieved on the grounds that they were uneconomic. Instead it showed only how new middle schools might be built or how they might be established within *primary* school premises (thus implicitly favouring the 8–12 option).

Taking all the evidence together, it appears that the dominance of the 8–12 pattern of provision can be explained not so much as a response to the findings and recommendations of the Plowden Report on *primary* education as to the new material constraints which followed from the raising of the school leaving age at the *secondary* level.

Conclusion

What conclusions can be drawn from this historical analysis of the middle school? Chapter 2 showed that middle schools provided an administratively expedient way of going comprehensive, a form of educational reorganization which could be launched within existing buildings on a limited state budget. As such a convenience, they were a consequence of a dilemma faced by the state of having to increase expenditure and intervention in order to boost productivity, while having to fund that expenditure by deducting revenue from the very profits it was designed to boost. Middle schools, as a kind of educational reform on the cheap were, in this sense, just one effect of the administrative irrationalities of the capitalist system.

Chapters 3 and 4 went on to argue that administrative convenience did not provide the whole explanation, though. Various other options, like split-site and junior high schools were just as or almost as expedient. The reason why the middle school option prevailed, at least in the West Riding, was because of its greater compatability with an upper school system whose curriculum was still strongly geared towards selective examinations at 16+. Middle schools, that is, in comparison with their Leicestershire Plan counterparts, offered a three rather than a two-year run-up to examinations. It was these top-down interests of selection within a meritocratically orientated system which dominated the middle school's development; much more so than any pursuit of egalitarianism, or romantic concern with spreading the gospel of primary school enlightenment. These other parts of the dominant repertoire of social democratic thinking of the time certainly helped legitimate the middle school to a broader public, but they were much less decisive in influencing the Ministry than was the middle school's fortunate compatability with meritocratic purpose and administrative constraint.

Yet the combination of secondary comprehensive and primary progressive arguments was very important ideologically for the middle school's development. Nor was this combination a chance occurrence. It was fixed in common historical roots. Each of these traditions had an altruistic reforming edge to it: the concern with egalitarianism, social justice and equal opportunities in the comprehensive debate, and the commitment to romantic philosophies of child-centred education among many self-styled 'progressives' in the primary sector. Each was given a vital stake in the creation of hoped-for prosperity in the British economy too. The meritocratic model of comprehensive schooling was most concerned with the efficient identification of talent in order to secure economic growth. Nor were the advocates of the 'primary revolution' altogether motivated by concern for the sweetness of childhood, or by the light of professional experience. The Plowden Report itself, no less, pointed out what it saw as an important connection between self-directed learning in childhood, and that flexibility and adaptability of adults which would be needed in the future as technological change required (paragraph 496). In this sense, the connection between the rise of educational progressivism in the 1960s and the emergence of patterns of comprehensive schooling on meritocratic lines at the same time was not altogether a coincidence. Each was born in a climate of social and educational optimism on the one hand, and out of a not unrelated interest in using education to produce the kind of labour force which could sustain an economy sufficiently buoyant to support continuing programmes of social and educational reform on the other.

Thus, there were two important concurrent developments in educational policy during the 1960s — one apparently pessimistic and constraining (administrative convenience), the other apparently optimistic and enabling (the drive to

openness) — which derived from the administrative irrationalities and the legitimation needs (the need to 'buy' mass consent through social and educational reform) of
British capitalism respectively. Once this central relation is grasped it is clear that the
restrictions of administrative convenience on the one hand, and the rise of
comprehensivism and educational progressivism on the other, were not a chance
combination of 'positive choices' and 'negative constraints' as Sharp (1980, p. 39)
puts it, but part of a common pattern of determinants rooted in the nature of the
British social democratic state at the time and the problems it faced in managing the
capitalist economy.

Of course, in detail, the pattern of the middle school's development and of
comprehensive reorganization more generally was a good deal more uneven than
this.[22] The structural looseness of the English education system — a system which
was decentralized in its principles of administrative and political control during this
period — meant that coordination between different parts of the system was less
tight than some might have wished. Purposes realized at the local level were not
always the same. They were not uniformly meritocratic — as the egalitarianism of
the Mexborough councillors showed. There were also often sharp differences
between national and local state and within the local state itself about the merits of
secondary reorganization or the best way to go about it. In some cases these
differences were matters of straight political disagreement, as in the resistance
mounted to centrally imposed requirements for comprehensive reorganization by
some LEAs; in Clegg's differences of opinion with the Ministry over the desirability
of junior high school schemes; or in the political enmity felt by the Castleford
Labour group towards the Chairman of the West Riding Education Committee and
the middle school policy with which he was seen to be associated.[23] In other cases,
the differences arose more from problems of communication and timing, as when
Berkshire neglected the middle school option of comprehensive reorganization
because it had underestimated the strength of government support for it in Circular
10/65 (Benn and Simon, 1970); or when Alec Clegg and Keighley's Education
Committee Chairman simultaneously presented conflicting proposals for educational reorganization, the one favouring junior high schools, the other (Clegg's)
opposing them.[24]

Lastly, state policy on education in general, and middle schools in particular,
was complicated by effects of historical lag, by what one ex-Minister of State for
Education has termed a pattern of 'disjointed incrementalism' — 'the maintenance of
established provision which is normally attracted to itself' (Fowler, 1983, p. 15). In
the middle school's case, its adoption or rejection in favour of some other alternative
was in this sense often decreed by the particular kind of building provision left by
history to the locality concerned.

Subject to political conflict and negotiation, to administrative disagreement and
misinterpretation, and to the local historical inheritance of building provision,
middle school and related policies of comprehensive reorganization therefore
exemplified the staccatto-like pattern of administrative intervention that characterized educational policy in the 1960s and early 70s. But if this structural looseness led
to gaps, inconsistencies, and variations of the kind just described, in many cases, it

also created a kind of *functional autonomy*, a high degree of local flexibility which helped centrally induced initiatives to be adjusted to local circumstances. And this was where the highly individualistic and creative contribution of Chief Education Officers like Sir Alec Clegg was vital.

Such people used their local knowledge and initiative to work out policies which would comply with central requirements and administrative restrictions. And they brought to that task of coordination the highest levels of persuasive skill. Clegg, for instance, as we have seen, skilfully combined and synthesized a wide range of arguments in support of the middle school case. He also shrewdly presented the middle school idea to suit the political and educational preferences of very different audiences — as when he attached covering letters to copies of his 1963 middle school report which he circulated to the press and elsewhere; one to the High Master of Manchester Grammar School arguing that middle schools would provide 'better quality youngsters' for the grammar schools,[25] one to *The Guardian* optimistically hinting at the possibility of a shift from a Conservative government,[26] and one to the Ministry implying no such thing.[27] Clegg also cleverly manipulated the consultative process to create an illusion of mass support. When he issued his 1963 report, he stated that he had 'consulted in writing 15 of the ablest and most experienced teachers in ... the Riding' (WRYECR, 1963, p. 2), but he failed to make clear how or according to precisely what criteria these chosen people had been selected — a point on which the teacher associations would later criticise him heavily.[28]

Yet in devizing appropriate solutions, in coping strategically with the constraints of national state budgeting by exploiting points of looseness in the system, officers like Clegg also operated off a network of educational and more broadly economic and political assumptions which were shared with their colleagues in central government and administration. In this respect, despite certain differences and problems of coordination, the outlooks of local and national administrators and politicians were often remarkably similar in the 1960s — a time of broad social democratic consensus about the purpose of education and its relation to the economy. We have seen the part that such assumptions played in Clegg's pronouncements on educational policy — the importance he attached to talent spotting, able pupils and examination preparation, for instance. And we have seen how central such meritocratic themes were to the choosing of the middle school option in the West Riding. In these things, Clegg shared much in common with the outlook and assumptions of his colleagues at the national level, as the findings of many crucial educational reports of the period — Crowther, Newsom, Robbins and Plowden, for instance — illustrate.

This tacit subscription to the dominant social-democratic hegemony, to the maintenance and improvement, but not the transformation of the existing social and economic system, helped reinforce the middle school's historical purpose; its realization of secondary rather than primary concerns, and of meritocratic rather than egalitarian objectives. The dominance of these particular objectives among the range that were brought into play during educational debate, and the unquestioned nature of the social and educational system they served were, along with the state-induced constraints of administrative convenience, the major factors which brought the middle school into being.

How has this historical inheritance, this lodging of the middle school not in the needs of the middle years or in primary school enlightenment but in meritocratic purpose and administrative necessity, affected it in practice? Has it succeeded at all in establishing a unique identity for itself, providing a smooth transition between primary and secondary education? Or has the middle school been cast more in the image of its historical predecessors? What patterns of curriculum, ability grouping and staff organization have come to characterize the middle school? Where have middle school staffs been drawn from and where have they been deployed to in the middle school setting, and with what consequences? It is these central questions that will be addressed in the remainder of the book which now gets to the heart of middle school practice.

Notes

1 This was an adviser who had particularly close connections with the two case study schools examined in the second part of the book.
2 Letter to L.R. FLETCHER, 3 May 1963.
3 It is not clear how this head was selected to offer his comments, or how representative of other grammar school heads those comments were.
4 Examples can be found in BRYAN (1980).
5 Letter to FLETCHER, 15 May 1963.
6 This evidence is laid out and cited in several West Riding documents. See, for instance, the Memorandum on 'Comprehensive' schools presented to the Policy and Finance Sub-committee, 12 January 1965.
7 West Riding *School's Bulletin*, November 1964.
8 Memorandum: 'The organization of secondary education in the West Riding' presented to the Policy and Finance Sub-committee, 9 June 1959.
9 Memorandum: 'Reorganization of secondary education: Castleford' presented to the Policy and Finance Sub-committee, 1962 (exact date unavailable).
10 Letter to FLETCHER, 3 May 1963.
11 Notes distributed to the deputation meeting Mr PRENTICE, 9 February 1965; and Memorandum on 'Reorganization in certain areas of the West Riding: visit of deputation to Minister of State, 11 February 1965' presented to the Policy and Finance Sub-committee, 9 March 1965.
12 Memorandum: 'Comprehensive schools' presented to the Policy and Finance Sub-committee, 12 January 1965 and sent to Hayter (HMI) and Leadbetter (Under-Secretary of State) at the Ministry, 8 January 1965.
13 See chapter 2. One of the major justifications of the importance of this 'educational argument' was that the idea of changing the age of transfer was not novel for the West Riding. In fact, CLEGG contended, it predated the proposal for middle schools by a number of years. Thus, in a postscript to his exploratory letter to FLETCHER at the Ministry in the middle of 1963 (3 May), CLEGG insisted that 'When some years ago we first considered a junior and senior high school scheme, we had in mind a transfer age of 9, but I never went forward with it because of the law of the land'. And in his second letter to

the Ministry on the middle school idea, just twelve days later (15 May 1963), CLEGG asserted even more emphatically that his preference all along had been for transfer at 9 and 13 rather than 11 and 14.

> Some years ago when we were first considering junior and senior high schools, our conviction was that we should break at 9 and again at 13, but we concluded that this would not be permissable because of the definition in Section 114 of the 1944 Act of a senior pupil.

Yet while there is no way of confirming or refuting whether CLEGG and his colleagues had ever privately toyed with the idea of transferring at 9, there is no documented evidence available to substantiate such a claim. Indeed, according to BRYAN (1980, p. 55), CLEGG had, by his own admission, never heard of middle schools until he visited the United States at the beginning of 1960 — a visit which, it should be added, *post*dates the commencement of discussions about junior high schools schemes in the County.

On the evidence available, then, it seems unlikely that even if the 9–13 proposal was considered at all before 1963, that it was anything more than a passing whim. This is not to deny the existence of very real doubts in the West Riding about transfer at 11 which stretched back as far as the 1940s. But the seeds of such doubt were sown in an environment quite unlike that of the 1960s, an environment dominated by concern with the technical efficiency of selection at 11 — one in which the merits of primary school practice were of little importance.

14   53.2 per cent as against 46.8 per cent of all middle schools.

15   63.9 per cent as against 36.1 per cent of all middle and first-and-middle combined schools.

16   Calculated from the raw figures returned on Form 7 to the Department of Education and Science by LEAs for their numbers on roll in each school. Supplied courtesy of the Department of Education and Science.

17   53.5 per cent as against 46.4 per cent of all middle school pupils.

18   The restored advantage is to the level of 5 per cent.

19   *Statistics in Education, Vol. I Schools*, published annually by the Department of Education and Science.

20   Ironically, Brighton is one of the LEAs which has now made arrangements to unscramble its middle school system.

21   The Southampton middle schools discussed by Freeland are, interestingly, part of Hampshire LEA.

22   There is only space to review these complications very briefly here. For a more extended discussion of these issues see HARGREAVES (1985) chapter 5.

23   This is reported in GOSDEN and SHARP (1978).

24   Keighley's proposal was presented in a draft memorandum 'The Leicestershire Plan in Keighley' and accompanied with a letter from Keighley's Borough Education Officer, F.H. PEDLEY to CLEGG 2 May 1963.

25   Letter to the High Master, Manchester Grammar School, 11 October 1963.

26   Letter to the News Editor, *Manchester Guardian*, 1 October 1963.

27   Letter to TOBY WEAVER, Ministry of Education, 7 October 1963.

28   These criticisms were expressed in 'Observations on the West Riding Committee's Pamphlet, "The Organization of Education in Certain Areas of the West Riding, Five to Nine, Nine to Thirteen, Thirteen to Eighteen"', Joint Committee of the Four Secondary Associations (West Riding), June 1964.

Part 2
School Organization

'And if a house be divided against
itself, that house cannot stand'

(*The Gospel According to St Mark*, 3, 25)

Introduction

Methods

The approach adopted in the rest of the study is predominantly, though not exclusively, of a case-study or ethnographic nature. It consists, that is, of a detailed study of two particular middle schools, their life and internal processes, the character of the day-to-day experiences offered within them, and the backgrounds, orientations and career aspirations of their teachers. This is the particular strength of the case study method — its capacity to get to grips with the qualitative aspects of educational experience; with the strategies, cultures, actions and perspectives of the people involved.

The two middle schools (one 9–13, one 10–13), located on the commuter fringe of a northern conurbation, were studied during the whole of the summer term in 1975. For the usual reasons of confidentiality, the schools are given pseudonyms: Riverdale and Moorhead. I would like to stress the importance of that confidentiality. This study is not an evaluation of the effectiveness or special characteristics of these particular schools; still less of the schools as they are now with all the changes they have undergone since the study was conducted. Rather, it is an attempt, through the case study method, to identify problems and issues faced by middle schools as a whole. If, therefore, you find that the study leaves clues as to just where these schools might be, I ask you to pursue your investigations no further.

In each school, observations and/or tape recordings were made of classrooms and of meetings of staff, governors, parents, year group teachers etc. Interviews were conducted and recorded with all thirteen staff at Riverdale and thirteen of the twenty-six staff at Moorhead (selected at random), and with a sample of twenty fourth-year pupils — ten boys, ten girls — from each of the two.

Full details of the conduct of the case study work are published elsewhere in a biographical account of the project (Hargreaves, 1986a). For now, three issues require brief comment. The first concerns the duration of the fieldwork. In comparison with many other case studies in education, the time spent in the field seems unusually brief (a term, as against a year in many other cases). In this instance, however, the ethnographic work did not make up the entire study but only one part of it, albeit an important one. Moreover, the fieldwork itself was unusually intensive: a full five days per week throughout the study compared to two or three days per week in most others.

A second issue is whether the study is now out of date, having been published a decade after data were collected. In some senses it clearly is, though this is, in part, an unavoidable difficulty of all social research. The real world does not stand still while the research process moves from data collection to analysis, to writing up and finally to publication. Because of this, research is often overtaken by events even before it reaches the printers. In qualitative research, the delays tend to be greater still, because of the sheer volume of data and the time and difficulties involved in analyzing it. A period of six to ten years is not an unusual timescale for completion of this kind of work — and the inclusion of further elements (like the present historical one) tend to extend that timescale still further. But excuses (however reasonable), do not satisfactorily answer the basic point — is the study out of date?

In some senses, middle schools have had to face new developments and pressures since this study was completed — falling rolls, financial cutbacks, staffing difficulties, and a whole set of expectations and pressures that have followed in the wake of the Great Education Debate in 1976 — expectations about the need for greater attention to be given to subject specialism, differentiation, improved standards and basic skills, for instance.

These sorts of special issues and problems as they affect middle schools now will be raised in the concluding section of the book. But a clear grasp of their importance, and of how and why middle schools have responded to them in a particular way can only be understood, I want to argue, by appreciating not only the early historical development of middle schools, but the kind of character and ethos, the patterns of staffing, organization and curriculum, the dominant educational priorities which those schools came to develop in practice — priorities and forms of organization which became the linchpin of middle schools' practical (rather than ideal) identity and which would shape how they would respond to new pressures and expectations in years to come.

But more than this, while some of the issues facing middle schools in recent years have changed, other aspects of middle school practice have clearly retained strong elements of continuity, as we shall see when the case study findings concerning the nature of the middle school year system, and patterns of setting and subject specialism, are compared with more recently published national survey findings on these very same questions. And even where some middle school issues clearly *have* changed, the selection of different middle schools for intensive study (one large and overcrowded, one small and short on specialist staffing) — enables us to anticipate some of the consequences of matters like falling rolls (a dominant issue at the time of writing), and expansion too (an issue that will affect middle schools in years to come, and that they are already experiencing in new towns and other areas of expanding population).

A third issue concerns the typicality of the cases studied. I can make no confident claims here that Riverdale and Moorhead are typical of middle schools more generally either then or now. Nor was it possible to deal with this question at the time fieldwork commenced, for what would have been required to select a 'typical' case would not only have been national survey evidence of the organizational characteristics of middle schools (not then available), but also foreknowledge of what the important and relevant organizational characteristics were — precisely the thing one would expect the exploratory case study work to discover. However, with the benefits of hindsight, four things at least can be said in defence of the selection of Riverdale and Moorhead as cases.

First, as with the historical work, the value of the findings of these case studies depends in part on the production of other cumulative work. In this respect, as we shall see, findings from other scattered case studies offer some support for the ones reported here (for example, Ginsburg *et al*, 1977; Bryan, 1980; Meyenn and Tickle, 1980; Wallace and Tickle, 1983; Wallace 1985), and available survey findings provide interesting points of comparison with the results reported here too (Taylor and Garson, 1982; HMI 1983a).[1]

Second, the two schools were located within what was once the West Riding of Yorkshire LEA and were each established by that Authority. This was the LEA selected for historical study and the siting of the case study schools within it therefore makes them particularly suitable for tracing the effects of educational policy on middle school practice.

Third, the establishment of these schools in the early 1970s places them, in historical terms, *beyond* the first flush of middle school reorganization and all the 'halo' effects of special interest, extra LEA support etc. which that tended to induce, and *before* the onset of deep economic recession and all the additional and often depressing constraints which this often placed on middle school aspirations and practice. The two middle schools were, in other words, studied when their identity and inner coherence was likely to be at its strongest — *after* the uncertainty and enthusiasm that accompanies the early days of innovation, but *before* the insecurity and pessimism wrought by cutbacks and recession.

Last, the one criterion by which the schools *were* consciously selected was that they were adjacent (separated by only two miles) and drew on similar catchment areas, while exhibiting clear differences in size, type of buildings and classroom organization. Thus, while most other case studies base their findings on a single case,[2] this one has an explicitly comparative element built into it so as to allow assessments of both differences and similarities between middle schools, along with the reasons for them.

The Schools

Moorhead

Moorhead Middle School was established in September 1970, when the Moorhead area of the West Riding reorganized on three-tier lines. It was planned as one of three middle schools in the locality which would form the base of a 'tight' pyramid of schools , at the apex of which would be the new 13–18 upper school, retaining its prestigious title of Moorhead Grammar. When Moorhead Middle first opened, though, its two fellow middles had not yet been built. Riverdale, two miles down the valley, did not open until two years later. Millbeck, a similar distance in the other direction, did not start receiving pupils until a whole decade later. When Moorhead Middle began, then, it had to cater for the pupil intakes of Riverdale and Millbeck as well as its own. Severe pressure on space resulted.

One temporary solution to the space problem was to begin taking pupils at 10 instead of 9, a pattern of organization which continued even after Riverdale opened in 1972, and indeed right up to the opening of Millbeck. Thus, Moorhead became one of the very few 10–13 middle schools at the time. Even with the exclusion of one whole year group, though, pressure on space remained strong. Numbers on roll were 585 during the period of research, rose to 614 the year after and had been as high as 635 before that, yet the school had been established within post-war secondary modern school premises which, as they stood, could cater for nothing like these numbers. The addition of a separate open-plan wing for the 10–11 year olds helped, but even so, the accommodation was still insufficient and many classes had to be taught in small 'terrapin' huts of the kind which became such a familiar feature of expanding comprehensive sites in the 1970s.

The Moorhead site, then, consisted of three parts: the post-war secondary premises themselves where staffroom, science/craft room, library, hall, music room and the many individual classrooms with their neat ranks of tables were dotted along the rather pristine looking check-tiled corridors; the relatively more spacious, airy and colourful 'junior' block for the 10–11 year olds with its home bases clustered round central areas (though with the crucial addition of concertina'd screens to create separate classroom-like environments when teachers wished); and the scattered terrapins which provided an annexe for two classes in the first year block and for many more in the main part of the school. There was, then, in these days before the onset of falling rolls, a general impression of overcrowding at Moorhead Middle, of a building where teaching space and specialist facilities were always in short supply. This issue, in fact, was one on which teachers, the head and the governors commented on many occasions.

The staff at Moorhead — seven men and seventeen women — consisted of a large group of teachers who moved to the middle school when the grammar, secondary modern and primary schools in which they worked disappeared under comprehensive reorganization in Moorhead, though such teachers were increasingly being supplanted by new appointments from 'outside', several of them fresh from training. Apart from the Deputy and Senior Mistress, all staff were organized in year teams, immediately accountable to their heads of year.

Moorhead's Headteacher, Mr Butcher, had been with the school since its opening. A university graduate in economics, he decided, he recalled, that opportunities for teaching economics were limited, but that he did want to teach and indeed, wanted to become a headmaster 'because I had certain ideas on education, certain ideas on organization of schools which I thought I would like to have the opportunity of experimenting with'. After teaching a mixture of economics and general subjects in a secondary school, he then took a deputy headship of a primary school — 'a ridiculous appointment', as he put it, since his experiences at that level then consisted solely of 'a few courses on primary education'. After two years he moved to a headship of a larger primary school from where, after a further six years, he progressed to Moorhead Middle.

Much of the reason for this last appointment, Mr Butcher reflected, could probably be put down to the fact that during his headship of the large primary school, that school was used as a pilot for *Nuffield Junior Science* which 'focussed a lot of attention on the school and, I suppose, incidentally a lot of attention on me . . . and I got involved then with the extension of the primary age range right up to the age of 13 since this was the age range that this was designed to cope with'. 'It was then', he went on,

> that the whole question of middle school education was being raised in the West Riding . . . and so I got interested in it and it was then that I decided that if the oportunity came along for me to become head of a middle school, that's what I would like to do. And that's how I came into it. This one came up and that's how I got here.

Once in the middle school, Mr Butcher's view of it was that it

> should be an *entity in itself.* Initially, it depends, I suppose, what the background of the . . . uh . . . each member of staff as to what, how it functions initially. But it's got to have *its own identity.* It's *not just a transit camp* between the primary school on the one hand and the secondary school on the other. But nevertheless, it's got to take account, I think, of the *best practices of primary* education and also the *desirable practices for the lower end of the secondary school* which secondary schools were not always able to implement, because of all sorts of other factors. And it should be *an amalgam* of these two things. But it's got to have *its own ethos* and it's got to have its own objectives. (my emphases)

This vision of the middle school was presented not just in interview to me but on paper and in talks to parents and other public bodies also.[3] It was a vision based very much on the *invention* model of middle schooling — one which emphasized and oscillated between both its unique and transitional aspects.

Riverdale

Riverdale Middle was much smaller than Moorhead. Established in September 1972, and catering for an equally well insulated but not nearly so large community as Moorhead, it had but 255 pupils on roll in the year the research was conducted. This amounted to something like a two-and-a-half form entry, rather than the six or seven forms per year group that were to be found at Moorhead. By middle school standards, Riverdale was, for that time, very small indeed, although with the later onset of falling rolls, many more middle schools have subsequently shrunk to three-form entry or less (an indicator of Riverdale's relevance to current middle school issues).

When first set up, Riverdale was located in temporary accommodation in another part of the village, with no facilities for craft or other specialist areas of the curriculum. In view of these difficulties, Mr Kitchen, the Head, initially opted for a curriculum based on what he called 'the primary extension principle', with a heavy dependence on outside studies and community visits. Exciting as this often was in the short term, Mr Kitchen recalled that the general shortage of facilities, tensions between himself and the outgoing head of the village primary school, and the location of some of Riverdale's pupils two miles away at Moorhead, all had disruptive effects on the learning and adaptation to school of the two top year groups in particular.

At the beginning of the next school year, September 1973, half the pupils — the third and fourth years — moved into the new buildings. But staff and pupils in general were still split between two sites and the third and fourth years had to be housed in the first and second year blocks since their own block was not yet available, and had to spend all term surrounded by the continuing noise and disruption of building alterations — 'a particularly damaging situation', the Head recalled.

By January 1974, all pupils were on the one site, but many of the specialist facilities (for drama and school meals, for instance) were still not completed and there was much ferrying of pupils to and fro between the school and various church and village halls. Nor had all the building defects been removed either. No wonder, in the midst of all this turmoil, that Mr Kitchen saw one of his prime tasks in this period as trying 'to establish an identity for the school against adversity'.

None of these disruptive influences in the school's history were immediately apparent to visitors such as myself approaching the school for the first time in early 1975. The school was in an attractive location, sheltered by mature trees at the front and backing on to an expanse of playing fields at the rear. The building itself, despite its rather unimaginative grey exterior was light and spacious within, an impression that was enhanced by the colourful and carefully mounted displays of childrens' work that could be found all around the school. Physically, the school was divided into two large blocks for 9–11 and 11–13 year olds respectively, linked by the staffroom, library and hall areas along with the Head's and Deputy's office and a storeroom or two. The upper school block was further divided into third and fourth year units, a wedge of specialist craft and home economics facilities being placed between them. In all blocks, though, general teaching space and classroom furniture were organized in a similar fashion. What could be found in only the junior block at Moorhead applied at Riverdale throughout: a clustering of home bases around central shared working areas with movable screens between them formed by only the flimsiest of curtains and concertina doors. Barring one or two important exceptions, during French lessons for instance, there were no neat serried ranks of uniform tables here of the kind that could be found in the top two years at Moorhead, but a mixture of circular and rectangular ones organized in no obvious geometric pattern. This was as true, almost, of the senior block as the junior one. Throughout the school in fact, the patterning of seating and the movement of children around working spaces left the person making but a casual inspection with a powerful impression of openness and diversity in the school's educational approach.

The Riverdale teaching staff — five men and eight women — were, in the words of two members of Her Majesty's Inspectorate who visited the school in early 1975, 'young and consequently inexperienced'.[4] Of a full-time staff of twelve (excluding the Deputy Head, who was on secondment), there was only one appointment — the Senior Mistress and Acting Deputy, Mrs Weaver — on a scale 3 post or above. The remaining five posts of responsibility in the school were all on scale 2. The occupants of four of these, moreover, had less than five years' teaching experience each at the time of the research. This inexperience brought benefits as well as drawbacks, for one factor which accounted for it was that only one of Riverdale's teachers, Mr Banks, had been directly involved in and redeployed because of comprehensive reorganization in Moorhead. The rest of the staff came to Riverdale by their own 'free' choice; six direct from training and four of the rest from other parts of the County. By contrast, at Moorhead, even five years after the school had been established, as many as five of the thirteen staff interviewed had moved from local primary and secondary schools on reorganization.

As at Moorhead, Riverdale staff were organized for teaching purposes into year-based teams. The small size of Riverdale, though, meant that Year Leader responsibilities had to take in two years combined — first and second, and third and fourth respectively.

Riverdale, then, was a new school, in a new building with a new, young and somewhat inexperienced staff. In the main, it was just these things, in fact, which, according to Mr Kitchen, attracted him to this particular appointment. Having had experience of teaching in an 11–14 junior high school in the Midlands, Mr Kitchen was doing advisory teaching work at the Teacher's Centre in a nearby area that was also taking an interest in middle schools, when he 'fancied having a crack at a middle school'. His access, in his advisory position, to information concerning the kinds of buildings in which middle schools were being established helped him decide on the kind of school he would prefer. As he put it in interview, comparing his own school with Moorhead:

> If I'd wanted a converted secondary-school type middle, I would've applied for one. In fact, at the same time as applying for here, there was one going which was twice the size of this one and I may have stood a chance of getting it, I don't know. But I opted for the smaller one and the purpose-built one because the purpose-built one attracted me. It was the one that would approximate to a primary school, quite frankly.

In this, Mr Kitchen was revealing his commitment to the primary *extension* model of middle schooling, a model which he had valued in his own school's formative days and the importance of which he continued to stress at the time of the fieldwork. As he put it in interview:

In terms of how I saw the middle school, I've often argued at the time that change was *how much secondary, how much primary*. I think that having its *own identity* is concerned at this point. But if my back was against the wall, I would say I would have a primary middle and *extend* the primary influence as opposed to a secondary set up. And so perhaps my idea of a middle school is my idea of a *good primary school extended* to meet the needs of children who are a little older and slightly more complex in their make up. (my emphases)

Summary

The staffing details and major characteristics of, and differences between, the two schools are summarized in the following two tables. You may find it helpful to refer to these tables later, at various points, when looking at the schools in more detail.

On the face of things, Moorhead and Riverdale appear to be very different schools indeed. Overall, Moorhead seems rather 'traditional' in its architecture, staff composition and internal appearance; and Riverdale strikes one as much more 'progressive', an open plan institution cast very much in the Plowden mould. Nor do these differences appear to be related to the nature of the schools' respective pupil intakes either. On the basis of information drawn from a sample of fourth year pupils, both schools seemed to be skewed towards middle class entry (72 per cent of heads of household had non-manual occupations at Moorhead, 56 per cent at Riverdale — both significantly different from patterns of national distribution.[6] Nor could any differences between the schools be explained by their catering for different

Table 2: Staff List — Riverdale and Moorhead

	Moorhead		
	Deputy Head: Mr Greek		
	Senior Mistress: Mrs Spinner		
Year 4	*Year 3*	*Year 2*	*Part-time*
Mr Jefferson*	Mr Bird	Mrs Keen	Mrs Smith
Mr Thomas	Mr Mowbray	Mrs Erikson	Mrs Cezanne
Mrs Baggins	Miss Lamb	Mr Johnson	
Mrs Masters	Miss Curie	Mrs Lake	
Mrs Close	Mr Moor	Mrs Handyman	
Mrs York	Mrs Plant	Miss Orson	
Mrs Bone	Mrs Priestley		

	Riverdale		
Year 4	*Year 3*	*Year 2*	*Year 1*	*Part-Time*
Mr Driver	Mr Stones	Mrs Fletcher	Miss Gough	Mrs Littlejohn
Miss Rogers	Mrs Speaker	Mrs Home[5]	Mrs Raines	
Mrs Weaver				

Mr Button

'Floating' Teacher: Mr Banks
Craft Specialist: Mr Home[5]

Table 3:   *Riverdale and Moorhead: Major Characteristics*

Moorhead 10–13	Riverdale 9–13
Large (N.O.R. 585)	Small (N.O.R. 255)
Converted secondary building	Purpose-built, open-plan
Established 4½ years	Established 2½ years
Many 'reorganized' staff (just under half interview sample)	Only one 'reorganized' staff member
'Mature', experienced staff	Young, inexperienced staff
'Formal' appearance of 11–13 classrooms	'Informal' appearance of 11–13 work areas

kinds of middle class pupil either — proportions of 'old' as opposed to 'new' middle class parents (parents, that is, who produced or traded in goods, property or money, as compared with those who dealt with language, symbols and communication) were virtually identical.[7]

Despite intake similarities, then, the schools appeared different in certain respects. Yet appearances can often be deceptive. They can certainly draw attention away from equally important similarities. For instance, while Moorhead had a Head who aspired to an invention model of middle schooling with its emphasis on transition and uniqueness, and while the Head of Riverdale leaned more towards the primary extension principle; neither seemed to want a split, schizoid middle school with primary and secondary identities resting uncomfortably alongside one another. And while Mr Kitchen did seem to favour some percolation upwards into the middle school age range of primary methods and philosophies, neither wanted the secondary school tradition to play a major, more dominant role in the middle school's identity.

How successful were they in realizing their educational visions in this respect? Were their schools unique, transitional places, or even upward extensions of primary models, or were they divided or secondary dominated? The next three chapters examine three aspects of middle schooling at Riverdale and Moorhead in an attempt to answer these questions: the organization of year groups, and the existence and distribution of setting and subject specialism in the top and bottom halves of the middle school respectively.

Notes

1   It is regrettable that quantitative studies have not explicitly built on or developed their instruments in relation to available qualitative work. TAYLOR and GARSON's (1982) survey is written as if existing case studies of middle schools do not exist. Her Majesty's Inspectorate, of course, never refer to research and writing other than that produced by themselves or by affiliated bodies.

2   For example, the studies by WOODS (1979), BALL (1981), SHARP and GREEN (1975), EDWARDS and FURLONG (1978) and BURGESS (1983).

3   Most notably, such views were expressed in a document *Some Thoughts on the Middle*

School produced for parents and staff during the first few years of its operation; which concluded as follows:

> In general, therefore, the middle school will be neither totally primary nor totally secondary in character, nor will its function be simply to provide a gradual change from the former in the first year to the latter in the final year, although it should undoubtedly make the transition less abrupt. The ideal middle school should provide an amalgam of all that is best in both types of school and should have a character which is peculiarly its own.

4   As reported by the Head in conversation.
5   Mr and Mrs HOME were husband and wife.
6   Full statistical details are included in the thesis (HARGREAVES, 1985). The school sample was of 134 fourth years. National figures were taken from the *General Household Survey*, 1974 — the nearest date available to the study reported here — documented in *Social Trends*, London, HMSO, (1976) p. 76. The difference between the social class distribution of the two middle schools together and national social class distribution was found to be significant at the .01 level (Kolmogorov-Smirnov, one-sample test).
7   The categories of new and old middle class were derived from the work of BASIL BERNSTEIN (1975) who argued that the new middle class were particularly strong supporters of what he called the 'invisible pedagogies' of the open-plan, progressive primary school. His criteria for identifying the two groups are not altogether clear, though. Some occupations — farmer and radiographer, for instance — proved particularly difficult to place. The majority, though, presented less problems than this; there being very many teachers and lecturers in higher education, for instance. Categorized this way, the relative proportions of old as against new middle class parents differed by just 0.3 per cent between the two schools.

Chapter 5

The Year System

Introduction

One of the most common patterns of organization within 9–13 and 10–13 middle schools is the year system; the grouping of teachers and pupils for organizational purposes in year-based teams (National Union of Teachers, 1979, p. 8). It was precisely this system, in fact, which the Department of Education and Science (1970b), in their *Education Pamphlet No. 57* recommended as the basic unit of organization for middle schools.[1] Whereas the dominant unit of staff organization in large 11+, and indeed 13 and 14+, comprehensive schools is the individual subject department or larger faculty (HMI, 1978a; DES, 1978), middle schools are generally too small and their specialist staff in any particular area rather too thin on the ground to make it possible to set up coherent subject departments as such. In part, then, the year group system in middle schools has arisen by default, for want of those schools being able (even if they wished) to emulate the subject–departmental model of their secondary counterparts. However, more positive reasons behind and justifications for year group systems in middle schools should not be underestimated. The grouping of staff in teams under year group leaders can do a great deal to coordinate the academic, social and pastoral aspects of educational experience for the pupils in any particular year, and can contribute greatly to the establishment of that balance, breadth and coherence of curricular provision which, as HMI (1978a, 1981 and 1983b) have recorded, can prove so difficult to achieve elsewhere in the seondary sector.[2]

Whatever the merits of the year system in terms of establishing lateral coordination of educational provision, though, there is also a very real danger that year groups might become insulated from one another to such an extent that vertical continuity of curriculum provision and teaching method would be seriously prejudiced as a result. As HMI (1983a) put it in their survey of 9–13 middle schools,

> too great an emphasis on the year group did sometimes have disadvantages. In some cases, the curriculum and teaching approaches lacked adequate continuity from year to year because of the undue emphasis given to separate year groups. (paragraph 2.26)

The year group system, that is, while promising improved lateral coordination also endangers the maintenance of vertical continuity. Against an ideal of gentle transition, it counterposes the ever-likely threat of abrupt breaks and, from the pupil's standpoint, not a smooth but a stacatto-like movement between the tightly insulated, rigidly stratified levels of a strictly age-graded system. But more than this even, depending on just how the years are organized and staff are deployed to them, the year system also increases the middle school's chances of perpetuating a division between what might loosely be called primary and secondary approaches at the conventional demarcation line of 11.

How were the year systems organized at Moorhead and Riverdale? Were they arranged and staffed in such a way as to foster continuity, or did they operate as tightly sealed organizational compartments? And if the breaks from year to year *were* somewhat abrupt, where did the sharpest breaks of all occur? I will look at Moorhead first, paying particular attention to five indicators of the role of the year system in the organization of that school — the head-teacher's remarks, the responses of staff to interview questions about the influence of colleagues on their approach to teaching, staffroom seating patterns, the distribution of teacher time between different years, and the arrangement of year groups within the school building itself.

The Moorhead Year System

The Head

Mr Butcher, the Head of Moorhead, put a great deal of weight and responsibility on the shoulders of his year teams and their leaders. This was reflected in the fact that the three year leaders held higher scale posts — the only scale 3s and above in fact — than anyone else below Deputy. This tendency to allocate the more senior posts to year heads in middle schools is not just peculiar to Moorhead but is a common practice elsewhere also (Bornett, 1980). At Moorhead, it was these three year leaders, and not the subject heads, who were drawn into all the major discussions with the Head and his deputies on aspects of school policy. 'I attach a great deal of importance to the senior members of staff', said Mr Butcher, when asked how he ensured that his aims and objectives were taken up by his staff. He went on:

> I have regular meetings with senior members of staff without an agenda so that we can just throw ideas at each other. And certainly, there's no doubt about it, that the way in which we approach the work here is very much a team effort.

A team effort this may have been, but it was also a team whose membership, except for the Head and deputies themselves, was confined to the year leaders, the holders of the senior scales. Moreover, according to Mr Butcher, it was this lateral year system and not any vertical system of subject departments which prevented members of staff going too far adrift in their curriculum and methods from the accepted 'line'. The opportunities for particular members of staff to carry on in their own way regardless, Mr Butcher argued, 'are limited, since the year group system demands that there is a good deal of consultation between teachers within each year'.

Staff Interviews

Heads' intentions are not always translated into practice, however. It is therefore important to look at what staff themselves have to say too. I asked all staff I interviewed whether any of their colleagues had influenced the way they taught at all. Seven teachers — among the most experienced in the school — did not cite anyone as being especially important in this respect.[3] They valued their classroom autonomy very much. But other members of staff not only claimed to be influenced substantially by certain of their colleagues, but attributed most of this influence to their year heads and year teams. Mrs Erikson (year 2) picked out her year head 'because, you know, she's so competent: sort of a model for what you could achieve if you'd been doing it for twenty years'. Miss Lamb (year 3) also mentioned her year head 'because I've turned to him for advice where classroom subjects are concerned ... I would say he's had quite a bit of effect on me already and I've only been in school a few weeks'. Similarly, Mrs Close (year 4) and Miss Curie (year 3) spoke more generally of the importance of being part of 'a team'. And Mrs Spinner, the Senior Mistress, interestingly *denied* being influenced by her colleagues on the grounds that she 'was not really a member of a team'.

These findings are worth comparing with the responses to a second interview question. Were teachers happy with the amount of control they had in deciding what children learned?[4] Once more, experienced staff drew particular attention to their own highly valued sense of independence and autonomy through such remarks as 'I've always been my own master in the classroom' (Mr Bird), 'I get my own way, more or less ... one is to a large extent a free agent' (Mr Thomas) and 'we've got a free hand in what we do, so it's really up to us' (Mrs Handyman). Of the remaining six clearly decipherable responses[5], two contained positive comments on the helpful guidance of the year team — Mrs Erikson in connection with 'the integrated studies area that was democratically agreed by the second year teachers' and Miss Lamb who, outside her own specialist area of home economics was

> rather glad I don't have an awful lot of say ... for obvious reasons that they're not really my subjects so I'm glad that I've got somebody to turn to and say 'Right, what do I do now? Give me some ideas to follow!' For example, the year head gave me a list of topics I could cover in each of the subjects.

The remaining four members of staff were deeply critical of what, to them, appeared to be an absence of vertical continuity and general support in the specialist subject areas. Mrs Masters pointed out the need for more discussion on the social studies syllabus; Mr Moor stated 'there are some occasions when I would like a little bit more advice in certain things; a little bit more advice from people who are supposed to be specialists within their subjects'; and Mrs Close even in her own area of English where she held a good deal of responsibility (she coordinated the 'set' English in years 3 and 4), drew attention to the need for more coordination and staff discussion — a need which, she felt, pervaded other areas of the curriculum too. On the subject of vertical continuity, though, Mrs Priestley was the most severely critical:

> I think the year head is giving as much as he can, but I feel that the school is not integrated. There's definitely a second year and a gap, and a third year and a gap, and a fourth year and I don't think we work together. I'm thinking of subject material. I mean we do such odd things, say, in history. I mean it's not integrated at all in terms of continuity.

One thing these staff responses appear to indicate is that the year team and year head exercised a substantial and often much-valued degree of influence, particularly on less experienced members of staff. Alongside this ran expressions of some regret about the *lack* of influence exerted by vertical subject-based groups and a resulting failure to secure continuity of educational experience across the years. There is a good deal of evidence to suggest, then, that the year teams were much more influential upon the curriculum and teaching of Moorhead Middle than were the subject coordinators.

The Staffroom

These year-based patterns of influence, appeared to be reflected in the social structure of the Moorhead staffroom too. Although I collected no systematic data on the content of staffroom talk at Moorhead, I did make notes on where teachers normally sat. The following seating arrangement at a full staff meeting is fairly typical (figure 2). The year membership of each teacher present is placed after his or her name. In staffrooms, just as in classrooms, if choice is 'free', then where people sit and who they sit next to says a great deal about their choice of friends, the groups to which they belong, with which they identify, and to which they aspire. The social organization of Moorhead staffroom, in this sense, appeared to have a strong year basis to it. There are, as one might expect, some exceptions to this pattern. Mr Jefferson, the Year 4 Leader, for instance sat among his second year colleagues at this particular meeting, a fact which is probably explained by his late arrival, for at other times, if he was not, in his capacity as Head of Music, giving instrumental tuition or leading choir practice, he usually sat with other members in his own year team. Mrs Baggins, the fourth year art teacher, chose to associate with the more child-centred and innovative teachers of the second year team because, like many art teachers (Bennett, 1985), she felt somewhat marginal to the traditional subject specialist concerns and pedagogical approaches which were shared by many of her fourth year colleagues.[7] And Mr Thomas, the other intruder in the second year half of the staffroom on this particular occasion, rarely entered the staffroom at all at other times, much preferring the clutter of his craft workshop. Aside from these

Figure 2: Seating Arrangements at a Moorhead Staff Meeting

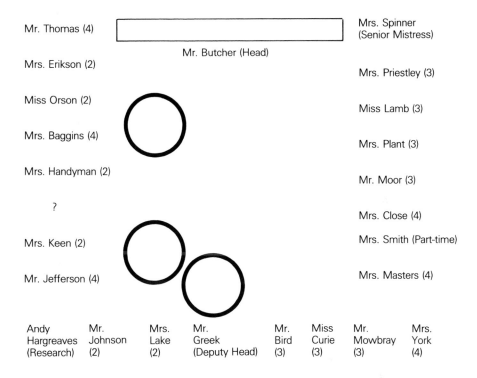

Mr. Thomas (4)

Mr. Butcher (Head)

Mrs. Spinner (Senior Mistress)

Mrs. Erikson (2)

Mrs. Priestley (3)

Miss Orson (2)

Miss Lamb (3)

Mrs. Baggins (4)

Mrs. Plant (3)

Mrs. Handyman (2)

Mr. Moor (3)

?

Mrs. Close (4)

Mrs. Keen (2)

Mrs. Smith (Part-time)

Mr. Jefferson (4)

Mrs. Masters (4)

Andy Hargreaves (Research)   Mr. Johnson (2)   Mrs. Lake (2)   Mr. Greek (Deputy Head)   Mr. Bird (3)   Miss Curie (3)   Mr. Mowbray (3)   Mrs. York (4)

exceptions, though, the Moorhead staffroom was split into two very distinct halves; the second year, primary age-range teachers seated down one side, and the third and fourth year secondary age-range teachers down the other, with Mr Greek, the first Deputy, acting as a symbolic bulwark between the two.

Thus, while in interview, the experienced members of the Moorhead staff disclaimed any influence of their colleagues upon their teaching, there is a strong likelihood that such influences may have accumulated nonetheless in a tacit, routine and unnoticed way, through the day-to-day medium of staffroom culture. If the seating arrangements of the Moorhead staffroom are anything to go by, these sub-cultures had a strong year basis to them. This, it seems, not only fragmented the Moorhead staff into year-based sub-groups in general, reflecting and perhaps reinforcing a wider year-based fragmentation within the school as a whole, but also marked a sharp difference, a veritable split in the social organization of the Moorhead staff between the bottom 'primary' year and the top two 'secondary' ones. Was the staffroom unusual in manifesting this kind of split? Or were other aspects of the organization of teaching at Moorhead characterized by similar tendencies too?

Teacher Time Allocations

Much can be deduced about the internal organization of a school simply by inspecting the allocation of those two precious resources — time and space — within it. In this respect, school timetables are not just informative managerial guides to who is where and at what time, but also highly significant documents of a school's organizational priorities (Simper, 1980; Brookes, 1980; Johnson, 1980).

Moorhead's timetable said a good deal about the extent to which the different years and their teachers were separated or insulated from one another. The allocation of each member of staff's teaching time between the three different years is the crucial source of data here.

Table 4: *Percentage Allocation of Teacher Time Between Different Year Groups at Moorhead.*

	Percentage Time Spent With Each Year Group		
Year Team	*Year 2*	*Year 3*	*Year 4*
2	100.0	0.0	0.0
3	7.1	72.5	20.4
4	3.3	24.2	72.5
Deputy Heads	11.1	29.6	59.3

These data raise several interesting points. First, most teachers' time was spent within their own year groups. This is, of course, probably justified if the principle of year attachments and year teams is to have anything more than paper significance. But while there is always likely to be some disagreement about the exact proportions of time teachers should spend inside and outside their own year groups if lateral coherence and vertical continuity are *both* to be preserved, the degree to which teachers were enclosed within their own years appeared excessive at Riverdale and Moorhead if hopes for any continuity of educational experience at all between the years were to be retained. The second year team was, in this sense, the most extreme case of year-based insularity; its staff spending their entire teaching time within their own year group.

Most teaching at Moorhead was therefore year-based, and for the second year team this was exclusively the case. A third point, following on from this, is that while there appears to be a substantial crossover of teaching responsibilities between the top years, with teachers in both years 3 and 4 having contact with pupils in their 'other' year for at least 20 per cent of their teaching time, there was hardly any crossover of teaching expertise at all involving year 2. Fourth, and related to this, while there was some 'downward' movement, however small, of third and fourth year teachers into second year classes, there was no 'upward' movement at all of second year teachers into years 3 and 4. Fifth, and last, the Deputy Head and Senior Mistress spent most of their teaching time in years 3 and 4 also.

To sum up, at Moorhead, teacher time allocations were largely confined to particular year groups; exclusively so in the case of year 2, a situation which will likely have created the basis for a set of shared and distinctive problems on which year-based staffroom sub-cultures could then feed. Not only is it probable that this will have generated a system of organizationally separate and culturally reinforced year teams which seriously threaten the goal of smooth transition that Mr Butcher deemed to be so central to the middle school concept, but the existence of greater gaps and sharper breaks between years 2 and 3 than years 3 and 4 strengthens the likelihood of there being a fundamental primary/secondary split in the middle school's identity. More than this, if the distribution of teacher time allocations is at all a reliable indicator, then the greater downward permeation of year 3 and 4 teachers into year 2 than vice versa gives some support to the view that 'secondary' influences are stronger than 'primary' ones in shaping the middle school's character.

Buildings

One last indication that something approaching a primary/secondary split was imported into the year system at Moorhead Middle is to be found in the very layout of the school buildings themselves. Of course, school buildings do not completely determine the curricula and teaching methods that go on within them (Cooper, 1983; Wallace, 1980). But, by opening some possibilities and closing off others and through the educational assumptions which are implicit in their design, they do help shape and influence the way in which those schools become organized (Eggleston, 1977). Now here, as Blyth and Derricott (1977, p. 55) have noted, the Department of Education and Science boldly advised middle school heads to steer clear of the potential organizational hazard of a sharp break at 11 by placing their second and third year classes in particularly close proximity so as to encourage the sharing of experience between middle school staff across the customary primary/secondary divide. Indeed, Ginsburg and his colleagues (1977, p. 35) found that the heads of two of the five middle schools they studied had established just such a 1–2–1 pattern of organization for these very reasons. More often than not, though, as Blyth and Derricott (1977, p. 55) themselves observe, the DES's advice has been disregarded.

So it was at Moorhead where, terrapins apart, all third and fourth year classes (along with specialist craft, science and home economics facilities) were housed in the original two-storey secondary modern school building. The open-plan wing which had been added to adapt and extend the old secondary school for middle school purposes was given over exclusively to the second years, not only segregating them, in effect, from the rest of the school, but in an environment whose very construction suggested and implied very different methods and approaches than did the classrooms and corridors of the old buildings. The very architecture of the school, then, with its separation of 'secondary' and 'primary' areas, suggested a continuation of a division at 11.

Summary

Moorhead staff were organized into year teams where they spent by far the greater part of their teaching time. Moreover, the place where transfer and sharing of staff expertise was at its least was between years 3 and 4 on the one hand, and year 2 on the other. These arrangements were reflected in and reinforced through year-based staffroom sub-cultures and through the very architectural design of the school itself with its creation of a separate, distinct and relatively insulated 'primary' unit.

Mr Butcher put a great deal of weight on his year heads as a source of educational leadership within the school and felt they would produce a real coordination of effort and integration of experience across the curriculum. But for all this, it seems, he paid a price. While he strove to achieve a unique indentity for Moorhead as one distinctive school with a special educational purpose, in practice his school was divided into a number of separate year-based organizational units and staff sub-cultures which not only generated serious problems of vertical continuity but also created, or rather, sustained a particularly sharp break at 11. Moreover, the data on teacher time allocations indicate that if there was any exertion of staff influence across this divide at all, it was the downward influence of the 'secondary' age range teachers in years 3 and 4 that counted most. In short, in terms of its patterns of year organization, Moorhead Middle School was characterized not by smooth transition but by overall *fragmentation*, by a particularly sharp *division* at 11, and by a marginal dominance of *secondary* over primary influences.

The Riverdale Year System

In some respects, the Riverdale year system was less well defined than the one at Moorhead. For one thing, given the shortage of scale points in a school with only a two-and-a-half form entry, there were only two, instead of the usual four year leaders one might otherwise expect to find in a 9–13 middle school. Moreover, the staff was so small that there were insufficient numbers of teachers in the staffroom — rarely more than eight at any one time — to provide any firm basis for the development of well-defined staff sub-cultures.

In addition to the school's small size, the recency of its establishment also had a tempering effect on the influence of its year system. As we saw earlier, Mr Kitchen, the Head, often spoke about the school's recent past, about the previous fragment-ation of its staff, about the disruptive effects of continuing building work within the new premises, and so on; and he repeatedly drew attention to what, because of all this, he regarded as a major priority of school management — the collective establishment of an agreed curriculum and purpose for the school as a whole with which the staff could readily identify. Against these pressing school-wide concerns, the fortunes of the particular year groups were presumably of much less significance: he rarely mentioned them either in interview or more general conversation.

Notwithstanding these various factors and their potentially weakening effects upon the formation of a system of tightly segregated and strongly insulated year groups, though, there are many other counter-indications that divisions between the year groups were at least as well-defined as those at Moorhead, if not more so. Take the simple matter of buildings, for instance. Although, unlike Moorhead, there were no striking differences in design between the 'upper' and 'lower' parts of the school at Riverdale, the teaching spaces in each being organized in terms of home groups clustered around central shared areas, nevertheless, the school was architecturally divided into two completely distinct halves, between which stood the staffroom, the hall and library. The very design of the building, that is, suggested the placement of years 1 and 2 in one part of the school and years 3 and 4 in the other.[8]

Patterns of staff deployment further contributed to Riverdale's recreation of a divide at 11. The school had two year heads, Mr Driver and Mrs Fletcher, each of whom held responsibility for two year groups. The boundary between their designated areas of responsibility fell just at the point which would otherwise have separated primary from secondary education, Mrs Fletcher being the leader of years 1 and 2, and Mr Driver of years 3 and 4. Of the remaining staff, all but three- Mr Home who taught specialist craft throughout the school, Mr Banks who assisted in the library and with small group maths tuition (though mainly in years 3 and 4) and Mrs Littlejohn, the part-time French teacher who taught in years 3 and 4 only — were formally attached to particular years. One partial exception to this, Mr Button was, at the time of the research, attached to *two* years (1 and 2), but again, it is of interest that these did not straddle the 11 + divide.

This grouping of teachers by years was reinforced through the balance of (or, rather, imbalance between) their teaching commitments. An analysis of the Riverdale timetable reveals that just as at Moorhead, teachers spent their time in school almost exclusively with their own year group. If anything, the boundaries between the years were, in this respect, even more clearly defined than those at Moorhead. Teachers in years 1, 2 and 3 at Riverdale taught outside their own year group for only 5 per cent or less of their time, and even in year 4 where the figure was as high as $22\frac{1}{2}$ per cent, this was still not so high as the admittedly modest percentage of out-of-year teaching that took place among fourth year teachers at Moorhead.

Table 5: *Percentage Allocation of Teacher Time Between Different Year Groups at Riverdale*

| Year team | Percentage time spent with each year group | | | | |
	Year 1	Year 2	Year 3	Year 4	General
1	98.15	1.25	0	0	0
2	2.8	97.2	0	0	0
1 + 2	40.0	55.0	5.0	0	0
3	0	0	100.0	0	0
4	1.7	1.7	17.7	77.5	1.6
Others	7.5	7.5	30.0	27.5	27.5

Most strikingly of all, when 'lower' school (years 1 and 2) teachers are compared with 'upper' school (years 3 and 4) ones, no more than 2 per cent of teaching time in either case was spent outside teachers' own half of the school (table 6).

Table 6: Percentage Allocation of Teacher Time Between 'Upper' and 'Lower' School Parts of Riverdale

| Year Groups | Percentage time spent in each 'half' of the school | |
	Years 1 + 2	Years 3 + 4
1 + 2	98.9	1.0
3 + 4	2.0	96.9

If the findings from this analysis of teacher time allocations are combined with what is also known about the strict architectural and geographical separation of the 'upper' and 'lower' parts of the middle school from one another, then it is reasonable to conclude that 'lower' school pupils probably saw very little of the staff attached to the 'upper' part of the middle school, and that likewise, third and fourth year pupils had little contact with those teachers whom they had come to know during their first two years of middle schooling. This raises serious questions about the school's capacity to meet the requirements for achieving smooth transition upon which the credibility and claims for distinctiveness of middle schools have in large part rested.

Even more than at Moorhead, then, it seems that the architecture and staffing arrangements at Riverdale combined together to produce a fragmented year system, the most dominant feature of which was an almost total insulation of the 'primary' and 'secondary' ends of the middle school from one another. In this way, despite its recency and despite the purpose built nature of its accommodation, Riverdale Middle School helped recreate within its own walls the abruptness of a split at 11 which had once occurred and in many places still does occur between primary and secondary education. That staff were aware of this hiatus and of the insular nature of their year-based teaching can be discerned from the remarks they made in interview.

As at Moorhead, I asked teachers whether any of their colleagues had an influence upon their teaching. Four placed a great deal of emphasis on the effect that colleagues in their year team had upon them. Mr Stones, for instance, though keen to point out that his colleagues 'don't have that much of an influence' — a situation which might in part be explained by the temporary (one-year) nature of his appointment — nevertheless did concede that where any influence *was* present, it was the people around him, particularly Mrs Speaker, who had the strongest effect. Mrs Speaker herself, Mr Stones' third year colleague, put the point this way:

> I suppose in the set up we have here one is most concerned with the person working with you in your particular year group . . . and obviously their ideas and their abilities and their way of doing things do affect the overall teaching within that year group.

'It's very much a team thing', she went on, 'there's a great deal of cooperation goes on; a great deal of help one to the other.'

Mr Stones' remarks in particular illustrate the importance of propinquity in shaping colleaguial relations among middle school teachers on year team lines — the more you see of someone and work alongside them, that is, the more likely it is you will be influenced by their approach to teaching. The comments of Mrs Raines, a first year teacher in her probationary year, add weight to this view. After pointing to the influence exerted by two of her fellow first and second year colleagues, Miss Gough and Mrs Home, upon her work, Mrs Raines continued, 'Perhaps in the first and second year, I'm much more affected by the other teachers than, say, further up the school because I don't see much of them. Very much divorced, in a way!' For Mrs Home, one of the second year teachers, this divorce was in many respects evidently a most unhappy one. Having talked approvingly about the influence of her year head upon her teaching, Mrs Home went on to make some critical remarks about the year system in general; remarks which were tinged with more than a hint of resentment. Other than the influence of her year head, Mrs Home argued,

> the first and second years come into very little contact with the third and fourth year. In this school, it's very much first and second — stop — third and fourth, which I personally don't think is a good thing ... First and second years, I think we feel very much aggrieved that the third and fourth years are helped out as much as possible. You know, any extra staff then they get it. And yet we're battling down here with the larger classes and we get very little help. I mean, for a whole two terms, my class couldn't get up to the cookery area and science area because we just take our class and our class alone. Nobody has come down to help. So this is a grievance and a problem really as well.[9]

Separation, division and insulation between the primary and secondary ends of Riverdale; these were central themes of Mrs Home's critique, a critique which also contained a strong sense of status deprivation[10] not only in explicit complaints about inferior staffing and such like, but also in her apparent awareness of an age-based hierarchy as revealed in her routine references to 'down here' and to getting 'up to' the specialist facilities in the senior block of the school.

There were some apparent exceptions to this rule of year-based influence and to the gaps and forms of insulation which it generated. Mr Button and Miss Rogers, for instance, recently transferred to their respective year groups from 'the other half' of the school, would admit to being influenced only by people in that previous year attachment. And the staff who were not explicitly attached to any year group at all — Mr Home and Mrs Littlejohn in particular — denied being influenced by anyone. Yet, if anything, these exceptions helped prove the year-based rule, rather than undermining it. For one thing, as recent recruits to their year teams, it is perfectly understandable that past loyalties and affiliations should continue, in the short term at least, to have a stronger pull than present commitments on the teaching of Miss Rogers and Mr Button. And while Mr Home the craft teacher, and Mrs Littlejohn, the part-time French specialist were, to be sure, not influenced by any particular year group, they were not part of any clearly delineated alternative or complementary pattern of staff organization or affiliation either, be this on subject lines or any other. Mrs Littlejohn apparently suffered the fate of most part-time teachers complaining that she 'never sees anyone else',[11] and Mr Home was, in his own words, 'not working with anybody' which while making him his own master, also thrust him to the margins of the system whose staff organization and basis of cooperation was predicated almost entirely on year-based principles. This system, as we have seen, led at Riverdale, to a fragmented, divided and insular pattern of school organization with some consequences for feelings of status deprivation among teachers within the 'lower' part of the school.

Conclusion

Various studies of comprehensive schooling have revealed that when grammar/secondary modern reorganization takes place, teachers have a tendency to hang on to and form staff sub-cultures around their previous educational identitites; a process which, if anything, is reinforced through headteacher policies which award high status positions to ex-grammar school teachers at the expense of their secondary modern colleagues (Riseborough, 1981). Moreover, even in established comprehensive schools, while heads may speak with passion and commitment about their school's overall identity and purpose, studies have revealed that significant divisions, conflict and competition occur between the academic and pastoral systems (Burgess, 1983; Evans, 1985) and, in the academic system itself, between different subject departments. (Ball, 1981)

All these studies point to important gaps between the managerial rhetoric of institutional unity and somewhat murkier realities of conflict, competition and division within a school's organizational pattern and sub-cultural life. Similar gaps have been highlighted in this analysis of the year systems at Riverdale and Moorhead. But at least one important point distinguishes the findings of this study from previous ones. In studies of 11–18 or 11–16 comprehensive schools, the divisions that have been identified have been vertical in character; they have been divisions between subject communities or between academic and pastoral work which have run throughout the entire age range of the school. In this study of Riverdale and Moorhead middle schools, though, divisions on vertical subject lines appear to be weak or virtually non-existent — this being due to the small numbers of teachers, usually no more than two, who are specialists in any one subject, and who might, if they were in the company of several other like-minded colleagues, otherwise form the basis of identifiable subject communities.

Instead, the divisions at Riverdale and Moorhead, and, it seems, in middle schools more generally, are lateral in character, the lines of demarcation and cleavage in organization and teacher sub-cultures occurring *between* different year groups. Thus, in contrast to the headteachers' espousal of an ideology of smooth transition in educational experience between primary and secondary education, I have identified a pattern of year organization in both schools characterized by fragmentation, division and a particularly strong degree of insulation between the 'top' (secondary) and 'bottom' (primary) ends of the middle. According to HMI (1983a), this is a pattern that extends far beyond these two schools alone. It is a pattern which poses significant threats to those aims of vertical continuity of educational experience which have figured prominently in claims concerning the distinctiveness of the middle school identity.

Notes

1 So too did various speakers at the Warwick conference covered by the Schools Council in 1967. See SCHOOLS COUNCIL (1969).

2 Thus, while secondary schools also often employ year systems as part of their organizational arrangements, the purpose is in their case almost exclusively pastoral (BEST *et al*, 1980). They do not contain that additional brief for curriculum coordination which is essential to the middle school year system.

3 There are several possible reasons for the absence of claimed influence among this group of experienced teachers. It may be that the more the teaching career lengthens, the more that awareness of any influence diminishes as that influence itself becomes routine and taken for granted. This is how many experienced secondary teachers often respond to examination constraints, for instance, seeing them increasingly over time not as a constraint at all, but as a taken-for-granted 'fact of life', as it were (SCARTH, 1983). Equally, it may be that more experienced members of staff are likely to treasure their classroom autonomy more than do their more junior colleagues, and thus to see the admission of influence as a possible threat to their competence and expertise. This may make them reluctant to concede the existence of any such influence in interview. Lastly, of course, more experienced staff may be genuinely less pliable in or more confident about their own educational views and approaches than colleagues at an earlier point in their careers, and therefore less likely to solicit or respond to advice from others.

4 The details of the staff interview schedule can be found in the appendix.

5 Two responses were unclear or untranscribable. One of the respondents (Miss CURIE) was so vague in her answer to this question, that interpretation was very difficult. Another response — Mr MOWBRAY'S — was muffled and therefore untranscribable.

6 The question mark indicates an unidentified visitor.

7 These views were revealed to me in informal staffroom conversation.

8 An arrangement which is further fixed by not-so-trivial matters such as size of toilets and height of coat hooks.

9 It is worth noting that such aggrieved responses — as all the responses about the year system and, later, about setting and specialism — were produced not in response to questions directly focussed on these issues, but in response to more general questions about likes and dislikes, strengths and weaknesses, etc. — questions of a general character designed to elicit teachers' working perceptions of educational issues in their schools *as they saw them*.

10 See HARGREAVES (1967) for an account of status deprivation as experienced by working class pupils.

11 For research on the isolation and detachment experienced by part-time teachers, see NEEDHAM and TROWN (1980).

Chapter 6

Setting

Introduction

Two of the distinctive features of British secondary schools, as compared to their primary counterparts, are the practices of grouping pupils by ability between classes and of organizing the majority of teaching on subject specialist lines. This distinction is not a hard and fast one. There are many secondary schools which have adopted mixed ability grouping as a dominant feature of their school organization (Kelly, 1978) and a number which have developed programmes of integrated studies, particularly with their first and second years (CCOSS, 1984). Equally, though streaming by ability is less common than it once was in English primary schools, it still persists in a small minority of cases (HMI, 1978b) and there are signs too that topic work and the integrated school day are by no means as popular as they once were and are now facing a clear, DES supported challenge from some teachers and heads who prefer a stronger subject specialist orientation within the primary curriculum (DES, 1983). Despite these important areas of overlap, though, the differences between the two spheres are still sufficiently great to allow the existence and distribution of ability grouping and subject specialist teaching within middle schools to be used as reasonably valid indicators of secondary-type influences there. The purpose of the next two chapters is to map out these two key interrelated features of middle school practice in the top and bottom halves of such schools respectively as a way of establishing the primariness, secondariness, uniqueness or divided nature of the middle school identity. This chapter focusses on the first of these features; the nature and distribution of ability grouping in middle schools.

The National Picture

Apart from mixed ability grouping, there are three major ways in which schools can and do sort their pupils into classes on ability-based grounds: streaming, banding and setting.

Streaming and banding are not especially widespread in the 9–13 middle school system. Streaming, the allocation of pupils to classes according to what is presumed to be some general measure of intellectual ability, is operated in just over 4 per cent of 9–13 middle schools at the top end of the primary phase — at 10 +, that is (Taylor and Garson, 1982, p. 128; HMI, 1983a, p. 24) — a figure that closely resembles the 6 per cent produced by HMI for the primary sector (HMI, 1978b, p. 28).[1] Further up the middle school, with the 12 + age group, for instance, the proportion of schools that stream is somewhat greater: 13.3 per cent in the Taylor and Garson survey (1982, p. 128), 25 per cent in the more losely sampled and less precisely documented HMI survey (HMI, 1983a, p. 24). These figures might at first strike one as being rather high when compared with ones of 7½ per cent for the first year of secondary school and 13 per cent for the second year (HMI, 1980, p. 26).[2] But it is as well to note that in the secondary sector streaming has often been superseded by systems of banding, ones which entail much broader divisions of pupil groups by ability, and that this alternative arrangement for educational differentiation has not been available to most middle schools, depending as it does on the schools concerned having a large number of forms of entry.

When banding is taken into account in conjunction with streaming, middle schools no longer seem more selective in their grouping arrangements than their secondary counterparts. According to the HMI 9–13 middle school survey, 'In two schools (out of forty-eight), banding was employed in all four year groups: this form of organization was used in seven schools in the third year and four in the fourth year' (HMI, 1983a, p. 24). These modest figures compare with a substantial proportion of 25½ per cent of 11–16/18 comprehensive schools which band their pupils in the first year and almost 31 per cent which band in the second year (HMI, 1980, p. 26).[3] When the figures for streaming and banding are combined, some interesting comparisons emerge between 9–13 middle schools and conventional primary/secondary systems involving transfer at 11 +.

Table 7 reveals that just over 8 per cent of 9–13 middle schools operate one of these systems in their first and second years (slightly *more than* their primary counterparts) and around 30 per cent operate them in years 3 and 4 (a good deal *less than* their secondary counterparts). What this would appear to mean is that if one wishes to use streaming and banding as indicators for distinguishing primary from secondary patterns for organization, then middle schools seem to soften the

Table 7: Percentage of schools which operate systems of streaming or banding with different age groups.[4]

| School type | Age Group | | | |
	9 +	10 +	11 +	12 +
9–13	8.3*		29.2*	33.3*
Primary/secondary		6.0†	33.2‡	43.8‡

Sources: * HMI (1983a) p. 24.
 † HMI (1978) p. 28.
 ‡ HMI (1980a) p. 26.

differences between the two phases: an item of support, one might imagine, for their claims to being genuinely transitional institutions.

Two cautionary points should be noted at this stage, however. The first is that the figures for streaming and banding refer to their incidence in the middle school system as a whole and not to their distribution within individual schools. In other words, it is not that individual schools employ some banding or streaming with younger pupils then gradually increase the proportion with older age groups, but that some middle schools band or stream thoughout, some do not do these things at all, and some institute them suddenly, as it were, with pupils in, say, years 3 and 4. In this sense, the transitional impression afforded to middle schools by aggregating these different possibilities together in the streaming and banding figures for all schools is misleading.

The second point is that there is another pattern of ability-based pupil grouping which has not yet been discussed but which is exceedingly common in middle and secondary systems alike: that of setting. Setting, the grouping of pupils subject by subject according to what are presumed to be specific abilities in each of those subjects, is a common feature of middle school organization, particularly in the top two years. At that point — what might traditionally be regarded as the secondary phase — the frequency of subject setting seems remarkably similar in middle and secondary systems alike. It is difficult to make strict comparisons, age by age, between the two sectors — for there are almost no recent national figures available on setting with pupils aged 11–13 in 11–16/18 institutions — but the setting statistics produced by two HMI surveys on middle and secondary schools respectively, albeit with different age groups, are illuminating here:

Table 8: Percentage frequency of setting among the 12 + age group in 9–13 middle schools, compared with the 13 + age group in secondary schools[5]

Subject	Age Groups and Sectors	
	12 + Middle[6]	13 + Secondary[6]
Mathematics	87.5	90.6
English	60.4	62.0
Modern Languages	68.8	45.8
Science	27.1	28.1

Sources: HMI (1979) p. 17 and HMI (1983a) p. 31.

What the figures in table 8 reveal is that in proportional terms, almost as many middle schools set their pupils for mathematics, English and science at 12 + as do secondary schools one year later at 13 + . If we also bear in mind a further point made by HMI (1979) in their secondary school survey, that setting is more common in this third year of secondary schooling than in the preceding two, then it seems very likely that age-for-age, 9–13 middle schools are setting their pupils just as much as conventional secondary schools are, and possibly even more than that. There is just a little evidence to substantiate this claim, in fact, in the form of statistics concerning one of the most commonly setted subjects in the secondary as indeed in the middle school curriculum — mathematics. In a separately published appendix to their secondary school survey, HMI (1980) outline the ability grouping arrangements for that subject in the first, second and third year of secondary school. What is interesting here is that even if one adopts a generously inclusive definition of ability segregated teaching in mathematics at the secondary level as everything (setting, banding and streaming) that is *not* purely mixed ability, and even if one then compares these figures with the results of that national middle school survey (Taylor and Garson's) of the two currently available which reveals the *lowest* proportion of setting for mathematics in such schools, it still turns out that at the top end of the middle, many more 9–13 schools are setting their pupils for mathematics at age 11 and slightly more at 12 than are secondary schools at the same stage (table 9).

Table 9: *Percentage frequency of setting in mathematics for pupils at 11+ and 12+ in 9–13 midddle schools and 11–16/18 secondary schools[1]*

	Type of School		
Age Range	Middle	Middle	Secondary
	Taylor and Garson	H.M.I.	H.M.I.
	(1982, p. 129)	(1983, p. 31)	(1980, p. 26)
11+	83.3	73.1	49.8
12+	87.5	75.6	73.4

It seems, then, that not only have 9–13 middle schools commonly adopted an organizational pattern of ability grouping in their upper years which bears a strong stamp of the secondary school tradition, but they have employed that practice on a wider front even than the secondary schools themselves. The 9–13 middle school, that is, appears in one important respect to have become more royal than its 'secondary' king.

A second point that emerges from national figures on the amount and distribution of setting in 9–13 middle schools is the existence within them of a sharp break rather than a smooth transition in ability grouping practice in certain subjects at the customary primary/secondary dividing line. As both Taylor and Garson's (1982) and HMI's (1983a) survey show, the onset of setting in three of the four most commonly setted subjects in the middle and secondary school curriculum occurs more frequently at the beginning of year 3 than any other year (figure 3); a point also supported in Meyenn and Tickle's (1980) case study of two contrasting 9–13 middle schools.

These figures for setting in middle schools and secondary schools respectively offer substantial support for the argument that secondary-based conventions and pressures influence important areas of middle school practice greatly in the higher years and in doing so help perpetuate the long-standing division between primary and secondary education at age 11. But what of the early years of the middle school? Setting is certainly less common there than in the later secondary-like years: but just how widespread is that organizational pattern with pupils of 9+ and 10+, and how does its occurrence compare with ability grouping arrangements in the equivalent last two years of primary schooling?

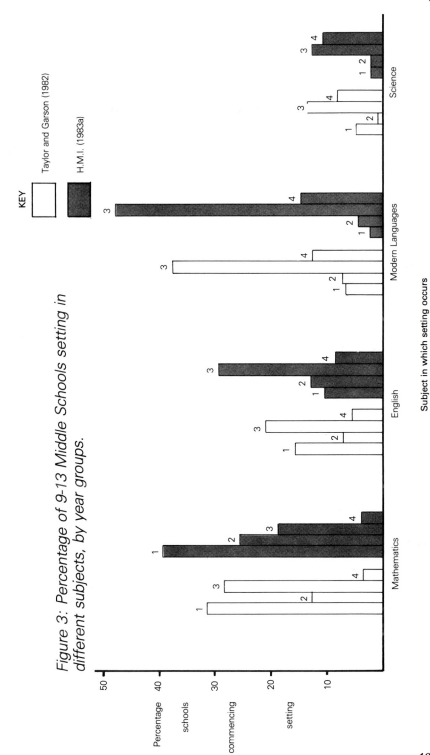

Figure 3: Percentage of 9-13 Middle Schools setting in different subjects, by year groups.

Once again, strict age for age comparisons are difficult to draw here. For instance, while the HMI primary report notes the arrangements for ability grouping *within* classes and for streaming between them, it makes no mention of setting at all. The reason for this omission may be that setting is actually exceedingly rare in primary schools. Of course, it is possible to argue that streaming has similar effects to setting and that figures for streaming at the primary level should therefore be taken account of too. But even if this is done, it still turns out that only 17 per cent of primary schools that are large enough to stream their pupils do so; this being barely 6 per cent of primary schools overall (HMI, 1978b, p. 28). These figures are still substantially smaller than the 22 per cent and 45–64 per cent of 9–13 middle schools that set their pupils at 10 + in English and maths respectively: a comparison which suggests that in one important aspect of their organizational arrangements, 9–13 middle schools are, in their lower years, remarkably out of tune with current primary practice. Moreover, that comparison also suggests that 9–13 middle schools do not just have a strongly secondary character in their upper years, but that they are also susceptible to the downward permeation of secondary influences and organizational patterns into what might otherwise be conventionally regarded as the primary phase of their work too.

Such are the trends of discontinuity and secondary domination that can be inferred from national survey data on setting arrangements in 9–13 middle systems. These figures were not, of course, available at the time that the case studies of Riverdale and Moorhead were conducted. At the commencement of the case study work, and in the absence of previous substantial research on middle schools, the presence and significance of setting was an issue that awaited discovery. However, drawing on the benefits of statistical hindsight, it is now useful to see how far the national secondary-like trends in ability grouping practice were in evidence at Moorhead and Riverdale, and to examine the detailed form they took there. More than this, the case studies also allow us to identify some of the reasons for and principles underlying the setting, in a way that existing survey evidence does not.

Setting at Moorhead

From the point of view of setting, Moorhead Middle School, like middle schools nationally, had a pattern of discontinuity between the year groups, though it is worth adding that in this particular school, the change at 11 was no more abrupt than that at 12. From having no setting at all in year 2, Moorhead setted its pupils in the high status subjects of French and mathematics for 25 per cent of the timetable in year 3, and continued to do so for these subjects in year 4 also (table 10). At that later point, an additional group of subjects was included in the setting arrangements too — some English, most science, and also, for reasons which might be less immediately obvious, music, P.E., housecraft and art. In the final year of the middle school, that is to say, Moorhead pupils were set for about half their timetable.

Table 10: Subjects in which setting occurred, and proportion of timetable setted at Moorhead middle school

	2	3	4
Percentage timetable set	0	25	50
Subjects set		French Mathematics	French Mathematics .33 English .67 Science Housecraft/Art Music PE

When asked to explain 'the nature of ability grouping in the school and (his) particular reasons for the system which (he had) adopted', Mr Butcher, Moorhead's Headteacher, responded as follows:

> The system which we adopt isn't based on a particular educational philosophy but it's based on what we believe, I think, to be the most efficient way of teaching a particular subject. I'm not a person who believes in mixed ability groups necessarily, nor do I necessarily believe in setting and streaming. The areas of the curriculum which we choose for setting or streaming are chosen *simply because we think that we can teach those particular subjects more efficiently in one way or the other.*
>
> We set for French and mathematics in our third year simply because we think *we can teach French and mathematics at that level more efficiently in sets* than we can in mixed ability groups. We don't set at all in the second year simply because we think that *we can teach as efficiently in mixed ability groups in that year as we could in sets,* and what we gain by mixed ability teaching more than compensates for any possible gains in efficiency by setting or streaming at this particular level. Now as we go higher up the school, the pendulum swings the other way and what we gain in efficiency in teaching in sets more than compensates for what we lose in terms of the social engineering factors, if you like, of mixed ability teaching. (my emphases)

This kind of talk, with its frequent question-begging references to 'simple' matters of efficiency recurred in an address to parents of the following year's pupil intake, though here there was an additional hint that the 'efficiency' to which Mr Butcher so often referred suited not just pupils' interests but staff interests too.

> In the third year, we set for mathematics and French because we think that they can be taught better in sets in those subjects than any other way. It seems not only to be in the childrens' best interests but in our best interests also.

One way of interpreting Mr Butcher's use of 'efficiency' here might be in terms of the usual definition of setting as a system which groups pupils by subject-specific abilities in the particular subjects concerned so that teaching can be more accurately and easily pitched at an appropriate level for *all* pupils in that group. Efficiency in this sense would be an efficiency of pupil learning produced by concentrations of ability on subject-specific grounds. This was not the case at Moorhead, though. Timetabling difficulties, exacerbated by a shortage of trained specialists in the chosen setted subjects — maths and French — meant that while pupils were indeed placed in different sets for mathematics and French depending on their mathematical and second language ability respectively, setting had to take place in other subjects also and on the French and maths criteria. In the third year, as table 11 shows, setting was able to be limited to French and mathematics only: three sets (1, 2, 3) within each of two parallel bands (X, Y); plus a 'remedial' group (3R).

Table 11: Setting arrangements for third year pupils at Moorhead[8]

Set	11.20–11.55 Subject	Set	11.55–12.30 Subject
1X	Maths	1X	French
2X	Maths	2X	French
3X	Maths	3X	French
1Y	French	1Y	Maths
2Y	French	2Y	Maths
3Y	French	3Y	Maths
3R	Maths/French/English	3R	Maths/French/English

In the fourth year, with the inclusion of some setting in science and English *against* French and mathematics, the grouping system transgressed the usual rationale for setting; that it is a flexible system for grouping pupils according to their specific abilities in different subjects. Nor did it conform to the rationale normally offered for streaming: that it groups pupils according to some general measure of intellectual ability. The Moorhead system, that is, was neither fish nor fowl: it employed measures of attainment drawn from two subjects — mathematics and French — as a basis for grouping in other subjects also. This scarcely seems a system likely to produce the most efficient grouping arrangement for maximizing pupil learning. Table 12 shows these timetable arrangements for fourth year 'set' groups on Monday mornings.

Table 12: Setting arrangements for fourth year pupils at Moorhead — Monday[9]

Set	9.55–10.20 Subject	10.30–11.05 Subject	11.20–11.55 Subject	11.55–12.30 Subject
1X	Maths	French	Science	Science
1Y	French	Maths	Music	Class Period
2X	Maths	French	Housecraft/Art	
2Y	French	Maths	English	English
3X	Science	Science	Maths	French
3Y	Maths	French	PE	Music
4R	English/French/Maths		Science	Science

In effect, in Moorhead's fourth year there was not one kind of setting but at least two.[10] These two forms of setting which I shall call *principled* and *residual*, differ from one another in terms of the administrative intentions underlying their establishment. *Principled setting* arises from a commitment to ability grouping in particular subjects where that kind of arrangement is thought to be particularly appropriate on educational or pedagogical grounds: most usually in what are usually known as the 'linear' subjects of French, mathematics, science, etc.[11] *Residual setting*, by comparison, is a form of pupil grouping arranged out of the administrative necessity for subjects to be found which can be 'set' against the ones initially selected for principled setting. Thus, when small schools (as middle schools are when compared with most of their secondary counterparts) with limited staff resources, especially in particular subject specialisms, have a strong *principled* commitment to differentiation by setting in high status subject areas such as French and mathematics, a further set of difficult pragmatic decisions must then be made regarding other subjects to be set against them at the same time; subjects where setting would not otherwise be a serious consideration. In Moorhead's case, this meant that in addition to the principled setting in French, mathematics and the like, there was also residual setting in PE, music, housecraft and art. Together, the two forms of setting accounted for some 5 per cent of the fourth year timetable overall; a good deal more, indeed, than we might expect in many comparable secondary schools at the same age level.

Setting at Riverdale

At open-plan Riverdale, setting was not nearly so overt and public a feature of school policy as it was at Moorhead. For one thing, Riverdale's Headteacher, unlike his Moorhead counterpart, made no mention of setting in his report to the joint governing body of the two schools. In addition to this, Moorhead staff were apparently unaware of the presence of setting at nearby Riverdale as was evident in their surprised retort — 'Do they set, then?' — to my informing a small number of them during staffroom conversation towards the end of my research about Riverdale's setting arrangements. Finally, student teachers on school placement at Riverdale were equally unaware of the existence of setting there even after four preliminary one-day visits. It was only when teaching practice proper commenced that Sue, one of the two students, realized that 'virtually everything ended up being setted in the fourth year', including craft and home economics, because of the available pupil groups. Just how accurate Sue's judgment was here can be seen by examining table 13 which lists the overall percentage of the timetable which was set and the particular subjects in which setting took place in each of the four year groups at Riverdale.

This table makes interesting reading when compared with the interview response of Mr Kitchen, Riverdale's Head, to a question concerning the nature of ability grouping in his school. He began by asserting that

Table 13: Subjects in which setting occurred, and proportion of timetable setted at Riverdale middle school

	Year			
	1	*2*	*3*	*4*
Percentage timetable set	0	15	50	80
Subjects set		Mathematics	Mathematics French English Swimming PE Science Project Music	Mathematics French English Swimming PE Science Project Craft Housecraft Some Integrated Studies Some Drama

> The vast ability grouping's mixed ability. If I didn't believe it, I don't think I could do otherwise really. As a two-and-a-half form entry school one's limited to the sort of ways one can tackle things and I think inevitably one of them's got to be mixed ability. This is my philosophy anyway, so I'm quite happy with it.

In one sense, this judgment was a fair one. Averaged out across the four years, the majority (63½ per cent) of the teaching was indeed organized on mixed ability lines, though this proportion scarcely merits the use of the adjective 'vast'. When the proportions of mixed ability grouping are averaged out for the top and bottom halves of Riverdale school respectively, however, the unhelpfulness of an overall school mixed ability ratio becomes apparent; for while in years 1 and 2 some 92½ per cent of the grouping was organized on mixed ability lines, in year 3 and 4 only 35 per cent of the grouping was organized in this way — echoes yet again of that sharp division between primary and secondary modes of organization at 11 which seems to be such a persistent feature of the middle school system.

Having made this general statement about the overall importance of mixed ability grouping, Mr Kitchen then went on to talk about two important exceptions to his overall educational philosophy and school policy. The first of these was French.

> As certain children move through the school, in certain areas perhaps we need to look at their differences. In particular I'm thinking of French. It seems to me now a nonsense that every child in the middle school pursues a four-year course in French. The slow learner very often has tremendous difficulties in other spheres. For a certain time, French is a welcome, refreshing relief. It's something new. It's something we can well cope with at the audio-visual stage. But once they switch to written French, then they have great difficulties. They can become disruptive and make too great demands upon the French teacher and so already I leave a few out. But next year I'll certainly do much more of this. I've got to make a judgment on

children about half way through their French course. Is it beneficial to them? Not only to them, but is it also beneficial to a class grouping or the people who take them to have these children in? We are thinly covered here and I've got to think of this for them and for the teachers quite frankly.

Here, Mr Kitchen provided a *principled* justification for setting in French which might, in his view, even involve the exclusion of some slow learning pupils from that subject altogether. In this sense, Mr Kitchen appeared to be adopting an educational posture that French specialists often adopt elsewhere (for example Ball, 1981; Evans, 1985): namely that the intrinsic difficulties of the subject require pupils to be segregated for teaching purposes on ability-based lines at an early stage.

If Mr Kitchen supported *principled* setting in French, his observations on the ability grouping arrangements for mathematics — the second subject he recognized as being outside the mixed ability system — were of a rather different order.

In mathematics, I would hope that ultimately we will get to the point where we do not need to set ... but I have no real mathematicians on the staff at all. People are very much afraid of mathematics on this staff. At the moment, mathematics tends to be used in a way, really, to keep children quiet, rather than any true purpose, which is a convenient way of keeping half the class occupied. There's a very thin standard that goes into the mathematics work.

Clearly, Mr Kitchen did not support the setting arrangments in mathematics in his school on any principled grounds to do with the intrinsic organization of and accompanying difficulties posed by the subject. On the contrary, he was anxious to unscramble setting in mathematics, but was also aware of one important area of difficulty: that the teaching of that subject in his school was currently undertaken by non-specialists. In line with more recent observations made by HMI, not least in their *9–13 Middle School Survey* (1983a), Mr Kitchen's remarks revealed a worry that the absence of trained mathematics specialists in the school and the resulting necessity for mathematics to be taught by non-specialists tended to lead teachers of that subject to adopt conventional and rather unimaginative teaching approaches and grouping arrangements with their classes. Setting in mathematics was, in this sense, seen to arise not from the strong commitment of subject specialists to their subject and to principles of ability segregated teaching that commonly go with it, as in French: but from subject insecurity and perhaps even subject incompetence on the part of those non-specialists asked to teach it. What we have in such cases, is a form of setting which arises from what has recently (DES, 1983) been termed *subject mismatch*: from a lack of fit between a teacher's qualification and training and the subject he or she is now required to teach. I therefore call this kind of grouping arrangement *mismatch* setting.

In practice, *mismatch* setting is difficult to distinguish from *principled* setting in any particular instance; for whatever a group of teachers' motivation for setting, an appeal on their part to the criteria embodied in principled setting, to the claimed special difficulties of the subject they teach, offers a much more plausible and publicly defensible justification for what they do than does any confession of insecurity or incompetence. Yet if Riverdale's Head is right, and if HMI are also right in their observation that subject mismatch exerts unfortunately restrictive effects upon teaching method and classroom organization, then it is likely that given the difficulties faced by 9–13 middle schools in recruiting an adequate compliment of specialist staff, and given the resulting amount of specialist teaching that must then be performed by non-specialists (81 per cent of middle school mathematics teachers are not trained or qualified in that subject, according to HMI (1983a, p. 30), *mismatch* setting in mathematics and possibly also English and science may be an exceedingly common feature of English middle schools. This is a matter that would certainly benefit from further research.

Mr Kitchen therefore seemed to value *principled* setting in French and conceded, though he also regretted the existence of *mismatch* setting in mathematics. He said nothing at all, however, about the large amount of *residual* setting in his school in the physical and practical subjects of physical education, swimming, housecraft and craft. The precise reasons why this residual setting was so extensive and why it affected these subjects in particular, take us into the intricacies of school timetabling and are far too complex to explain in detail. Basically, though, three major factors appeared to be at work:

(i) The need to find subjects to set against the principled and mismatch setted subjects of French, English and mathematics; particularly against French where only one specialist (a part-timer) was available.

(ii) The restrictions imposed by the school having two-and-a-half classes in each year group. This meant that, in effect, year groups could not be organized as two or three distinct class units, but only as five half-class units.

(iii) Problems in the design of the practical areas. Restricted space only was provided for craft and housecraft to the extent that no more than twelve pupils could use each area at any one time. Had the school been entirely or predominantly mixed-ability in the way that the Head claimed, this arrangement would probably have presented few special difficulties: indeed, the half-class status of these practical groups might well have suggested a 'natural' solution to the organizational and timetabling difficulties brought about by the school's two-and-a-half-form entry status. But once the commitment to principled or mismatch setting had been made, as with French, and three half-groups then needed to be found to set against that subject, the choosing of one conveniently available half-group for setting in, say, craft then entailed setting in the other practical half-group also, with one further half-group in mathematics, integrated studies or whatever remaining.[12]

In this way, because of the commitment to principled and mismatch setting; because of shortages of specialist staff, particularly in French; because of the restrictions imposed by the school's peculiar two-and-a-half form entry status; and because of the limited provision the architects made for the practical subjects, residual setting became a widespread feature of the Riverdale curriculum.[13].

Conclusion

Both case study and national survey data have pointed to the fact that for reasons of academic principle and of pedagogical insecurity arising from the difficulties associated with subject mismatch, 9–13 middle schools are inclined to set their pupils by ability in what are commonly regarded as the high status areas of the secondary school curriculum. Furthermore, because of organizational problems created by their small size, by accompanying staff shortages in specialist subjects, and by limitations on specialist facilities, such schools also employ a good deal of residual setting in subjects of somewhat lesser status too. The significance of this finding concerning the causes and extent of residual setting in 9–13 middle schools may well stretch beyond the particular case study schools from which it first emerged. One problem with existing national data on setting in 9–13 schools is that they make reference only to the mainstream, high status subjects of French, English, mathematics and science, and thereby reflect, rather uncritically, existing professional assumptions about where setting is most likely to occur. The incorporation of precisely such assumptions in national survey procedures has, due to the failure to consider the impact of residual setting at all, almost certainly led to a serious *under*-estimate of just how pervasive setting is throughout the middle school system as a whole.

If we take the three forms of setting together — principled, mismatch and residual — it becomes clear that not only is the extent of setting in 9–13 middle schools equivalent to, but in a number of respects it actually exceeds the amount of setting to be found among comparable age groups in the secondary sector. More-over, in most subjects, the onset of setting occurs more frequently at 11, the conventional starting point of secondary education, than at any other point. If setting is at all a valid indicator of the primariness or secondariness of the middle school identity, than the data available draw us to the conclusion that the 9–13 middle school is not unique or transitional but divided, and that within this overall division, second-ary pressures and influences exert a greater effect than primary ones.

Notes

1   The operative definitions for streaming, banding and setting are taken from the Glossary in HMI (1979) *Aspects of Secondary Education.*
2   The secondary school figures are those which HMI supply for what they call 'full' and 'restricted range' comprehensives. The figures are based on the organization of teaching groups for mathematics only — so they supply a minimal criterion for one subject only, albeit a high status one.
3   Again, the figures are for grouping in mathematics in full and restricted range comprehensive schools.

4 The data in this table are compiled from three different surveys, using three different samples. Because the basis of the sample in all three surveys (as most HMI 'illustrative' surveys) is neither systematic nor clear, it is not possible to know the sampling errors which are involved in each case, and therefore not possible to subject the data to tests of statistical significance.

5 Again, it is not appropriate to apply tests of statistical significance to these data (see note 4).

6 These figures are for full and restricted range comprehensive schools.

7 *Ibid.*

8 This arrangement operated daily.

9 In this instance, the mixture of subjects was similar for each day, but the actual allocations to particular classes varied from one day to the next.

10 We shall see later that, in effect, a third principle of setting may well have been in operation also.

11 Questions concerning the purportedly 'linear' nature of these particular subjects will be raised in chapter 7.

12 Moorhead, like many other middle schools, had similar problems with specialist facilities: the craft and science areas having to be shared. This created further 'fixed points' on the timetable around which setting arrangements then had to be made. Where timetables have a high number of such fixed points, then once a commitment has been made to some setting and specialism, a good deal more setting and specialism almost inevitably follows as an unintended consequence.

13 The discussion here focusses predominantly on the Headteacher's interpretation and perceptions of the setting system. Teachers' perceptions of setting at Riverdale and Moorhead will be discussed in chapters 8–10.

Chapter 7

Subject Specialism

Introduction

One of the greatest areas of difficulty for middle schools intent on establishing their own unique identity is the tension they have to resolve in their curriculum provision between specialism and generalism. This difficulty was expressed very clearly during a staff meeting at Riverdale

Mr Driver: O.K. Well. Things haven't been perfect this year. You see, the trouble with specialism ... at secondary schools, is that you can only use one tenth of a person's intelligence. They're teaching their particular subject and they know quite a lot about other things and they could help a lot. They could give encouragement and be very interesting over a wide field, and because of the subject divisions, they are restricted to a narrow field which eventually becomes boring to them. You know, you eventually find that your own narrow field is rather repetitive, rather boring and so on. So if you have some sense, you come to a middle school where you can be a bit wider.

Now at primary schools you have the opposite problem. You have people who have knowledge over a much wider field and are expected to use it over a wider field but in certain circumstances their knowledge is not sufficient for that particular field. So here you have a problem. You have a contradiction between having to do everything and not knowing enough about certain things, or having to do one thing, knowing about other things and wasting that knowledge.

Mr Kitchen: Well, here you've put it. The agony of the middle school, isn't it?

Mr Driver: The agony of the middle school! The basic dilemma!

How have middle schools, and the case study schools of Riverdale and Moorhead in particular, resolved this difficulty, this agony or basic dilemma? What balance between specialist and generalist approaches have they managed to establish? Have they secured a smooth transition in curricular experience at age 11, or have they perpetuated a sudden break?

Timetable Allocations and Priorities

In their 9–13 survey, HMI (1983a) found that while a mere 12.5 per cent of the schools had a mainly specialist pattern of organization in year 2 in the view of their heads, no less than 64.6 per cent had adopted such a pattern by year 3: an increase of over 50 per cent. Case study work has also revealed the existence of sudden increases in specialist commitments in middle schools at age 11 (Meyenn and Tickle, 1980). Table 14 provides some indicators of specialist as against generalist orientation at Riverdale and Moorhead. The indicators have their limitations — they are measures of timetable allocation and priority between different kinds of curriculum provision and different forms of teacher contact, and in that sense do not purport to reflect subtle variations in the presentation of the curriculum at classroom level (though such matters are touched upon later).[1] And even at the level of timetabling, serious difficulties still remain. Does a timetabled subject (as opposed to open timetabling, leaving curricular choice to the teacher's own discretion) indicate a commitment to specialism? And among these timetabled subjects what inferences should be drawn from the inclusion of lessons devoted to things like 'integrated studies' or 'talks': do these show commitment to specialism by virtue of being separated out, or generalism, due to the integrated character of their content? Difficulties and limitations such as these will be borne in mind as the analysis proceeds; but by examining a *range* of indicators, it is hoped that some sense can be gained of managerial and organizational priorities in the two middle schools, and thus of the broad balance or imbalance between specialist and generalist forms of commitment in the different year groups.

Moorhead

One of the features that characteristically distinguishes primary from secondary modes of organization is the close and extensive contact that pupils have with a single class teacher ('their' teacher) in the first case and their exposure to a much wider range of teachers practising different subject specialisms in the second. At Moorhead, pupils in the 'top primary' year (year 2) in the open-plan part of the building spent only 17.3 per cent of their time on average with teachers other than 'their' own, meeting between five and six other teachers in total during any one week. This non-class teacher contact took place in French (taught by two members of the year team), music, science and sessions devoted to pupil 'talks' — the latter two being seen as opportunites for the Deputy Head and Headteacher respectively to

Table 14: *Analysis of timetable allocations for different kinds of curriculum provision and different forms of teacher contact at Moorhead and Riverdale Middle Schools*

SCHOOL	Year	Percentage time spent with non-class teachers	Percentage time spent on timetabled subjects	Number of subjects taught by specialists	Number of subjects timetabled in total	Mean number of other teachers met
MOORHEAD	2	17.3	25.9	3	6	5.6
	3	45.6	41.8	7	11	10.5
	4	55.3	74.7	10	14	10.5
RIVERDALE	1	7.5	27.5	2	7	5
	2	7.5	47.5	3	8	5
	3	27.1	65.0	5	14	6
	4	27.9	61.3	4	11	5

have some teaching contact with the year group. This distribution of teacher contact in the 'primary' year of Moorhead corresponds closely with the pattern generally found in primary schools at the same age — primary pupils being taught by teachers other than their own for 20 per cent of their time or less in most cases. (HMI, 1978b, p. 34)

Looking at the number of subjects given specific timetable slots in Moorhead's second year timetable, only six were officially separated out from the rest of the curriculum: French, music, science, PE, integrated studies and talks, and the latter two of these are scarcely 'subjects' in the conventional sense. These periods occupied just over 25 per cent of the second year timetable. Of course, these teachers, like many of their primary colleagues, often constructed the remainder of their own personal timetables with particular curriculum slots in mind for particular parts of the week — mathematics usually taking place in the morning, for instance. But in principle, and often in practice, there was a great deal of scope for curriculum flexibility on the part of the second year class teacher.

Matters were somewhat different in the third and fourth years. In general, the discontinuity in specialist teaching arrangements and in the amount of contact pupils had with one as against many teachers, was greater between these two years and the second year than between the second and third years together and the fourth. In the top two years at Moorhead, contact with non-class teachers, for instance, was much more extensive than in the second year: 45.6 per cent and 55.3 per cent in each year group respectively. By this point in their middle school careers, pupils were meeting almost double the number of teachers (between 10 and 11) than they had in their second ('primary') year.

The allocation of time to specialisms in these top two years was also considerably greater. Eleven subjects in the third year and fourteen in the fourth were timetabled in total (though these too included integrated studies and 'talks'), compared to only six in the second year.

The overall percentage of time spent on timetabled subjects, however, showed no greater gap at the end of year 2 than elsewhere — the increase being greater one year later, in fact. But a glance at just one third year class's timetable (3M) suggests that this indicator may well be misleading, for many of the spots which were left blank on the general staff timetable were, in fact, given specific subject allocations at class level.[2] Thus, Monday, before break, which was blank on the staff timetable was labelled English (oral, grammar and creative writing) on 3M's. Similarly, the first period on Monday afternoon, again blank on the staff timetable, was allocated to geography at class level. And again when, on the first part of Tuesday afternoon, 3M was taken by Mr Bird, the third year leader, while no specific subject was identified on the staff timetable for this period, the one for 3M clearly designated it as history. Both these curricular specialisms of history and geography, it is worth adding, were not just offered according to the whims of the class teacher either, but in fulfilment of the requirements of the history and geography syllabuses laid down by the head. The third year curriculum at Moorhead was therefore rather more specialist than the staff timetable led one to believe.

'Integrated' or 'open' curriculum slots were not always what they seemed, therefore. This point was further illustrated by the fourth year arrangements for social studies. The two double periods per week allocated to this in practice amounted to history one day and geography the next. Mr Butcher assured the parents of his incoming pupils of this when he told them that in the third and fourth year 'there will be things like social studies, which is nothing more than another name for history and geography'. Nor was this just an attempt to assuage doubts and appease potential opposition among prospective parents. For as one fourth year teacher, Mrs Close, explained to me as she guided me through the staff timetable

> Oh yes, well, this afternoon's history, then drama (for English) . . . Ah, and that (pointing to the social studies slot on Tuesday) is geography.

Pupils too apparently saw social studies as discrete units of history and geography. In one social studies lesson, for instance, pupil folders were labelled history and contained subheadings such as 'The history of railways' inside them. When asked about homework by me, one of the class responded, 'No, we don't get history homework'. And in the interaction that passed between teachers and pupils in such lessons, the teacher made remarks like, 'Now John, what's your problem — to do with your history?'

If these two points are taken together — the covert specialist nature of the third year timetable at class level and the strict segregation of social studies into separate periods of history and geography in both years 3 and 4 — then the curriculum in the top two years at Moorhead was even more specialist than analysis of the staff timetable suggests, in general showing a sharp break from the more generalist, class teacher based principles of curriculum organization in the second year.

Riverdale

Such differences were not nearly so well defined at open-plan Riverdale. Some indicators suggest the existence of something approaching an abrupt change at 11, others point to the presence of a rather more gradual transition. How might these differences be explained?

Take the indicators which suggest the absence of a smooth transition first. From the column on teacher contact, it is apparent that first and second years spent little time meeting teachers other than 'their' own — though it is important to point out here that given the pattern of shared teaching that existed within the year groups at Riverdale, I have interpreted time spent with non-class teachers very broadly as time spent with teachers outside the year team. Using this criterion, pupils in years 1 and 2 met only the craft teacher, the music teacher and, briefly, the Head, in addition to the teachers within their own year group. By years 3 and 4 though, the proportion of contact pupils had with other teachers had increased significantly to around 27 per cent. Much of this increase is accounted for by the fact that French was taught daily in years 3 and 4 and therefore much more extensively than in year 2, and that this subject was, at this point, placed in the hands of a part-time French specialist, all of whose teaching duties fell in the top two years. Despite this notable increase in pupil contact time with teachers other than their own at the top end of Riverdale, though, the overall amount of such contact in those years was still substantially less than in the equivalent years at Moorhead and scarcely deserves the label *specialist* at all.

A second measure — the number of subjects timetabled in total — seems to give a much stronger indication of specialist emphasis at the top end of Riverdale school, and of a somewhat sudden shift towards such an emphasis at 11. Table 15 shows the subjects that were timetabled year by year at Riverdale and correspondingly indicates which subjects were *not* separated out for specialist treatment in particular years, these usually being dealt with under the rubric of integrated studies (IS).

Table 15: Subjects taught separately in each year at Riverdale Middle School

	Year			
Subject	1	2	3	4
Mathematics	x	x	x	x
PE/swimming/games	x	x	x	x
Craft	x	x	x	x
French	not taught	x	x	x
Music	x	x	x	not taught
Drama	IS	IS	x	x
Cookery/housecraft	IS	IS	x	x
Science project	IS	IS	x	x
English	IS	IS	x	x
Integrated studies (IS)	IS	IS	IS	IS
Art	IS	IS	x	IS
Reading	x	x	x	IS

Even this table gives a misleading impression of specialist emphasis in the top years of Riverdale, though. There was, to be sure, an abrupt increase in the number of subjects taught, particularly between years 2 and 3. This was not, however, accompanied by a dramatic increase in the actual amount of *time* devoted to those subjects between those two years. Indeed, an inspection of the second column in table 14 reveals that the percentage of time spent on timetabled subjects other than integrated studies rose more sharply between years 1 and 2 than between any other two adjacent years — a fact which can be explained by the commitment among the fourth year team to a 'block timetabling' approach to the curriculum where large blocks of time were set aside for pupils to work on and allocate their time between various exercises and projects.

On paper at least, then, the timetabled Riverdale curriculum, while certainly revealing a growth in specialist commitment from years 1 to 4, did not show the same sudden changes at 11 as Moorhead. There were, of course, other sources of real discontinuity at Riverdale, particularly in terms of the amount of setting, as we saw earlier. But the official organization of the Riverdale curriculum showed undeniable tempering effects on the conventional distinction between generalist and specialist forms of provision that otherwise so often divides the middle school into two relatively discrete curricular units.

This softening of Riverdale's specialist orientation may be due to a number of possible influences: the implied messages contained within its open-plan architecture, the Head's preference for a middle school of the primary 'extension' type, or the kind of staff the school was able to appoint. These points will be explored more fully in the next part of the book. But a further factor is the school's unusually small size. The restricted size of the school staff of just thirteen placed severe constraints on curriculum flexibility and particularly on the school's specialist capability. Without wishing to draw attention from the very real commitment of Riverdale's Head towards a middle school of the extension type, it must be recognized that, in part, the school's softening of its specialist commitment was therefore a pragmatic response to the staffing constraints imposed by its limited size.

Summary

In summary, there was a split between generalist and specialist patterns of curriculum orientation at 11 in one of the schools and between mixed ability and setted patterns of pupil grouping in both of them. The differences between primary and secondary modes of organization in the top and bottom parts of the two schools respectively were therefore sharp, consistent and extensive in the case of Moorhead; rather less sharp and somewhat more patchy in the case of Riverdale. Moorhead, in that sense, appears to be more typical of the national 'average' pattern of substantial increases in specialist commitment at 11 in middle schools than does its Riverdale counterpart, although the less specialist form of curriculum organization adopted by Riverdale is one which many middle schools have found themselves having to contemplate in the 1980s as pupil rolls have fallen and specialist capability has weakened. (Wallace and Tickle, 1983; Hunter and Heighway, 1980)

High Status Subjects and the Middle School Curriculum

Insofar as a specialist orientation does dominate the character of many middle schools in their upper years and sometimes even earlier than that, it is worth asking whether some of these specialisms have a greater influence on the shape of the middle school curriculum than others.

One group of subjects which do appear to be strongly represented in the upper years of the middle school curriculum are those which, following the work of M.F.D. Young (1971), might be called *high status subjects* — subjects which have a high social value and legitimacy placed on them by 'dominant' groups in society. In line with the much valued academic tradition of which they are a part, such subjects are normally academic in character; not practical or vocational. Be they subjects that 'tend to be abstract, highly literate . . . and unrelated to non-school knowledge' (Young, 1971, p. 38), that give pupils access to the privileged enclaves of what Musgrove (1979) calls 'gentry culture'; or be they ones like maths and science that play a technically useful role in 'wealth creation', in the development or restoration of capitalist economies such as our own (Apple, 1979, p. 38); high status subjects play a key part in giving access to and maintaining the position of dominant groups and the social order in which they thrive.

High status subjects are therefore associated with a particular conception of secondary education where the dominance of the academic, grammar school curriculum persists and where the part played by this curriculum in the business of educational and social selection remains largely uncontested (Hargreaves, D. 1982). In that sense, the continuing dominance of high status subjects even after comprehensive reorganization is very much tied to the meritocratic conception of comprehensive schooling discussed in chapter 3, with its emphasis on conventional academic achievement, the promotion of able pupils (defined in academic terms, that is), and the orientation towards examination success. Is there any evidence that specialist subjects located in this high status sphere exert a greater influence on or are more strongly represented within the middle school than other kinds of specialism: that academic subjects are credited with more importance than practical ones, for instance?

Setting

One indicator is the distribution of setting. Chapter 6 pointed out that setting is widely employed in middle schools, particularly in the upper years, and that in this respect, middle schools appear to be even more royal than their secondary kings. Moreover, setting — especially principled or mismatch setting — was most common in a small number of subjects only: namely maths, French, English and science.

Such findings are very similar to those produced in case studies of mainstream comprehensive schooling where the wish to maintain ability grouping has been put most forcefully by teachers holding an *academic perspective* that emphasizes standards, academic excellence and the importance of the subject (Ball, 1981). These teachers, it has been found — teachers, in the main, of French, or science, or maths — tend to believe that the intrinsic linear ordering and difficulty of their own subject demands the segregation of pupils into ability groups so that the subject material can then be closely geared to their conceptual needs and capacities. Part 3 of the book will examine the role that such beliefs play in the perspectives and wider biographies and careers of individual middle school teachers. For now, it is worth noting one important criticism of the academic perspective and of the basis on which high status knowledge rests in general — that it rests more on conventional assumptions held by members of subjects communities orientated to promoting academic excellence and to teaching able pupils than on any special difficulties or peculiarities of their subject matter (Ball, 1981; Young, 1971). For instance, subjects in the aesthetic domain like music and drama can and do make equally reasonable claims to having 'linear' properties (sound experimentation before melody; mime before speech etc.), but these do not enjoy the same high status as their intellectual–cognitive counterparts. Moreover, what are claimed as intrinsic properties of particular subjects actually vary over time — the linear claims now made by modern linguists, for instance, were once made for English when it had a more strictly grammatical emphasis. (Ball, 1982)

In middle and secondary schools alike, then, setting appears to receive its firmest support from those academically orientated teachers most numerous in influential high status areas of the school curriculum which dominate the secondary sector. In either case, attitudes supporting ability grouping and subject specialism in high status areas tend to go very much together.[3] By that token, principled setting in middle schools actually rests on a culturally arbitrary principle that masquerades as an academic one.

Liaison

A second indicator of the influence of high status subjects on the middle school curriculum is the pattern of *subject liaison* between middle and upper schools. The extent of such liaison varies a great deal as does the attitude of teachers and heads regarding its desirability (Ginsburg *et al*, 1977, p. 39; Ginsburg and Meyenn, 1980; Taylor and Garson, 1982, chapter 7; Stillman and Maychell, 1984; Gorwood, 1981). Whatever the variation in the overall pattern, though, it is interesting that where liaison arrangements *do* operate, they appear to do so with an extraordinary unevenness between different areas of the curriculum. Only some subjects are evidently regarded as needing strong continuity between middle and upper schools, while others are accorded much lower priority, vertical continuity presumably being perceived as not such an urgent necessity in their case.

Table 16 lists a number of subjects where there are liaison arrangements of different sorts between middle and upper schools.[4]

Table 16: Percentage of 9–13 Middle Schools engaging in various subject liaison arrangements with their receiving Upper Schools[5]

Subject	HMI (consultation)	Taylor and Garson (meetings)	Stillman and Maychell (meetings with most/all upper schools)
French	96	88	73
Mathematics	98	88	57
Science	92	83	47
English	85	75	—
Geography	60	—	—
History	54	—	—
Humanities	27	57	—
PE	60	—	20
Art	56	—	16
CDT	54	—	32
Home economics	54	—	34
Needlecraft	42	—	25

Sources: HMI (1983a) p. 49; Taylor and Garson (1982) p. 139; Stillman and Maychell (1984) p. 24.

While there are some clear disparities between the different survey findings regarding the overall frequency of liaison in each case,[6] it is nonetheless evident that one group of subjects — mathematics, French, science and English — is systematically accorded higher liaison priority than any other. Whether one is looking at the existence of consultation in general, the setting up of specific liaison meetings, or the transfer of pupil records, these are the subjects that repeatedly receive preferential treatment (HMI, 1983a, p. 45). By contrast, liaison arrangements in the physical, practical and affective subjects are much less common and in some cases negligible or absent. On the Isle of Wight, for instance, Stillman and Maychell (1982, p. 17) found that 'the majority of the middle school heads claim no liaison in either art or craft'.

The position at Moorhead and Riverdale conformed closely to this national picture. In French, the arrangements for continuity were very closely defined in both schools. Miss Curie, Moorhead's French coordinator, reluctantly adopted *Le Francais d'Aujourd Hui* for much of her teaching in years 3 and 4 in order to fit in with the upper school French curriculum, and Mrs Littlejohn, her counterpart at Riverdale, despite her complaints of being 'hemmed in' by the upper school's French requirements, did likewise. Similarly, in mathematics, both schools adopted *Schools Mathematics Project* to dovetail with what their common receiving upper school required. Science liaison arrangements were more provisional, for while meetings *were* taking place no agreed curriculum or set of concepts, skills or understandings had yet been agreed across the two tiers. In humanities, arrangements were even more tentative than this, discussion being at a very preliminary stage indeed.[7] As far as I could detect, though, there were no liaison procedures at all, still less any agreed curriculum or scheme of work, for the practical subjects like craft, for the affective subjects like drama, or for physical education, though there were plans to get liaison arrangements under way in home economics.[8]

Once again, then, it appears that just four subjects in the middle school curriculum — mathematics, French, English and science — systematically command the attention of heads and teachers in terms of vertical continuity needs, while subjects outside the high status, academic domain, do not.

Syllabus Requirements and Curriculum Flexibility

The extent to which syllabus requirements are perceived to be mandatory and the perceived scope for pupil choice in different subjects are also indicators of those subjects' status. At Riverdale and Moorhead, pressures to conform to curricular requirements imposed from outside were most apparent in the high status subjects of French and maths. In French, both middle schools had complied with the upper school's 'request' that they should 'fit in with the syllabus that (the receiving school) has devized' (Miss Curie). Neither Miss Curie, nor Mrs Littlejohn, her counterpart at Riverdale, were entirely happy with this arrangement. Miss Curie suggested that she would not have selected *Le Francais d'Aujourd Hui*, given a free choice. It had insufficient back-up exercises for consolidation work, she said. Mrs Littlejohn complained that the course was very difficult but 'felt pressurized by the upper school into doing it'. Some of the consequences of this, she argued, were extremely unfortunate. She confessed to 'hating teaching the second set now' because 'they've given up. They lark about. They realize they're too far behind'. But she still felt the need to 'rush them on from one level to another' because of the upper school's course requirements. Miss Curie also felt ill at ease with the course's effect on her lower ability pupils, but had dealt with this by continuing with *En Avant* in their case — a less ambitious, more orally based course.

Perhaps, then, it was these direct syllabus pressures from the upper school as much as any 'academic' inclinations on their own part (see chapter 9) that led these teachers to adopt pedagogies of whole-class teaching plus individual seatwork within their subject. The Head of Riverdale pointed out that French, along with maths, was very much 'anti the rest of the way we teach', with what he called 'formal' approaches being adopted in the main. Certainly, neither of the French teachers seemed to give much emphasis to pupil choice within their subject. For Mrs Littlejohn, it was a matter of course design: 'The third year this year haven't had much freedom. . . . It's just the way the course is. There isn' t much freedom in the course the way I've planned it and the way I've got it.'[9] And when Miss Curie was asked how much choice she offered pupils, she did not mention French at all, even though this was her major area of teaching responsibility, but cited examples only from geography (as she called it) and integrated studies.

The position in mathematics was much the same. As we have seen, both schools, following liaison agreements with the upper school, adhered closely to *Schools Mathematics Project* syllabuses. Asked how he planned his work, this is how Mr Bird, Moorhead's Mathematics Coordinator replied

> There is planned in conjunction with (the second year leader) at the moment . . . a detailed syllabus following the SMP scheme . . . I follow the scheme fully — pretty well do everything that's in the scheme but a lot more besides. So by the end of the fourth year, they will have had three years of that scheme of work which has been carefully worked out not only syllabus-wise but in some detail as to how each topic or set of topics is tackled.

This left little room for pupil manoeuvre. Apart from one additional session of practical maths per week at Moorhead, where pupils were allowed (at least in some classes) to choose from a wide range of work-cards, 'setted' mathematics lessons in the mornings were heavily teacher-dominated: chalk and talk exposition being aimed at the middle of each set, with individual follow-up work afterwards. At Riverdale, the groups were smaller and the number of sets accordingly greater, but the principle was much the same: individual progression through the workbooks with interspersed sessions of more directly teacher-led activity.

To sum up: in French and mathematics — those two high status subjects which are most commonly assumed to have a special 'linear' character — pupil choice was seriously restricted by syllabus constraints, by being bound to patterns of organization and selection of knowledge which were built in to the very texts they were following. It is interesting to note that, in terms of middle school-upper school liaison, although these subjects sometimes encounter difficulties like any other, especially where the links are widely dispersed across an LEA (Gorwood, 1981), nevertheless, they are the subjects where curriculum continuity is most likely to be established through the adoption of a common, published scheme (Stillman and Maychell, 1984). Certainly, these subjects appear to be the ones where curricular prescription is at its tightest, and given the extent to which the organization and selection of knowledge is prespecified through packaged schemes, they are the ones which appear to offer least scope for pupil choice and initiative.[10]

Just how far pupil choice is inversely related to the status of the subject, to its 'academic' stature, can be gauged by looking at the very different case of craft. Craft is commonly separated out for specialist treatment not because of any presumed 'linear' attributes, but because of practical difficulties concerning tools and machinery and because of shortage of staff expertise in handling them. We have already seen that liaison in craft is much more rare than in mathematics or French. It is a low status not a high status subject; more practical than theoretical in character.[11] It was for these very reasons, in fact, that when asked about pupil choice, Riverdale's craft teacher, Mr Home, was able to say, with some pride

> I let the children always work under their own steam. I *never* put a deadline on things . . . Now if a child doesn't finish a job, I don't say 'Right, down tools, no more!' I let them carry on afterwards. They may get a job behind and they may miss one of the jobs out, but they've seen how it's done. They've worked alongside children who've been doing that particular job, so they've seen it at first hand, even if they're not doing it . . . Cos' if we pressurize them at this stage, it could be a bit awkward. Especially, let's face it, craft subjects are more relaxation than pressurized work in a classroom . . . and to pressurize them, I think, could always put them off, so I just let them go at their own pace.

To this relaxed attitude to pupil control over pacing of their own work, Mr Home added a further measure of choice regarding the selection of jobs that pupils could do, always offering them 'two or three' choices.[12]

Mr Thomas, Moorhead's craft teacher, adopted a similar approach. In his case, the adjacency of the craft workshop to his own classroom meant that during periods like integrated studies, he had even greater scope for fostering pupil initiative — 'So I might have kids model-making in the craftroom and doing drawing and written work in my classroom and nipping up and down to the library.'

In the lower status subject of craft, then, pressures to meet the immediate needs of the upper school, the demands and restrictions of a prescribed syllabus, were at their least, and substantial latitude was given to pupil choice. In the high status 'linear' subjects of mathematics and French, however, syllabus restrictions, deriving from upper school pressures, were at their greatest and curriculum constraint won out over pupil choice.

Time Allocations

A fourth indicator of the priority awarded to high status subjects in the middle school curriculum is the way in which *time* is allocated between different subjects in the top two years there (table 17).

Table 17: *Percentage of time officially allocated to particular subject areas in Middle and Secondary School sectors*[13]

| | Maths/English/French/Science | | | Physical/Practical/Creative | | |
	Riverdale	Moorhead	All Secondary	Riverdale	Moorhead	All Secondary
Age Range						
11–12	39.2	55.0	52.1	24.9	22.5	30.1
12–13	37.5	55.0	52.6	23.8	20.0	30.8

According to DES statistics (1980, table 8), around 52 per cent of the curriculum in the first two years of secondary school is taken up with the high status subjects of mathematics, English, science and French, while only 30 per cent or so of the curriculum is allocated to subjects outside of the intellectual–cognitive domain as a whole; to the physical, practical and creative subjects, that is. Taking these figures as a yardstick in the equivalent (i.e. top two)years at Moorhead, the pattern is again more secondary than the secondary system itself; 55 per cent of the curriculum being devoted to the 'big four' high status subjects, and as little as 20 per cent being spent on physical, practical and creative ones.[14]

At open plan Riverdale, the physical, practical and creative subjects were also, apparently, of lesser importance too, receiving well under the already scant allocation of 30 per cent of curriculum time that is customary at the secondary level. On the other hand, Riverdale does, once more, throw up some important timetable differences. In particular, under 40 per cent of the curriculum there was formally devoted to the 'big four' subjects of mathematics, English, French and science; much less than the secondary system as a whole and certainly than its sister school at Moorhead. Much of the reason for this can again be found in Riverdale's official policy of curriculum 'blocking', where many of the time allocations between subjects or projects were, in principle, left to the pupils to sort out on a day to day basis. There is a catch here, though. For within this apparently open and fluid system, teachers nonetheless managed to communicate to their pupils expectations that certain kinds of work were more important and pressing than others. Thus, while several pupils pointed out to me that they did, in fact, get 'set art' to complete in their own integrated studies time (indicating, perhaps, that the time allocation for creative, practical and physical subjects was greater than table 17 suggests), when I talked to a group of pupils who had been set a plaster of Paris model to complete, noticed that not all of them had done it, and that some of them appeared to have little intention of doing it, I was told 'we do have set art, but you don't have to do it if you don't want'. Similarly, when I asked a group of third year pupils who had handed in their mathematics, English and topic work, whether they had done the same with their art, the conversation went as follows:

Author: And what about your art?

Pupil: Haven't done it for ages, actually.

Author: Haven't you?

Pupil: No. I don't like it very much.

Pupil: I did it last week.

Pupil: I did it last week. Um ... we've got a choice. If you haven't done your English, that comes before art, so you've got to finish English before you do art.

Pupil: Yeah.

Author: In your art, then, you can leave it if you don't want to do it?

Pupil: Yeah.

At Riverdale, then, there was evidence of a tacit subject hierarchy operating within what was officially a pupil-choice system, with optional art coming after compulsory English. Moreover, as the extract illustrates, not all the integrated studies time was by any means exclusively devoted to integrated topic work. Rather, pupils spent a good deal of their time completing formal assignments already begun during set periods (as, for intance, with maths), or carrying out English work which was often of a routine 'traditional' kind — exercises, comprehensions, dictionary work, and the like (see also Delamont, 1983). The day to day world of classroom life was therefore much more skewed towards work in the 'big four' subjects of mathematics, English, French and science, than the official timetable suggested; and where pupils were given some choice between completing different projects, work in high status subjects prevailed, taking priority over those outside the intellectual-cognitive domain.

Conclusion

In 1967, the authors of the highly applauded Plowden Report argued that:

> experience in secondary schools has shown that teaching of rigidly defined subjects, often by specialist teachers, is far from suitable for the oldest children who will be in the middle schools. This is one of our reasons for suggesting a change in the age of transfer to secondary education. (paragraph 538)

Sixteen years later, the voice of educational officialdom had changed its tune somewhat. Now, in their 9–13 middle school survey, Her Majesty's Inspectorate (1983a) were arguing that the accommodation and staffing of middle schools must be such as to enable the schools to offer an education that, within the one school, moves from the organic whole of class teaching to the introduction and establishment of specialist subject teaching across the range of the secondary curriculum. (p. 130)

Just how specialist middle schools *should* be is clearly open to dispute. At this stage, I do not want to arbitrate between these pro- and anti-specialist lobbies — though I shall do a little of that later. My purpose at this stage has been descriptive, not prescriptive; an attempt to assess how far, in practice, English middle schools have been primary-like, secondary-like, genuinely transitional or deeply divided in their organization. I have used two indicators as a basis for that assessment: the preference teachers show for mixed ability grouping or setting, and the slanting of the curriculum towards a generalist or specialist pattern in different years. On the basis of this kind of evidence, it seems that up until the late 1970s at least, when middle school pupils reached the traditional age of transfer at 11, they could normally expect to be exposed to substantially greater amounts of specialist teaching, especially in the high status subjects, and to be placed in contact with this knowledge in segregated ability groups. By these criteria, that is, the traditional meritocratic concerns of the secondary sector seem to have exerted a great influence on the middle school curriculum, especially in its top two years, reinforcing the conventional divide in pupils' experience of schooling at age 11. Moreover, this divide, this separation, has been further strengthened by the highly insular character of the middle school year groups; their strict compartmentalization into separate units of curricular and pastoral organization.

Riverdale school, it was found, provided an important, though partial exception to this overall trend. While its year system was very tightly insulated indeed, and while the setting in its upper years was extensive, the tempering of the school's specialist orientation in its top year in particular, where large chunks of curriculum time were blocked together, was, on paper at least, substantial. However, at least some of these differences turned out to be cosmetic. Riverdale may not have had as overtly a specialist curriculum as the top two years at Moorhead, but at classroom level it offered what was still essentially a subject-based and subject separated diet; the boundaries between subjects and the teachers' control over the selection and organization of knowledge being fulfilled through the details of classroom interaction rather than through organizational procedures of timetabling.

Why should the middle school be divided in this way? Why should the concerns and emphases of high status subject areas dominate the curriculum, particularly for 11–13 year olds within the middle school system? Upper school pressures, we have seen, play some part in this, but one other obvious place to turn in looking for answers to these questions is to the middle school teachers themselves, for it is they who teach the middle school curriculum. And it is they who provide the prime human resource with which heads have to work when trying to create an identity, an ethos, a distinctive organizational pattern for their school. Part 3 of the book therefore looks closely at the staff of Riverdale and Moorhead; their biographies, careers and perspectives; and the effects of all these things on their classroom practice. It asks, in other words, how far the identity of middle schools is a product of the people they have recruited, the nature of their professional experience and the direction of their educational commitments.

Notes

1   DELAMONT (1983) also presents case study data on levels and types of specialist commitment within six middle schools. Timetable differences, she points out, can be misleading, for *at the level of the classroom*, subject matter tends to be very similar, despite the differences in timetable categorizations and allocations. Even if this is so, however, formal timetable differences are not ephemeral; they can have important consequences for teacher-pupil relationships and pupils' experience — not least in terms of the number of teachers they meet and their chance to develop close relationships with them.

2   In this respect, the arrangements were different from year 2. In year 3, particular subject contents for specific periods were written in — not least because these were often presented by another teacher.

3   There is one puzzling difference between middle schools and Beachside on the matter of setting: that of English. Whereas in middle schools, English is one of the subjects most likely to be set by ability, at Beachside the members of the English department were the most vociferous opponents of the banding system. One possible reason for this apparent inconsistency is that the English department at Beachside was unusual. This is backed up by further research of BALL's on four English departments, of which Beachside was one (BALL and LACEY, 1980). Two of these departments (one being Beachside's) had a tight consensus on English teaching policy, particularly on the adoption of an individualistic approach. This was largely due to the fact that the departments were staffed entirely by subject specialists who felt closely involved in the formulation and interpretation of departmental policy. In the other two schools, however, much of the English teaching was undertaken by non-specialists who had little sustained involvement in departmental policy. Here, there was less overall agreement on English policy, many non-specialists in particular diverging from the creative, expressive aspects of English teaching and choosing instead to adopt a 'basic skills' or textbook-bound approach. This may have been because they felt ill at ease with creative and expressive approaches to English when these did not form part of their teaching in other subject areas, or because their teaching responsibilities in other areas of the curriculum made them more conscious of the need to give emphasis to basic skills. BALL and LACEY offer us no evidence which would allow us to arbitrate between these possibilities. Clearly, though, teachers of English in middle schools who practise ability setting are likely to share much more in common with non-specialist secondary departments than with the English department at Beachside. One reason is that, like other subject specialists in the middle school, they are likely to be the only practitioners of their specialism there. And, as BALL and LACEY's work indicates, isolation from a subject sub-culture inclines English teachers more towards a basic skills-centred approach.

In the case of other high status subjects, such as French and mathematics, however, where the subject community as a whole is more agreed on matters such as setting than are English teachers, the grouping practices of middle school teachers fall more in line with most of their secondary colleagues, at least in the upper years of the middle school.

4 Because the data in this table are compiled from three different surveys, they involve different types and degrees of sampling error and are therefore not susceptible to tests of statistical significance.

5 Dashes in columns indicate that no data on these subjects are available in the surveys concerned.

6 There may be various reasons for these disparities — the differences between the samples, the dates at which the different surveys were conducted, or the criterion used as an indicator of liaison in each case, for instance.

7 After the end of fieldwork, humanities staff from the upper school visited Riverdale for the first time and, according to the Head, subsequently modified much of their own syllabus in order to eliminate repetition.

8 These plans were revealed in interview with Miss LAMB, the home economics teacher at Moorhead.

9 The only concession was with fourth-year pupils where one day per week was devoted to a French project in which pupils could study a famous French historical figure, a region of France, food and drink in France, and so forth.

10 See the work of APPLE (1982) for an argument outlining the technical control implications of curriculum packaging.

11 Recent shifts towards the development of a more broadly defined area of craft, design and technology within the curriculum may well infuse a stronger and more overtly theoretical element into craft teaching.

12 There are close parallels here with the middle school art and design teachers studied by TICKLE (1983).

13 Again, problems of uncertain sampling error render tests of statistical significance unhelpful.

14 Critics might want to argue that what goes on within specialist periods is very different and much more open and flexible in middle schools than in secondary schools; that much 'affective' drama takes place within the ostensibly 'cognitive' category of English for instance. Consequently, it might be argued, comparisons based on timetabled commitments to subject specialisms are likely to make middle schools appear much more specialist than they really are. In response to this, it is conceded that the indicators of specialist teaching are indeed exceedingly crude and imprecise. However, it must also be said that the imprecision applies to middle and secondary schools alike — history lessons contain cartographical (geographical) skills, science lessons contain mathematical ones, and so on. If we were to examine specialist commitment on the basis of subject-related skills, this would require an extremely sophisticated, cross-curricular, systematic observation study of the skills employed in middle and secondary schools respectively. All the present indicators can do is reveal the extent to which pupils are exposed to particular subject specialisms as organized (albeit differently organized) bodies of knowledge, concepts and skills, within discrete, compartmentalized parts of the school day.

Part 3:
Cultures of Teaching

'What teaching does to teachers, it does
partly by furnishing them those roles
which habit ties to the inner frame
of personality and use makes one with
the self'

(Willard Waller (1932) *The Sociology of Teaching*.)

Introduction

Headteachers, it is commonly claimed, have a major influence on the tone or ethos of their schools (HMI, 1979; Rutter *et al*, 1979). Her Majesty's Inspectorate (1983a, p. 18) made this point in their *9–13 Middle School Survey*, for example. However, while this view undoubtedly has a great deal of validity, the quality and impact of a head's leadership is also significantly influenced and often severely limited by the kind and quality of his or her teaching staff (one which the Head usually inherits with the taking up of his or her appointment).[1]

This is particularly true during times of educational reorganization when the pursuit of new educational purposes must be achieved, in the main, with the staff resources available in local pools of teaching labour. We are now familiar with these problems as they affected mainstream comprehensive reorganization (i.e. with transfer at 11), when teachers with their roots in and commitments to two very different traditions of grammar and secondary modern schooling respectively were suddenly thrown into the same educational environment and expected to work together. The grammar school teachers, usually graduates, with their widespread expertise in and experience of teaching high status subjects to high levels of age and ability were able to command most of the prestigious posts as heads of subject departments in the new, meritocratically orientated comprehensives. The secondary modern teachers, meanwhile, normally college educated and more committed to and experienced in traditions of vocational, practical and basic-skills directed education with a heavy overlay of classroom control were, despite growing experience with some 'O' level teaching during the 1960s, unable to compete successfully with their grammar school counterparts for these high status, academically orientated posts (Hargreaves, D. 1980). Where the claims of the ex-secondary modern teachers to status and recognition were denied or neglected, this often bred resentment and resistance to the initiatives of their heads, setting secondary modern teachers apart as caucuses of opposition to school policy (Riseborough, 1981). Where such claims were accommodated by establishing alternative pastoral career structures, this often led to the development of an academic-pastoral divide, one which could present major obstacles to the achievement of agreed, whole-school policies (Warwick, 1974; Burgess, 1983; Evans, 1985). In either case, the pursuit of unity was hindered by a legacy of division.

One lesson which mainstream comprehensive reorganization has therefore taught us, is what happens when teachers with different professional biographies and perspectives come together in pursuit of what others would often wish to regard as some common educational purpose. It has taught us, in other words, about the close and intimate connection between teachers' biographies, perspectives, cultures and careers, and the implications of all these things for classroom practice and for the change process in schools. I shall outline what importance these things have for middle school teachers in particular, shortly. But before that, it is perhaps worth specifying a little more precisely what is meant by these terms — biographies, perspectives, cultures and careers — so that their interrelationship and implications for the development of middle schools might be more clearly understood.

Biographies, Perspectives, Cultures and Careers

A teacher's professional (and indeed personal) *biography*, her past and projected *career*, and her educational *perspective* form closely interwoven aspects of her professional development and have significant effects on her approach to classroom teaching. In this sense, the strategies she adopts in the classroom and her attitudes to change are very much bound up with the kind of person she has become, the professional experiences she has had, the perspectives on teaching and learning to which she has become committed and the particular groups or cultures of teachers with which she has identified and from which she gains support.

Perspectives are 'frameworks through which people make sense of the world' (Woods, 1983, p. 7). We do not, in other words, respond to every situation we encounter in a completely novel and totally idiosyncratic way, but we bring to those situations patterns of understanding and interpretation which give our responses some personal consistency. The problems created by a pupil's learning difficulty or a disruptive class, for instance, will not be treated by all teachers in exactly the same way. How a teacher deals with them, rather, will depend very much on how she interprets them. Is the class *really* disruptive or just exuberant? Are they in high spirits or 'trying it on'? It is a teacher's framework of interpretation, her perspective, that shapes these kinds of questions and suggests solutions to them. In many respects, in fact, it is that perspective which makes her the kind of teacher she is.

The frameworks of meaning, the perspectives which teachers bring to educational issues and events are established and modified through teachers' own professional *biographies*. That is to say, a teacher's definition of any particular situation and the broader perspective which informs it 'has its history; it is the sedimentation of all her previous experiences, organized in the habitual possessions of her stock of knowledge at hand' (Schutz 1973:9). These experiences may be traumatic, as in a teacher's first encounter with a rioting class (Waller, 1932, p. 400) or a student teacher's first experience of teaching practice (Lacey, 1977). Or they may be routine, recurrent and habit forming, part of the more mundane, day-to-day business of teaching. In this sense, as Becker and his colleagues point out, 'If a particular kind of situation recurs frequently, the perspective will probably become an established part of a person's way of dealing with the world' (Becker *et al*, 1961, p. 37). Either way, traumatic or routine, a teacher's biography, her own professional inheritance, is a crucial determinant of his/her educational perspective.

While some writers have emphasized the unique and personal aspects of peoples' biographies, and of the perspectives they generate (for example, Schutz, 1973; Elbaz, 1983), others have drawn attention to the shared character of many peoples' experiences and the perspectives arising from them; to the fact that group perspectives (as they are often called) are often developed in relation to commonly experienced problems among people placed in similar situations, facing similar difficulties (Becker *et al*, 1961). In this sense, teachers' educational biographies and perspectives are closely bound up with the particular occupational *cultures* to which those teachers belong — each with its own socially approved ways of thinking, feeling, acting and believing in relation to educational matters.[2]

These cultural divisions produce not only different identities and perspectives among teachers, but different opportunities for professional advancement too. Occupational cultures, that is, provide *career* routes for their members. The subject department, for instance, acts as one of the major anchorage points of a secondary school teacher's career. It is here that posts of responsibility are in greatest abundance (Goodson, 1983), offering teachers *objective* careers in the sense of 'a system of compartments or stages sequentially arranged' (Lyons, 1981, p. 9). It is here too that many teachers' *subjective* careers are established, their subjective senses of prestige and worth (Hughes, 1937) that derive from the status of the subject they teach. Furthermore, where teachers are, for whatever reason, excluded from this conventional academic subject career route, the pastoral system with its posts of head of year and head of house, may provide an alternative. Careers, both objective and subjective, organize teacher's biographies and both realize and result from their perspectives, creating and reinforcing the different cultural divisions within the teaching profession.

For these reasons, it should be clear that a sound grasp of the close associations between teachers' careers, cultures, biographies and perspectives is crucial to understanding the problems of staff recruitment and deployment that schools face when they innovate or reorganize; the difficulties they encounter when they seek to establish new identities for themselves which cut across the long-established loyalties, traditions, cultures and careers of the staff they employ.

In addition to this, an understanding of teacher cultures and the deep seated educational traditions in which they are rooted also enables us to connect the rich details of individual teacher biographies to the broader patterns of educational and social history, to those biographies-in-common which writers like Mills (1959) have rightly held to be central to the sociological enterprise. Looking at the case of middle schools in particular, such a study of teachers' lives, their backgrounds and orientations, should deepen our understanding of the relationship between the middle school's history and the difficulties it now faces; between its past and present, that is.

The Phase Match Thesis

A number of writers on the middle school have already remarked that the kinds of staff recruited to such schools have significantly influenced their development. Ginsburg and his colleagues (1977, p. 36), for instance, have argued that:

> Because of the relatively recent emergence of middle schools, the staffs are comprised largely by persons with either primary or secondary training and/or teaching experience as well as by persons who have had solely middle school training and experience. To the extent that primary and secondary teachers pursue different educational philosophies ... teachers' professional backgrounds may be quite important in structuring teacher relations especially to the extent that these background differences correspond to the age of the child the staff member teaches in the middle school setting.

Blyth and Derricott (1977, p. 73) appear to be making a similar point when they suggest that 'middle schools are ... prone to the subdivision of staff according to their pattern of training and consequent professional orientation'. Nor are such interpretations confined to published critiques of the middle school. Moorhead's Headteacher, for instance, put the problem as follows:

> Staff, I think, can teach most effectively when they are teaching the way with which they themselves are most familiar, and it's nonsense to think that you can change a teacher who has been teaching for many years in a particular way into an entirely different way of teaching without allowing him or her time to develop. And therefore, I think, we had one year or so of the primary school and two years in the secondary school here.... We simply had to use the teachers who were available. So those who opted to come to the middle school either opted to do so from the primary school on the one hand or from the secondary schools on the other and eighty percent of our staff were recruited in this way. They didn't necessarily have a burning desire to teach in middle schools, the burning desire being in fact to remain in Moorhead (the town). And it may well have been and certainly was the case that in some cases they just wanted a job and they found themselves becoming redundant in the primary schools or else they found themselves unable to get the sort of jobs which they wanted in the upper schools and so they had no alternative.

What is being proposed in these accounts, in effect, is that there is a strong degree of *phase match* between the training and previous experience of middle school teachers on the one hand and the current age range which they teach within middle schools on the other; and that the recruitment of teachers from what amount to two separate cultures of primary and secondary teaching inhibits the middle school in its quest for a distinctive identity.

Just how far this 'phase match' argument applies to middle schools as a whole is not known. While national surveys provide figures on the varied backgrounds of teachers recruited to middle schools (HMI, 1983a, p. 41; Taylor and Garson, 1982, pp. 43 and 125),[3] and while there is some evidence that educational attitudes differ significantly among ex-junior and ex-secondary staff (Taylor and Sayer, 1984, p. 25), there are no data which relate the backgrounds of middle school teachers — ex-primary, ex-secondary or otherwise — to the duties they then take on within the middle school. The exact relationship between recruitment and deployment remains a mystery.

At Riverdale and Moorhead, evidence relating to phase match was gathered from interviews conducted with all Riverdale teachers and from those thirteen members of staff who were interviewed at Moorhead, as well as from two of their colleagues on whom limited information was also available. The results are summarized in table 18.[4]

Table 18: *Percentage of Teachers at Riverdale and Moorhead who are phase matched or not by various measures*

| | **Phase Match Measure** | |
	Previous Experience	*Training*
Type of Match		
Phase matched	42	52
Phase mismatched	22	4
Mixed inheritance	37	44

What the figures indicate is a slight, but only a slight trend towards phase match between teachers' professional biographies and their teaching responsibilities in these two middle schools. For teachers with wholly primary or secondary backgrounds, previous training was strongly and significantly associated with present deployment.[5] By this measure, only one teacher was clearly mismatched. The association in the case of previous teaching experience was much less strong, however, and far from being statistically significant. But in either case, many teachers did not have a wholly primary or secondary background at all and because of this, whatever measure is used, when all the middle school teachers in the sample are taken together, scarcely more than half of them are phase matched. If these two schools are at all typical, then, the phase match thesis is not as powerful an explanation of the middle school's split identity as many have thought.

There are a number of possible explanations for this. Perhaps the cultures of primary and secondary teaching are less tenacious than has been imagined. Perhaps those cultures have been weakened by the recruitment to the middle school of large numbers of teachers with a mixed professional inheritance. Perhaps middle school heads have been more successful in drawing different occupational cultures together than their secondary counterparts.

To all these possibilities must be added a further one, though; that the criterion of primary/secondary teaching is almost certainly too crude to discriminate meaningfully between different teacher cultures in the middle school or indeed in any other school setting. In part, this is because the entire teaching community cannot be accurately divided into just two categories — be this primary/secondary, progressive/traditional or whatever. But if all dichotomies of teacher types are problematic, the primary/secondary one has its own special difficulties. As we saw in the introduction, there are important differences *within* secondary teaching between the cultures of grammar and secondary modern teachers, and of different subject communities, for instance. Equally, at the primary level, it was noted, following Blyth (1965), that there are at least three dominant traditions within English primary education — developmental, preparatory and elementary. And some traditions — most notably the elementary one — are clearly highly influential within both sectors.

Given these important disctictions *within* primary and secondary education, bald figures on phase match or mismatch are bound to give an insufficiently detailed picture of the relationship between teachers' professional biographies and their educational perspectives in the middle school setting. In order to get such a picture, we need to abandon the strategy of comparing likely categories of teacher types from 'above', as it were, and turn instead to the teachers themselves, to the lives they lead within the middle school and have led before it, and to the sense they make of that experience. We need, that is, to engage closely with teachers' own meanings and understandings of the middle school experience, and of their careers preceding it, in order to generate from the 'bottom up', meaningful categories for identifying the different occupational cultures that have a strong bearing on the middle school's character.

The following three chapters are therefore devoted to a more detailed analysis of the professional biographies and perspectives of the staff at Riverdale and Moorhead. These teachers, it is argued, fall into three different groups, each with its own distinctive cultural inheritance: the academic-elementary, developmental and middle years teachers.

Notes

1 It is interesting how many schools with strong records in and reputations for innovation on a school-wide front have been newly established, purpose-built institutions; schools whose heads have been able to pick and choose staff who would be sympathetic and committed to their aims from the outset; schools whose establishment is accompanied by an expectation of and commitment to change. See, for instance, the changing schools described in the edited collection by Moon (1983).

2 I am not, in this instance, referring to what is often termed *the* occupational culture of teaching, to alleged attributes of the teaching profession as a whole (Waller, 1932; Jackson, 1968; Lortie, 1975; Hargreaves, D. 1980 and 1982), but to the cultures of subgroups *within* teaching.

3 According to Taylor and Garson's (1982) survey, 17 per cent of 9–13 middle school teachers are middle school trained, 26 per cent have primary experience only, 36 per cent secondary experience only, and 21 per cent experience of both sectors.

4 More detailed information on the phase match data is available in Hargreaves (1985).

5 According to Fisher's Exact Probability Test, the phase matching among teachers by this criterion was statistically significant to a level of .0013.

Chapter 8

The Academic-Elementary Teachers

In terms of their backgrounds, beliefs, and aspirations, thirteen teachers in the sample at Riverdale and Moorhead belonged to what might be called the academic-elementary tradition of English education.[1] As its name suggests, this broad tradition consists of both academic and elementary elements. Each of these elements, I want to propose, spans the usual phase distinctions between primary and secondary education and can be found as much in the preparatory and elementary traditions of primary schooling as in the academic or control-centred traditions of secondary schooling. The main features of these traditions were outlined in chapter 1, though their nature will be clarified still further as this more detailed examination of academic-elementary teachers in the middle school proceeds.

The chapter is divided into two main parts — each devoted to a separate group of teachers who, by virtue of their backgrounds and careers, embody and express the characteristics of the academic-elementary tradition in a slightly different way. The first group — six mixed phase teachers — had experience which transcended the primary-secondary divide. Nonetheless, it is argued, this contact with different sectors made these teachers less ideal candidates for the unique, transitional middle school than many might imagine, for their beliefs and commitments appeared to be rooted in experiences and influences common to both sectors. This professional inheritance, I want to argue, equipped them not for the needs of the middle school as a whole but for one particular version of middle school teaching only, a version best suited to its upper years.

The second part of the chapter looks at a further seven teachers with a similar set of educational perspectives to their mixed phase colleagues but whose previous experience was wholly secondary, and indeed, mainly secondary modern in character. These two groups of teachers — mixed phase and secondary modern — it is argued, with their ingrained allegiances to the assumptions of the academic-elementary tradition, have had a substantial influence on the character of Riverdale and Moorhead middle schools, particularly in their upper years, and perhaps on the character of middle schools as a whole.

The Mixed Phase Teachers

Name	School	Age	Length career (years)	Responsibility	Year groups	Percentage time in upper years
Mr Bird	Moorhead	61–65	27	Maths/Year 3	3	100
Mr Greek	Moorhead	46–50	26	Deputy/Science	—	77
Mrs Spinner	Moorhead	51–55	24	Senior Mistress	—	100
Mrs Masters	Moorhead	51–55	25	Library	4	100
Mr Banks	Riverdale	46–50	22	—	3–4	55 (+ Library)
Mrs Priestley	Moorhead	51–55	25	—	3	80
Mean		53.0	24.8			

According to Taylor and Garson's middle school survey (1982, p. 125) just over 20 per cent of teachers in 9–13 schools have a mixed phase background of primary and secondary experience (of teaching in both primary and secondary sectors that is); a figure which rises to around 28 per cent in the case of 10–13 middle schools. At Riverdale and Moorhead, the proportion was slightly lower than this: just five of the twenty-seven teachers considered in the sample (18.6 per cent) having this sort of split-phase background.[2] Only one of these teachers (Mr Banks) was at Riverdale whose otherwise young and freshly recruited staff had, in the main, insufficient years of teaching under their belt to have accumulated any real variety of professional experience.[3] The other four teachers with a strictly mixed phase background were all at reorganized Moorhead and amounted to 30.8 per cent of the interview sample there (close to — indeed slightly above — the national trend in 10–13 schools identified by Taylor and Garson).[4] One teacher — Mrs Priestley — had an exclusively primary background but, for reasons which will become apparent, is included with her mixed phase colleagues on the grounds that the content of her previous experience and perspective is very similar to theirs and most unlike that of her purely ex-primary colleagues.

The presence of mixed phase teachers — a fifth or more of the 9–13 middle school teaching force — with their variety of previous experience, might be viewed by some as a particularly positive feature of the middle school's professional inheritance (Gannon and Whalley, 1975). It might also be regarded as a significant challenge to the phase match thesis. But this begs the question of just *how* varied that experience actually is and what impact it appears to have had on the teachers concerned. As a way of dealing with this question, I will focus, first of all, on just one of the teachers in this group — Mr Bird — to show in some detail how apparently disparate elements in the backgrounds of mixed phase teachers actually interlock in a more clearly defined pattern. Then I shall go on to show to what extent the biographies and perspectives of the other mixed phase teachers are similar to his.

Mr Bird

Close to retirement age, Mr Bird was Head of Year 3 and subject coordinator for mathematics at Moorhead, for which he held a scale 3 post of responsibility. In the mornings, he taught mathematics to years 3 and 4 in sets; the responsibility for that setting policy being his. In the afternoons, he taught history, expressive arts and integrated studies to mixed ability groups in years 3 and 4.

Mr Bird was a strong advocate of setting and streaming. Asked what aspects of teaching he disliked, he picked out mixed ability teaching as his only area of real concern:

> I'm not too happy about certain situations as compared to some other situations. By that, I mean, for example, that I feel happier in a streamed situation or a set situation than I do in a mixed ability situation. But then it's only marginal because I teach history in a mixed ability situation. But I feel, you know, if I was really put to the point, that I could teach even history better in a streamed or set situation.

In part, this support for setting seemed to stem from his subject-specialist orientation. That orientation might well have been established during Mr Bird's initial teacher training in the immediate post-war period, which was geared to secondary mathematics teaching. There is evidence, though, that Mr Bird's subject loyalty was fixed even before that point, for before the war, he had studied mathematics at university, even if he had to drop out 'for personal reasons' before completing his degree. Mathematics as a specialism was clearly a dominant feature of Mr Bird's teaching and educational biography and figured prominently in the first nine years of his career (1948–57) spent teaching the upper age range of a 5–15 all-age school. In answer to a question concerning his strengths as a teacher, Mr Bird stated that

> I have, in the main subjects I teach, a pretty clear academic knowledge without an actual qualification, you know. I know my subjects, although I've never taken any one of them to a final degree level.

This view of the centrality of 'the subject' and subject knowledge to his teaching applied not only to mathematics but also to his other great love, history. Although having no high level qualifications in this subject, Mr Bird felt able to refer to himself on one occasion as 'a historian' and indeed was a leading member of the Local History Society within the community. And while there was no fixed category of history as such on the timetable, Mr Bird, like many other members of staff (see chapter 7) interpreted the two afternoon sessions devoted to social studies to mean history one day and geography the next.

Mr Bird often construed this subject in strongly classified and strongly framed terms (Bernstein, 1971), as having its own subject-specific body of facts and knowledge which required strong and overt teacher direction in its transmission. Speaking about lesson preparation, he said:

> I do prepare history fairly thoroughly because although one has it all 'here' in a general sense, the background of facts are not stored in the mind. Dates, what they actually did, why they did it and the detail of what they actually did — this is important and you must read it up beforehand and make skeleton notes of what you're going to pin the whole work on.

To be fair, though, not all Mr Bird's history teaching was seen in these terms. From time to time, he also employed a more exploratory, research-centred model of the subject:

> When I teach the other way, I outline a topic on a theme and they have to do some research. What I do there is prepare ... skeleton notes with the main headings of the things they have to investigate and find out about and deduce and try and get some causal relationship.

However, this research model, devoted, as Bernstein (1971) puts it, to unlocking the 'mysteries of the subject' for the pupil, was only considered by Mr Bird as suitable for the academically able — for potential adult researchers, in effect. Consequently, when the research model of history was made available to pupils in a mixed ability situation, this created profound anxieties for him:

> What generally happens is, of course, as we have an unstreamed situation, one of my personal feelings about the unstreamed situation that disturbs me is that many children will spend a tremendous long time and do an awful lot of work and you could happily leave those to get on with it and they'll go on *ad infinitum*. Many will spend a long time and not produce much. It doesn't always follow that some of those haven't learned a lot, but they haven't churned it out again. But many will spend a long time and not produce much and they won't have done much either and, of course, many will not have the mental ability and resources of character and personality to persevere for very long on a long topic.

As with most history, Mr Bird also defined mathematics in terms of bodies of knowledge, but added to this the conceptual aspects of the subject which were said to be ordered in a necessarily linear, hierarchical way. Thus, in answer to a general question about marking, Mr Bird spontaneously turned to the example of maths:

> Mathematics has to be graded. This is true of any subject which has this sort of intellectual arguing, reasoning context to it, because they've got to learn and understand what has been done in order that next week, next month, next year they can develop that knowledge or concept in another direction and learn that. And that's the whole of maths, you see: if you don't know the first thing, you don't know the next.

These ideas about the intrinsic ordering principles of different subjects were in turn closely linked to notions of children having fixed intellectual capacities, requiring them to be separated into different ability groups where the subject matter could be pitched at appropriate levels of difficulty. Commenting on what in his opinion, were his weaknesses as a teacher, Mr Bird said:

> I am not at my best with children of not very high intelligence because perhaps I'm not patient enough with them, their difficulties. Or it may be because I'm more bored with the level of material that one has to deal with. But I must confess that in that context, you know, I have a lot of teaching

experience with 'backward' children. I know the problem. I did a course once on 'backward' teaching ... but I think I would admit that as a weakness with them.

In many ways, then, Mr Bird was the personification of what Ball (1981) calls the academic perspective — subject centred, orientated to teaching the more able pupil, and a firm believer in the special intellectual demands of his own subject and the need this created for ability grouping. In Mr Bird's case, much of this perspective seemed to derive from his acquaintance with mathematics in higher education and from his earlier career socialization in the secondary sector, though these 'academic' attitudes seem also, to a certain extent, to have been carried over by him into areas of equally strong interest but lesser formal responsibility such as history too.

Paradoxically, however, given these views, the curious thing about Mr Bird is that like many teachers of his age and generation, his teaching experience was not entirely confined to the secondary sector. When the all-age school where he first taught closed in 1957, he was redeployed to a new post in a primary school in Moorhead, where he stayed until middle school reorganization in 1970. Such a move did not involve a Damascus-like conversion in Mr Bird's educational thinking, though. Rather, on transfer, he took with him a great deal of biographical 'baggage' from his secondary school teaching days. This was shown in his preference for teaching particular age ranges ('The years that I was interested in ... were the top end'), and for particular ability groups (he took a top-year 'A' stream for most of his time at the school).

When Mr Bird moved to the primary sector, then, he discovered that the transition was less abrupt than he had imagined. In part, this was because life in the upper streams in the top years of many primary schools was, given their 11+ scholarship bias, not unlike that of secondary school regimes in many respects (Rubinstein and Simon, 1962). It bore strong vestiges of the preparatory tradition, that is. But as we saw in chapter 1, scholarship teaching, like all-age and secondary modern teaching, also contained strong traces of the elementary tradition too, not least in its emphasis on basic skills. These sorts of influences appeared to have persisted in Mr Bird's attitude to middle school teaching. For instance, when asked what children ought to know by the time they left Moorhead middle, he stated:

> We are in this business, like it or not, to prepare children to live. People cannot lose sight of this fact and I think perhaps some 'moderns' lose sight of this a bit in the tendency that it's more important to be happy than that they should actually gain some knowledge. They have got to live in a world where they have got to be capable and *numerate* and *literate* to a high degree to live successfully in a social organization within the economic system. (my emphases)

On to these elementary-like concerns with basic skills, Mr Bird superimposed an equally elementary-like preoccupation with firm, almost regimented classroom discipline. 'A bit of a tartar', his Head called him. While I had no opportunity to observe Mr Bird teaching social studies, he certainly managed to create an atmosphere in his mathematics classes not far removed from the drill sergeant and the parade ground (Webb, 1962). Here, between periods of chalk-and-blackboard aided exposition, and silent spells of seatwork, Mr Bird operated a 'recitation' style of teaching (Hoetker and Ahlbrand, 1969: Westbury, 1973), where he moved rapidly and somewhat fearsomely up and down rows of pupils, throwing out streams of short, mathematical questions and demanding immediate, correct responses.

In Mr Bird, then, we can see a certain affinity between the subject-based secondary influences in his training and in the niche he managed to carve for himself in 'A' stream primary teaching on the one hand; and the ideas and approaches he picked up from the elementary tradition within the primary sector and among low ability pupils in the secondary sector, on the other. This dual inheritance — academic and elementary — was also reflected in his classroom teaching: in his concern with his 'subjects', with able pupils and with high 'standards' in the first case; and with basic skills, drill and rote methods, along with firm discipline in the second.

Thus, when, at his own request, he was given a teaching load and influential responsibilities within the top half of the middle school, Mr Bird was returned to the habitat where he felt most comfortable, on the top side of the 11+ divide — a habitat where academic and elementary concerns could be comfortably combined, where there would be no need to engage or compromise with the developmental tradition that had more of a foothold only in the middle school's lower years.

Mr Bird's case richly illustrates how academic and elementary influences can interpenetrate in a middle school teacher's biography and career. However, it does not and cannot show how generalizable these patterns are among middle school teachers as a whole. To deal with this question of generalizability, we need to look at the other mixed phase teachers, their backgrounds and experiences. To what extent were they bearers of an academic-elementary inheritance also?

Mixed Phase Biographies

In their initial training all but two of the other mixed phase teachers had, like Mr Bird, been prepared for teaching students of secondary age or older.[5] One of them, Mr Banks, had also undertaken a primary course at a later point in his career but this had only lasted two weeks. The remaining mixed phase teacher — Mr Greek — had spent two years on a junior-secondary course but in practice this had been predominantly geared to one sector only; the secondary one. For him, as indeed for many of his junior/secondary trained colleagues also, the mixed-phase status of these courses had little more than paper authenticity. As Blyth and Derricott (1977, p. 155) have pointed out, while their titles perhaps implied a mixed phase orientation, in practice many junior/secondary courses in the 1950s and 60s often acted as a residual category into which students with aspirations to become secondary school specialists, but whose specialisms were not scarcity subjects, began to drift. 'Such students', Blyth and Derricott went on, 'often showed little interest in the general and primary aspects of the course'. There were distinct signs of this in Mr

Greek's case — for in the middle of his training he had transferred to a course preparing teachers for the secondary age range and above in further education and county colleges, only returning (with some reluctance) to his junior/secondary course when it seemed to him that the county college experiment would not materialize in the way he hoped.

In effect, then, all but one of the mixed phase teachers (the exception being Mrs Priestley, an 'emergency trained' junior teacher) had actually been professionally prepared for *secondary* teaching. Interesting as this finding is though, it would be unwise to place too much importance on it. After all, every one of these teachers had spent more than two decades in the profession and initial training was now a very long way behind them. Certainly, looking back, these teachers did not themselves see their training as being particularly important in shaping their current approach to teaching. What mattered, rather, was their subsequent practical experience; that depth and variety of classroom experience which often comes with a long teaching career.[6] What form did that experience take? What type, what blend of primary and secondary practice was contained within it?

Figures for length and recency of primary as against secondary experience among these teachers reveal no definite overall pattern. On the one hand, four of the teachers (Priestley, Bird, Greek and Masters) had taught for more of their time in primary schools than in secondary ones, and the mean time spent in primary as against secondary teaching was 11.6 compared to 8.6 years respectively. On the other hand, half the teachers had also taught in secondary schools on their last appointment.

Behind these inconclusive statistics, though, the interview responses of the mixed phase teachers, their own accounts and interpretations of their previous careers, told a more consistent story; a story of exposure and attachment not to any one phase, but to a single academic-elementary tradition.

For two of the teachers, primary teaching of whatever kind was but a minor feature of their professional background. In every other respect, they were secondary teachers through and through. Mrs Spinner spent just two years in the primary sector — immediately after her secondary training — and then only because of domestic pressure to return home following a family bereavement. The rest of her long career, until appointment as Moorhead's Senior Mistress in 1972, was spent as a secondary modern science teacher. Mr Banks had even less primary experience than this — a single year sandwiched between posts in grammar and secondary modern schools respectively.

The primary experience of the remaining mixed phase teachers was much more extensive. They had spent the better part — and in Mrs Priestley's case, all — of their teaching careers in that sector, in fact. What was particularly crucial in their case, though, was not the brevity or datedness of their primary experience (as in Mrs Spinner's and Mr Banks' case) but the particular form it took. None of these teachers were 'progressive', developmental educators in the sense outlined by Blyth (1965). Rather, they were 'scholarship' teachers, teachers whose primary experience had been formed, developed and completed before the advent of comprehensive reorganization in their localities, and therefore closely geared to the needs of the

11 + examination. Thus, Mrs Masters, an Oxford graduate, who had done twelve years of primary teaching between spells of teaching grammar school English, had spent most of her 'primary' years with what she called 'the grammar school pupils' in the final year. And Mr Greek, Moorhead's deputy, had taught for virtually all his 'junior time', in an 11 + set up too. Similarly, Mrs Priestley recalled her days as a junior teacher when she had 'enjoyed working towards something, preparing children perhaps for something more', 'We don't get that now', she added ruefully.

We have already seen what significance this 'scholarship' orientation had in Mr Bird's case, reinforcing the academic-elementary inheritance he had already acquired through his teaching of secondary age-range pupils. So it was with the other mixed phase teachers too. Their combined experience of secondary teaching and of 'scholarship' teaching in the primary phase had also fostered in them an academic-elementary orientation to matters of pedagogy, discipline, subject teaching and standards.

Mixed Phase Perspectives

Mr Banks, for instance, had always been inclined to adopt an 'adult' approach in his teaching, a point for which he recalled being criticized in his probationary year. Having been taken from Moorhead Middle after reorganization, following a period of professional difficulty, Mr Banks, though grateful for Riverdale's acceptance of him, remained critical of its apparently child-centred approach. The absence of black-boards ('I wish I had a few decent ones'), the seeming unwillingness to uphold decent standards of academic performance and behaviour; matters such as these were constant sources of worry and irritation to him. His own preference was for teaching able pupils, pupils who were motivated and wanted to be taught. Yet in his view, middle schools, like comprehensive schools generally, would 'not be able to cater for the able child'. 'The brightest children,' according to him, 'are not achieving as much as they would do at a grammar school'. The solution, he proposed, in a manner characteristic of the academic perspective, was to

> . . . group year children in some ways for at least the main academic subjects. You can either do it in sets, or you can do it in grammar schools, secondary modern schools or special schools or whatever you like, but you cannot teach in the comprehensive set up.

Mrs Masters also showed strong inclinations towards the academic perspective, as one might expect from someone with grammar school experience as extensive as hers. She expressed great interest in her subject, English, rating it the aspect of teaching she enjoyed most. She held strong reservations about mixed ability teaching, feeling that it only stood a chance of working in classes of fifteen or less, and identified this as one of the major problems with which she was confronted. And on matters of pedagogy, she had doubts that individualized or group-based work could be achieved in ordinary sized classes, and therefore tended to dislike teaching what she called 'the rather disorganized things like integrated studies'. The centrality of the subject, grouping by ability and conventional teacher-centred pedagogy: all these distinctive features of the academic perspective were the things which characterized Mrs Masters' approach to teaching in spite, or perhaps even because of the many years she had spent teaching primary 'scholarship' pupils, in addition to her grammar school experience.

Mrs Spinner, though holding a management position as Moorhead's senior mistress with particular responsibility for girls' welfare, had also, nonetheless, retained a strong commitment to her subject, science. She cited it as her greatest source of enjoyment; all but two of her many in-service courses had been devoted to it, and only two of her teaching periods (under 7 per cent) lay outside it. Such 'academic' subject-centredness might seem unusual in a middle school teacher of such seniority, but Mrs Spinner's management role, unlike the Deputy Head's, Mr Greek's, was an ill-defined one, particularly with regard to other members of staff. *He* had a clear interest in and responsibility for the management of staff relationships which he discharged in a quiet, avuncular style that was valued by many of his colleagues. Mrs Spinner's formal brief was much more closely confined to matters of pupils' welfare, however, and her relationships with and responsibilities regarding other members of staff were therefore uncertain, ill-defined and consequently often fraught.[7]

Having no formal responsibility for staff leadership, not even at the level of year leader, Mrs Spinner tried hard to expand her role into staff affairs on a less formal basis (as she pointed out to me at some length in interview), but these did nothing to enhance her prestige and popularity. She organized the staff tea funds, but the staff only bickered about it and resented her 'nagging': she took care of school furnishings by washing staffroom curtains in the holidays, for instance, though few people noticed; and she led vigorous one-woman campaigns in staff meetings on matters of school policy — with regard to tightening up regulations on school uniform, for example — only to meet with hostility and resentment from many of her colleagues.

Like many senior women teachers who are cast into the characteristically 'feminine' and therefore lower status aspects of school management (Lyons, 1981), ones which as Richardson (1973, p. 218) points out, are 'a reflection of ancient assumptions about masculinity and femininity', Mrs Spinner had some difficulty justifying her seniority among her colleagues. Little wonder, then, that she should hang on to the more clearly defined and publicly recognized identity which her subject expertise conferred upon her. And little wonder too, that she should also place a high premium on the disciplinary aspects of her role, for not only was this an area for which her secondary modern background had equipped her particularly well, but it was the one officially recognized part of her duties from which she gained colleaguial respect, especially where male teachers of 'difficult girls' were concerned.

Mrs Spinner had a brisk and sometimes brusque, 'no-nonsense' approach to school discipline. She counted this among the most enjoyable parts of her work — second only to the teaching of her subject. 'I like seeing what makes the naughty ones tick', she said. She preferred praise to condemnation where possible ('I certainly believe that a little sugar gets you futher along the way than vinegar'), but 'that doesn't stop me tearing a strip off one, you know, really frighten them to death, when necessary'.

When, in response to Mrs Spinner's lengthy description of her interest in discipline, I tried to summarize her argument as follows — 'So in that sense you derive your enjoyment from the building of personal relationships between you and the children' — my reference to 'personal relationships' served only to trigger a reaction to what she apparently took to be unpleasant associations with egalitarianism and child-centredness.

> Yes, but don't get me wrong! I don't subscribe to the feeling that we are all friends together and that we are all equal. I *never* encourage that! I am kind to children, I like to be open with them, but they are *there* (downward gesture) and I am *here* (upward gesture). I am not one of those that likes that sort of freedom in the classroom and I would no more ever bandy Christian names about in front of children than fly.

Coupled with her academic-centredness, this elementary-like approach to teacher-pupil relationships, a legacy of her secondary modern experience, produced an approach to classroom pedagogy very similar to Mr Bird's. Hers was predominantly a 'transmission' pedagogy (Barnes and Shemilt, 1974) with lengthy periods of exposition or demonstration, extended question-answer sessions where searches for 'right answers' through the provision of oblique clues predominated (Hammersley, 1977); and long spells of individual writing — much of this devoted to copying from the board, taking down notes from worksheets or summarizing what had just been talked about in class. Nor was Mrs Spinner unaware of the 'traditional' cast these activities lent to her work, for when I requested a worksheet on insect evolution she had just used in a fourth-year science lesson, she retorted, somewhat defensively, 'Of course, this factual basis isn't very fashionable is it?'

Mrs Priestley was no slave to 'fashion' and change either. An ex-primary teacher of many years experience, she had resisted what she construed as unwarranted interference on the head's part; his efforts to make her change from the pattern of 'traditional', 'formal' teaching she favoured:[8]

> He has to think of his position, I suppose, to put it tactfully, and he wanted a very free school while some of us didn't, and I think he's beginning to realise it doesn't pay ... I think they thought — and after all, this three-tier system is in its guinea pig state, or it was five years ago — and I think they were just feeling their way along. And, of course, we'd all to do this, we'd all to do the other. We don't, some of us don't change so easily!

Despite headteacher pressure, therefore, Mrs Priestley persisted in adopting a classroom approach which was characteristic of the old elementary tradition. She ran her lessons according to a strict timetable, even though many of her extended teaching periods were normally 'open' on the main school timetable. She put a great deal of emphasis on discipline, counting her ability to control a class her greatest strength, and pointed to competence in basic skills as the most important thing pupils could take with them to the upper school. She regretted the passing of the 11 + and the standards it set and held this change in large part responsible for the 'lack of discipline' she now saw all around her: 'because they've nothing to work for. Aimless! They're aimless'.

Given the strength of these academic-elementary orientations and the tenacity of her resistance to change, it is not surprising that Mrs Priestley should no longer be working alongside those second year 'primary' range colleagues with whom she had first begun the middle school phase of her career. Mr Butcher, her Head, had now allocated her to the third year team, and while she found this somewhat discomforting, particularly because of the difficulties she encountered in grasping the range of subject matter at this higher level, her academic-elementary perspective was at least more attuned to that of her colleagues here than it was lower down the school. Like Mr Bird, despite her primary background, her educational allegiances made her best suited to teaching the secondary age range. Far from being mismatched with her professional background, then, if we look at her case from the point of view of her educational perspective and the nature (not just the phase) of her previous experience it betrayed, the middle school had actually enabled a *closer* match to be established between perspective and age-range responsibility than the primary/secondary system had allowed.

The Age Factor

Perhaps it was something about the times when their careers and professional development were established that had fostered a high degree of pedagogical conservatism in all these teachers. Perhaps it was something about their secondary experience, often acquired in tough secondary modern schools, that made many of them watchful of innovations that appeared to concede dangerous amounts of freedom to pupils, thereby undermining the teachers' authority. But there was something about the age of these teachers that mattered as well.

Whatever else these teachers were, they were now old or ageing (their mean age was 53). In the latter stages of their careers, with few promotion prospects ahead, they were either contentedly 'prepared now to potter out to my own retirement' (Mrs Spinner), or resigned to an indistinguished fate as professional 'time server' (Sikes, 1985) — 'I'm quite prepared to unhappily continue as I'm doing' (Mr Banks). At the worst, these teachers, like the middle-aged secondary modern teachers described by Riseborough (1981, p. 253), became role-retreatists: they no longer invested any motivation in their teaching role.

> *Mrs Priestley:* I've considered doing part time work ... but it's almost impossible now with things as they are in this area. So I settled for the fact that you can't devote the time which I feel you would need to give to the job. So I'm settled now, I've abandoned all hopes! I'm just watching and letting things go.

At this late stage of their careers, there were few incentives to change the habits of a professional lifetime. Yet change threatened on all fronts. So these teachers became watchful of fashionable, 'trendy' innovations that looked likely to challenge their own definition of teaching ('I have a rooted objection to the gimmicky in teaching, the fashion' — Mrs Spinner; 'some of us don't change so easily' — Mrs Priestley). 'Tides' ran ominously against them ('The tide's against knowing Kings and Queens and things like that' — Mrs Masters). Standards of discipline appeared to be slipping all around. And, perhaps worst of all, professional standards were on the decline too: upstart young colleagues failed to show these experienced teachers reverence and respect, credited them with little professional worth, challenged their authority and wrote them off as 'past it' (Sikes, 1985). This generated irritation and resentment

> *Mr Banks:*   Most young teachers seem to think they're the bees knees and that without them, school life and civilisation would come to a stop.

and sometimes open hostility

> *Mrs Spinner:*   Quite frankly, some of them (younger members of staff) set out to put spanners in the works. There are some who would automatically say 'No' if somebody else said 'Yes! ... I give way if it means the teacher losing face in front of children. *We* were brought up with professional loyalties, with codes of conduct and *I* still follow them.

But it also bred insecurity and sapped professional confidence.

> *Mrs Masters:*   I should have a reasonable amount of confidence through experience, but on the other hand, I do think that as you get older in teaching these days, ... perhaps I'm extra sensitive, but you do definitely have a feeling that because you're a bit of an old has-been, and that youth is the only thing that matters, and that tends to sap one's confidence when one is getting a little bit older.

Summary

Guardians of tradition (Lacey, 1970), resentful of interlopers, suspicious of innovation and fixed in the assumptions of the academic-elementary tradition which time and experience had etched upon them, these time-serving, retirement-bound teachers in late career were among the least well placed in the middle school to forge any new identity for it, least of all one that would transcend previous educational categories and commitments. They were too old, too set in their ways, too professionally insecure for that. Mixed phase teachers (and in one case even a primary teacher) they might have been in name; but in practice they were firmly and irrevocably bound to the academic-elementary tradition: a tradition which emphasized the importance of able pupils, grouping by ability, subject specialism, basic skills, transmission-type pedagogies and 'firm' discipline.[9] Together, these things were ill-suited to the creation of a new middle school identity. Nor were these academic-elementary influences solely confined to this group of mixed phase teachers. They were also represented among those middle school teachers whose background was wholly secondary, though not in exactly the same way or for precisely the same reasons.

The Secondary Modern Teachers

Name	School	Age	Career length	Responsibility	Year group	Percentage teaching time in 'upper' years
Mr Thomas	Moorhead	41–45	20	Craft	4	83
Mr Mowbray	Moorhead	36–40	16	Resources	3	84
Miss Lamb	Moorhead	26–30	3	Home Economics	3	100
Mr Stones	Riverdale	26–30	6	—	3	100
Mrs Littlejohn	Riverdale	31–35	5	—	3–4	100
Mr Button	Riverdale	21–25	4	Mathematics	1–2	5
Mr Driver	Riverdale	31–35	5	Years 3–4 and Science	3–4	100
	Mean	32.3	8.4			

Of the seven teachers at Riverdale and Moorhead whose previous experience was exclusively secondary, five had taught in secondary modern schools in their last appointment, the remaining two having spent all or part of their brief previous careers in what, in their terms, were rather difficult 11–16 comprehensive schools, not altogether dissimilar from the secondary moderns they replaced. As we have seen, secondary modern schools were heavily imbued with the long-standing concerns of the elementary tradition, and, from the 1960s onwards, with academic-meritocratic ones too. What impact did this secondary modern experience (be it in secondary modern schools as such or in difficult 'secondary modern' classes within comprehensives) with its prevailing academic-elementary concerns, have on this group of middle school teachers? What contribution did it make to the middle school identity?

Secondary Biographies

Like many of those secondary modern teachers who fared badly in career terms when comprehensive reorganization took place, these ex-secondary modern teachers at Riverdale and Moorhead were in all cases but one, college-trained non-graduates.[10] Indeed, in many respects, it would not be unfair to say that the two most senior members of the group were casualties of or refugees from that change;

teachers whose careers had been threatened, opportunities frustrated, status and informal teaching rewards taken away in the upheaval that comprehensivization brought with it. Thus, Mr Thomas recalled how, as a secondary modern craft teacher, he had once enjoyed the rewards of teaching 'kids with real promise who'd slipped through the idiot's 11 + net, who obviously had the right kind of potential: late developers particularly and occasional kids who transferred'. Then, he had taught small groups for 'O' level and prepared a number of pupils for further education in the 'local tech' — 'and we'd some damned good kids went there'. When comprehensive reorganization happened, all this came to an end.

> My old school amalgamated with another one and the scope of my work diminished hideously. I found myself in a department with three of us all the same level of experience — not all the same qualifications, but that's a minor point (sarcastically)! — and I lost the opportunity to do my 'O' level work because my old secondary school became the junior end.

With the loss of examination work and of contact with older pupils — two of the strongest sources of informal status for teachers in the secondary sector — Mr Thomas decided to make a career move; a 'horizontal' one, if necessary (Becker, 1952) to a similar scale position elsewhere but in a more rewarding and status-enhancing environment.

> The scope (of the job) was diminishing and I was looking around and I thought 'Now, then, what are these middle schools you see that's developing? And Moorhead's a lovely place! 'Master in Charge of Heavy Craft', it said. So I came.

If Mr Thomas came to Moorhead out of a need to restore some of the status and professional dignity that secondary reorganization had taken from him, Mr Mowbray was left there as a matter of little option when Moorhead Middle was set up in the premises of its secondary modern predecessor, the school where Mr Mowbray had previously worked from the commencement of his teaching career in 1959. With few prospects, as a non-graduate, of career advancement in his subject in the new upper school and (given no clear strengths on matters of discipline), little chance of promotion through the pastoral system either, there were few places Mr Mowbray *could* go other than the new middle school. The change did little to enhance his already unpromising career prospects. The responsibility allowance he already possessed was, of course, protected, but for this, he was asked to take charge of resources and not his own subject, geography (which the Head organized instead). In these ways, then, the two middle schools either provided some temporary refuge from or became the probable end point of at least two 'spoiled careers' (Hughes, 1958) which had been brought about by the folding of the secondary modern schools.

The other five teachers in this group had not established their careers in secondary schools with anywhere near the firmness of their more senior colleagues. They had taken on no scale posts; invested no long-term career commitments (Woods, 1979) in such schools. What these teachers were leaving behind were not hard-earned objective career gains with recognized responsibilities and allowances, nor even long established positions of informal prestige and authority as sound disciplinarians or whatever, but various forms of tough and unrewarding low grade 'dirty work' (Hughes, 1958) with frequently rebellious pupils in a discouraging educational environment.

> *Mr Stones:* The (secondary modern) school was just horrible: one of the worst ones, I think.
>
> *Miss Lamb:* I had a lot of problems there, *and they were problems!*
>
> *Mrs Littlejohn:* My probationary year was a traumatic experience in this awful (secondary modern) school.

Mr Driver spoke at greater length about the bearing these matters had on his move to the middle school. After three years teaching in a comprehensive, then a direct grant school, followed by a research studentship in science at university, Mr Driver found himself in the position of supply teacher in a nearby comprehensive. One particular set of incidents stuck in his mind.

> To get this modest wage, I had to sort of fight with this boy and squash him. And he was a constant irritant. And I thought, 'Well,' you know, 'this could happen year after year. I could get difficult people who haven't really been brought up very well. They don't really come here to learn, they come here to fight and I don't really want to continue with this. It's going to be the same sort of thing. I'm going to get people of poor ability all the time and I'll have to teach them science which they're not interested in. Nobody's going to enjoy it. It's just going to be attrition.' So I thought I ought to get into middle schools.

For one of the teachers, Mr Button, this involvement with low-grade dirty work was also bound up with a sense of career frustration, of blocked opportunities. Although appointed to comprehensive schooling straight from teacher training, in Mr Button's view, as a non-graduate, he might just as well have entered from the secondary modern schools. He moved to Riverdale, he said, because he 'couldn't really see a career structure in the secondary school because it was gradually becoming a graduate dominated area in comprehensive schools', and although he was offered promotion at his old school, he felt 'it was probably better to move into a smaller school'.

All five of the younger teachers therefore got out of secondary teaching while the going was still good. The two women teachers temporarily 'escaped' into childrearing — a not uncommon pattern for female teachers who, for whatever reason, become disillusioned or battleworn by their job and the demands it makes upon them (Nias, 1981, p. 238) — before reentering the profession in the rather less intimidating environment afforded by contact with younger pupils in these two socially well-placed middle schools. A third member of staff, Mr Stones, passed through the 9–13 system on a one-year temporary post *en route* to another secondary appointment elsewhere; this time a scale post in a nearby 11–18 comprehensive. Mr Button and Mr Driver stayed rather longer, though substantial questions continued to hang over their future careers. Mr Button, for instance, though a scale 2 by the time the case study was being conducted, was nonetheless inclined to see his longer term career prospects in terms of secondary school geography teaching. His study for an Open University degree ('better qualifications for a teacher') was an integral part of this career strategy. And Mr Driver, disillusioned with his work (for reasons I shall clarify shortly), left teaching altogether shortly after the end of the study, to complete his PhD.

Teachers with spoiled careers, underqualified teachers switching career tracks, or teachers making horizontal career moves to schools with a more desirable catchment area and a less intimidating clientele: this was the inheritance the secondary modern schools left to these two middle schools. Only one teacher (Miss Lamb) gained a higher scale post by moving to the middle school; only two (Mr Driver and Mr Thomas) had been attracted there by anything approaching a positive vision of the middle school ideal, however conceived; only two (again Mr Thomas and Mr Driver) appeared to have in mind definite future career possibilities in the middle school sector and even here, Mr Driver, as we have seen, subsequently left teaching, while Mr Thomas was probably being overly optimistic in aspiring to deputy headships given his predominantly practical craft background. Thus, although there were some undeniably able and skilled people among these teachers, they were nonetheless a group whose comitments were on the whole more to leaving the secondary sector than to arriving in the middle.

Secondary Perspectives

Keen to leave as most of these teachers were, though, the secondary moderns and the low streams of comprehensives nonetheless left their mark upon them, particularly in terms of their approaches to *classroom discipline*. More often than not, the classroom regimes of secondary modern schools have been identified as tight and 'coercive' (Reynolds and Sullivan, 1979) with teachers commonly resorting to 'domination' strategies of control, not least for reasons of survival and self-presentation (Woods, 1979) in a state of virtual 'guerilla warfare' (Willis, 1977) with the most recalcitrant of their older pupils. This was certainly Mrs Littlejohn's recollection of her own secondary modern experience. Asked what most influenced her current approach to teaching, she replied:

> My probationary year (in a secondary modern school) was a great influence on me. My style changed in my second year of teaching because — I realize now that it was partly my fault — of being inexperienced and, as somebody also described it, 'too nice'. But on the other hand, I realized also that a lot of it was the school's fault. And I became harder in my second year simply because not only were the children difficult . . . but the staff were horrible. And so I had to become harder to be like them. So my first teaching experience influenced my attitude today.

Noise was one area in which that influence seemed to persist. In conventional, class-based school environments, teachers are very sensitive to noise levels as a public measure of their own and their colleagues' competence, not least, given the isolated and insulated nature of most classroom teaching, because of the absence of other clues to assess such competence (Denscombe, 1980). Mrs Littlejohn's present attitude to noise levels in open-plan Riverdale, she felt, were very much conditioned by her previous secondary modern experience, where they had done little to bolster public images of her classroom competence:

> I'm very nervous of letting the classes make a lot of noise so that other people think I'm having discipline difficulties. And that stems from my first school, actually, because at first I didn't mind when children made a noise until people started coming in to see if I was alright. And that worried me, so that in the end I got a bit of a complex about it.

Miss Lamb had had similarly traumatic experiences to these, and their consequences for her present approach to teaching had apparently been enduring too:

> *Miss Lamb:* My early days of teaching had a most marked effect on me as a person because of the area, because of the children. It marked me for life, if you like. I had a really hard time those first few weeks. I struggled, to put it bluntly. But I came out on top, I think, in the end.
>
> *Author:* And has this affected the way that you teach now?
>
> *Miss Lamb:* I think that I'm hard, if you like. I don't like to have children talking while I'm talking. It's all the discipline methods, you know. And when I come in, I expect everybody to be quiet — that kind of thing. So I suppose my discipline in class has been affected by the first few weeks of my teaching experience.

Mr Stones too made connections between past demands on his disciplinary skills and his present approach to teaching. Discipline, he stated, was his particular teaching strength, though he also confessed that this could make him 'slightly unbending', 'a bit straight' at times. What he valued most in his teaching was

> Being able to get good discipline whatever age I've taught. And I've been used to the older ones anyway, so that's a necessity with the older ones. And I think once you've got good discipline, then you can start to do something. I think that's one of my strengths.

And Mr Button recalled how he cut his professional teeth during his probationary year

> It was in quite a rough school. It certainly influenced my ways of acting with kids — how I would accept things. And in many ways, I've brought these sorts of attitudes to this area which perhaps are useful because I tend to demand a very high standard of behaviour from children.

To these concerns with firm discipline, concerns which, in most cases, were clearly and explicitly linked to previous secondary modern or near-secondary modern experience, some of this group of teachers added a preference for more '*structured*' *classroom environments*. This was especially true of the teachers at Riverdale, whose school, they felt, fell sadly short of meeting this criterion.

> I'm not too keen on the actual way the school is organised. At the top end of the school, I would prefer a more structured set up where they are being taught ... (pause) ... If you've got to teach them, teach the whole lot rather than being split up into groups and then you go round teaching the same thing about ten times during the day. And I find it very difficult to cope with them doing lots of different things at the same time. But we've cut this down quite a bit now so that at one time, then everybody's doing maths, and at another time, they'll be doing science or art or craft. (Mr Stones — on dislikes)

Mrs Littlejohn, Riverdale's French teacher — whose lessons, though decked with the modern linguist's armoury of flash cards, tape recorder and other audio-visual aids, were nonetheless strongly teacher-centred in a style that is customary among practitioners of her subject at secondary level (Ball, 1981; Evans, 1985) expressed similar sentiments to Mr Stones'.

> I don't like the way that sometimes classes are so small, you know, they're divided into little groups that you don't have a teacher watching them so that you find children actually not doing anything in the end. Several times I wander up and down, well, having to because the curtains are being disturbed or children are coming in and making faces round the curtains. Well, that's what I dislike. Why isn't the organization such that every child has something to do?

Mr Button longed for the isolation and independence of the conventional classroom teacher

> Often the things you want to do, you'd like to do as a teacher, you can't because you can't shut the door. And there are times in this school when I feel like I would just like to shut the door and get on on my own.... At times its very nice to have a formal lesson in a school. I think it does the kids a lot of good to actually sit back and listen and in the situation we're in, it's a virtual impossibility, because there's noise, there's disturbance. And at times, I would just like to slam a door and go my own sweet way for five to ten minutes.

And Mr Driver, who I observed several times delivering formal science lectures ('like a university lecture') to pupils in the third and fourth year, was most reluctant to have

> everyone doing different things simultaneously. I think its possible lower down the school but I think that when you're getting to fourth year, the

level ... to keep sane, I couldn't really be doing a science problem and having a look at a bit of creative English and make suggestions for a piece of Art and at the same time put somebody straight on SMP maths. My brain isn't up to it!

At Moorhead, Mr Mowbray, talking about his likes in teaching, also raised the matter of what he called classroom formality:

I enjoy the aspect of teaching when it is on a formal basis where a class is seated, where the responses one gets can be successful or less than successful but at least one is in the position of giving and taking. I enjoy that sort of working.

'Firm' discipline and 'structured' or 'formal' classroom environments; these things seemed to rank highly in the educational preferences of Riverdale's and Moorhead's ex-secondary school teachers. So too did *contact with older pupils* in the top two years of the middle school, those pupils within the conventional secondary span. Miss Lamb, for instance, confessed to feeling diffident at first about teaching even these two years, given that most of her previous secondary experience had been with pupils older than this. Mr Driver boasted that he thought older pupils were 'harder to teach, if you're doing it properly'; they challenged teachers' academic authority more. Mr Stones discussed the matter at greater length, invoking that prepositional use of 'up' and 'down' in relation to older and younger age groups which so effectively and, for many primary age range teachers, so infuriatingly pins status associations to the teaching of different year groups. Here, the lowest status of all attaches to those year groups where one is allegedly scarcely teaching at all, but simply 'mothering'.

I don't like teaching the ones down that end, the first and second years, who would be sort of top two years in junior schools. I find them too demanding. You have to be too much like a mother to them which doesn't appeal to me. I enjoy much more the older ones because I find them a little bit more mature, some of them, and also they are able to produce better standards of work and think on a better level than the younger ones.

Where academic-elementary teachers and their developmental, primary colleagues were tightly insulated in their different year teams in the top and bottom halves of the middle school respectively, these observations on and preferences regarding the teaching of different year groups were no more than sources of personal irritation. But where teachers holding these different perspectives were members of the *same* year group, this issue could give rise to serious staff conflicts. Such was the case when Mr Button was redeployed by his Head from the top end of the middle school where he first began his appointment, to the first and second year team. In conversation, the Head confessed that the experiment had not worked, that it had created a lot of friction among the members of staff concerned. Mrs Home too, one of Mr Button's year team colleagues, pointed out that she did 'have problems within the team teaching' with the year leader and Mr Button.

'Sometimes (Mrs Fletcher's) and my ideas go against Jim's (Mr Button's), and she pointed to the example of maths. 'It has come to a point where Jim has said 'Look I have the scale post for maths, this is what you do!'

Mr Button himself concurred with these views. As an ex-secondary teacher, he felt out of place with the lower middle school age group, he said.

> I too often aim too high with the children, particularly in the first year. I find the second year level I can get nearer to but the first year children I find it very difficult even to get down to their level ... I find children of that age too young for me to cope with. They're not mature enough for me and I think I'm in the wrong situation when I'm with children of that age.

This unease with teaching younger children was associated with the fact that 'my ideas are not the same and my attitudes are not the same' as the rest of the year team. Thus, where they spoke of relationships, he spoke of discipline; where they enjoyed each other's adult company during teaching, he wanted isolation and independence.[11] Because of the conflict this clash of educational perspectives and practice evidently generated, at the end of the school year, Mr Button was therefore returned to the third and fourth year team, to the place where, in terms of his academic-elementary perspective, he properly belonged: on the top side of the 11 + divide.

Two more things figured largely in the educational perspectives of this group of ex-secondary teachers: their attachment to their *subject specialisms* and the value they placed on basic skills. On the matter of subject specialism, many of the teachers, it should be said, showed a very definite, positive interest in other areas of curriculum work than their own subject. Mr Thomas, for instance, the Moorhead craft specialist, got a great deal from his second and third year French teaching. But, in the main, it was the teachers' own subjects that seemed to remain uppermost in their curriculum interests and commitments. Most of the teachers, for instance, when listing in-service courses they had voluntarily undertaken over their teaching career, mainly mentioned ones concerning their own subject specialism. The impression of subject-centredness this in-service record conveyed was reinforced through more general comments the teachers made. Thus, Mrs Littlejohn taught only her own subject, French, and understandably spoke of little else. So too did Moorhead's new home economics specialist, Miss Lamb. Even when she was commenting on the more generalist aspects of her new middle school role, she did this with reference to her hitherto exclusively specialist training and background. 'Class teaching', she said, 'is an awful lot different to specialist teaching and this is one of the problems I've found already ... but my specialist training doesn't cover classroom subjects'. Of the other teachers, Mr Mowbray spoke of the geography bias in his teacher training which 'has largely followed me through my career', as did Mr Button. And even Mr Thomas, who, we have found, was in many other respects rather unlike his secondary modern colleagues, conceded that 'you need your own speciality' in the middle school setting.

Mr Driver's position was more ambivalent. A university science graduate, with a PhD in progress and some experience of science teaching at a direct grant school,

Mr Driver came to Riverdale Middle School as a highly qualified subject specialist. Yet, while he did not wish to relinquish his science role altogether, he was certainly anxious to become more of a generalist, to contribute to the breaking down of subject barriers within the middle school. The very strength of his subject identity, though, the degree to which he embraced the academic perspective, made the achievement of his generalist ambitions problematic. The specialist science he taught was equivalent in many ways to what might be found in secondary schools at the same age ('I'm more or less teaching in science the stuff that I would have taught at a secondary school'). None of his colleagues, he felt, had sufficient command of specialist expertise to be able to handle competently the intrinsic difficulties of the subject matter. It was not just a matter of their being non-scientists, but of their being non-graduates, too. Proud of his own academic background ('I think I'm academically very good, you know, I think I know my onions'), he had little professional respect for his non-graduate colleagues.

> I don't think very highly of them in a professional sense . . . I don't believe
> that the training colleges are in fact turning out people who are up to the
> job. It's not an easy job. Academically, I think they've got great gaps.

Thus, while in principle, Mr Driver was keen to become more of a generalist, his practical reluctance to devolve some of his science teaching to other less qualified colleagues made this virtually impossible. His strong subject loyalty and his high commitment to the academic perspective more generally kept him trapped within his own specialism, to the probable detriment, as he himself realized, of his future career prospects.

Alongside this retention of commitment to the subject, Riverdale's and Moorhead's ex-secondary teachers also ranked the teaching of *basic skills* highly amongst their educational priorities. In response to a question concerning what children ought to know by the time they left Riverdale/Moorhead middle school, most of these ex-secondary teachers attributed greatest importance to the imparting and development of so-called basic skills, the hallmark of the elementary tradition. All but one of them, indeed, mentioned it either first or second when responding to this question. Good spelling, the ability to use a dictionary and to write in sentences; this was what the French teacher, Mrs Littlejohn, thought Riverdale Middle School should be emphasizing most. 'The main thing', Mr Stones asserted, 'is to get them fairly literate and fairly numerate'. 'Skills in number and spelling and all these things' were felt to be among the most important 'end products' of middle schooling by Mr Thomas, who then went on to describe how he tried to eradicate grammatical mistakes and spelling errors in his own lessons. And Mr Mowbray too, after outlining the important contribution made by his own subject to understanding the environment, went on to argue for more attention to be paid to the basic skills, to the use of dictionaries and the like. For Mr Driver it was being 'able to write sentences in English properly', and for Mr Button 'the ability to use numbers competently' that mattered most.

All in all, then, when considering what it was pupils should know by the time they transferred out of the middle school, these teachers were overwhelmingly concerned with the inculcation of basic skills, the cornerstone of the elementary tradition.

Summary

What, then, can be concluded about these seven ex-secondary teachers now at work in the middle school setting? As a group, they were undoubtedly a varied bunch. No two of them were the same; no two of their professional biographies and educational perspectives were exactly alike. Yet, between them, there appear to be sufficient shared themes and common patterns to suggest the existence of not just a secondary, but a predominantly secondary modern inheritance, one that has had a more than negligible influence on the middle school's character, especially in its upper years. At the heart of that inheritance, I have identified a set of rather unimpressive and unpromising objective teacher careers. Most of the group, that is, appear to have come to the middle school less for that school's positive educational attractions than as part of some kind of professional salvage operation, to repair spoilt careers, switch career tracks or escape from low status 'dirty work' within secondary modern schools.

In principle, some of these teachers might have been seeking a fresh start, a new professional beginning. But in practice, when they took up their new posts, they brought with them a number of practices and preferences that established strong forms of continuity between the character of the old secondary moderns and that of the new middle schools: a survival-induced preoccupation with firm discipline and more 'formal' or 'structured' transmission-like classroom relationships with lots of public 'give and take' as Mr Mowbray put it; a continuing preference for teaching older, secondary age-range pupils (no 'mothering' for them); a retention of interest in and commitment to the academic traditions of the specialist subject; and a valuing of the 'elementary' importance of 'basic skills'.

The exceptions to these academic-elementary influences among ex-secondary teachers only provided further support for the existence of the general rule. Mr Button had been made the subject of an experiment to counter these influences, to cross-fertilize staff expertise across the different years and blend different educational traditions and perspectives *within* one particular year team; but this had patently failed. The difference between his and his colleagues' perspectives had proved to be irreconcilable. Similarly, while Mr Driver had sought some broadening of his educational responsibilities into generalist class teaching, the assumptions and practices bound up with his academic perspective, particularly his reluctance to cede his own subject teaching to others, kept him very much tied to his own specialism.

Conclusion

Judging by the evidence of these case studies, the academic-elementary perspective appears to have exerted a powerful grip on the life and character of the upper years of middle schooling, making successful staff movement across the middle school age range exceedingly difficult, even for heads and teachers who in principle favour such a policy. Neither the ex-secondary modern teachers with their spoilt careers or flight from 'dirty work', nor the ageing mixed-phase teachers — the two principal inheritors of the academic-elementary tradition — therefore seem to hold out much promise for any reduction in the impact of secondary assumptions and practices on teaching and learning in middle schools; for easement of subject specialization, reduction in academic setting, or relaxation of disciplinary regimes. But what of those teachers whose background is wholly and recently primary? Have they exerted any compensatory influence on the middle school at all, any effect which would counterbalance that of their academic-elementary colleagues? It is to this group of people — the developmental teachers — that I want to turn next.

Notes

1   The analysis presented in the following three chapters covers all the teachers in the interview sample except two — Mr HOME, the specialist craft teacher at Riverdale, and Mr MOOR, a third year teacher at Moorhead. The reasons for Mr MOOR's exclusion are explained in the footnotes to Chapter 10. Mr HOME is excluded on the grounds that he was the only teacher in the sample who taught 'across the board' in terms of age range but within the specialist framework of his own subject —craft. A few words about his background and approach might be appropriate here.

Mr HOME was secondary trained as a PE and craft teacher and in that sense would normally be grouped with the secondary teachers described in the second part of this chapter — though Mr HOME had no previous extensive experience of secondary teaching, having come to Riverdale as his first appointment. A lover of his own specialism — craft ('I enjoy the craft; it's quite entertaining'), a believer in firm discipline ('I find myself here being a bit more disciplinarian than most other teachers; I like to clamp down on kids') and a sceptic of 'open' patterns of classroom organization ('obviously, being secondary trained, I prefer to see children doing things straight down the line so they know exactly where they're going'), Mr HOME was in many respects clearly tied to the perspectives and assumptions of the academic-elementary tradition. Like many craft teachers, though (for example, Mr THOMAS at Moorhead), the pedagogical approach adopted *within* his own particular specialism was, compared to many of his secondary-like colleagues committed to rather more 'academic' subjects, unusually relaxed, especially in the wide scope afforded to pupils in the choice, the selection and pacing of their own practical projects.

The atypically specialist nature of Mr HOME's position, though, meant that his contribution had little impact on any particular year group as a whole, as he himself recognized.

> With me being a specialist, I'm not in a class situation. I'm in my own area and I don't often get back into the classes to see — in fact, I'm not timetabled back into any class areas. All my timetable is blocked so that I'm either in the craft area or out on the field.

It is for this reason of specialized containment, of minimal impact on whole-year or whole-school organization, that Mr HOME is excluded from the main analysis.

2 This figure excludes the sixth teacher I have categorized as 'mixed phase' — Mrs PRIESTLEY — whose previous experience is confined to the primary sector only (see main text, following).

3 See the following two chapters and the final part of this one for further details of the Riverdale staff.

4 Again, these figures exclude Mrs PRIESTLEY.

5 If Mrs PRIESTLEY is included in this analysis, there are three exceptions, not two.

6 See HARGREAVES (1984) for further details on this point.

7 The different orientation of these two senior members of staff was reflected in their choice of in-service courses — Mrs SPINNER has opted for ones on girls' welfare (as well as those in her own subject); Mr GREEK had chosen ones on more general aspects of school management.

8 The categories of 'traditional' and 'formal' were Mrs PRIESTLEY's own.

9 Only one of the six teachers in this group stood apart from all this: Moorhead's Deputy, Mr GREEK. To be sure, there was enough in his background to fix him firmly to the academic-elementary tradition too. Though a primary teacher for most of his career, his teaching had been predominantly with 11 + classes 'so it tended to be quite traditional'. He also had a strong attachment to his subject — science — putting it second as a source of enjoyment and devoting 77 per cent of his timetable to it. Yet, in the later years of his primary career, the conversion of his school to the Thorne scheme of selection for grammar school by headteachers' assessments (see chapter 4) rather than an 11 + examination, had in Mr GREEK's view, 'eased the pressures a little and given a little more flexibility'. And although his school did not go 'completely open-plan', he was then able to experiment widely with systems of rotating four or five different groups doing different subjects at the same time: he became a 'group instructor' rather than a more conventional, transmission-like whole-class teacher, that is, (GALTON, SIMON and CROLL, 1980, pp. 122–3). Consequently, although his present middle school teaching duties were now largely specialist, his approach to science teaching was very different, than, say, Mrs SPINNER's. Whereas her fourth year lesson on earthworms, for instance, was heavily and explicitly teacher-dominated with much question and answer work, copying from the board and from books, taking notes from worksheets and so forth — his lesson on the same topic moved almost immediately into observational work, with children going off to hunt for library books, or moving excitedly to the front of the class to select, examine and ask questions about insect specimens of their own. Mr GREEK was, therefore, clearly something of an exception: a low key and reluctant disciplinarian, not an unyielding drill sergeant, a believer, in his own words, in 'democracy not dictatorship'.

Some of the explanation for this is undoubtedly to be found in the distinctiveness of his own professional biography, in the situations he encountered in his earlier career. But while most teachers are very much creatures of situation, pushed and pulled by the demands their own occupational circumstances make upon them, not all are constrained to the same degree. There is a sense in which, in other words, Mr GREEK was less a victim — perhaps because not a *willing* victim — of circumstance than his other mixed colleagues: a sense in which he was ever searching for opportunities to change, develop and grow whatever his circumstances.

Exceptions such as this are important. They remind us of the fallibility of social constraint, the underlying creativity of humankind, the ever-present possibility of innovation and change. Schools would be sorry places without such people.

10 All but one of the mixed phase teachers were also non-graduates. In total, then, 11 of the 13 academic-elementary teachers (84.6 per cent) were of non-graduate status. This

compares with a figure of 73.1 per cent non-graduate membership for the sample of teachers in the two middle schools as a whole. This latter figure is remarkably close to the figures for proportions of non-graduate teachers in 9–13 middle schools nationally of 74 per cent and 74.1 per cent produced by HMI (1983a, p. 140) and TAYLOR and GARSON (1982, p. 124) respectively. Thus, it would seem that in schools which already have very high proportions of non-graduates among their staff, the members of the academic-elementary tradition who dominate the middle school's upper years, are *even more* likely to have non-graduate status.

11 As we shall see in the following chapter, this friction between Mr BUTTON and the rest of the first and second year team was due not just to a straight difference of educational perspective, but to gender-related differences in professional approach too.

Chapter 9

The Developmental Teachers

Name	School	Age	Length of career	Responsibility	Year group	Percentage time in lower years
Mrs Fletcher	Riverdale	31–35	10	Year Leader (1–2)	2	100
Miss Gough	Riverdale	21–25	4	Reading	1	100
Mrs Raines	Riverdale	31–35	1	—	1	100

Three of the teachers in the Riverdale/Moorhead interview sample were phase-matched primary teachers. That is to say, they had a background that was exclusively primary in nature and now taught entirely within the lower years of the middle school. It also happened that all of these teachers worked at open-plan Riverdale; though this seems to have been less a comment on differences between the two schools than a chance result of the sampling (at least two of the second year team at Moorhead had come there straight from primary training, for instance — but neither appeared in the interview sample).[1]

The important thing about these teachers is that they were not just primary teachers, but primary teachers of a particular kind. They were not academic 'scholarship' teachers (they had almost no experience of teaching 11 + groups). Nor did they appear to have those 'elementary' preoccupations with drill and rote learning that were so important to their mixed-phase colleagues. Rather, they were, to use Blyth's (1965) terminology, *developmental* teachers, teachers more attuned to the recommendations and orientation of the Plowden Report than to the requirements of grammar school entrance.

There are many synonyms or near-synonyms for *developmental* teaching — progressive teaching (Hammersley, 1977), craftsman teaching, (Gracey, 1974), informal teaching (Bennett, 1976), process teaching (Blenkin and Kelly, 1981), and so on. In all cases the precise characteristics of this pedagogical orientation are much debated. In general, though, the adherents of this tradition, however labelled, are usually identified as embracing a broad set of educational values that are more centred on the child and the contribution of education to his or her continuing *process* of *development*, than on that child as someone being prepared as some future 'finished' educational 'product' in fulfilment of 'society's' demands (Blenkin and

Kelly, 1981). Thus, characteristically, developmental educators place little value on academic subjects and they de-emphasize the boundaries between them — it is the process of knowing, not the completed package of the 'known' that matters most to them. They also like to play down their role as instructors, favouring instead a more cooperative relationship between teacher and children in the learning process, one which allows and encourages children to take an active part in their own learning and development (for example, Blyth and Derricott, 1977, pp. 96–7). It was orientations of this kind that dominated the perspectives of the developmental teachers at Riverdale.

Developmental Perspectives

Curriculum

On curricular matters, for instance, these teachers spoke not so much of subjects but of 'centres of interest', topic work and projects. As Mrs Fletcher, the first and second year leader put it, 'we base most of our work around centres of interest, project work, which we try to aim at being centred round the childrens' interests'. The emphasis was much less on facts and on bodies of knowledge, than on finding out, on the study skills required to discover knowledge for oneself. Thus, speaking of what Riverdale children ought to know by the time they left the middle school, Mrs Raines said

> I don't think that there is a body of knowledge that they should know leaving Riverdale Middle School. What I would hope the children had learned at school is what education is about: that you take each thing as a fresh new day, you do the same things over and over again throughout your life but in a different way, to a different level. I'd like the children to be able to find out for themselves information that they require. I don't see much point in giving them facts to learn, because by the time they'll need the facts or they'll want to use them, the facts will likely be obsolete.

Similarly, in response to the same question, Mrs Fletcher said

> I think they ought to know how to use books. They ought to know how to find the answers and where to find the answers to questions. I don't think there's a body of knowledge that they ought to have because, I mean, they would never stop, we would never, ever, any of us stop.

Bodies of knowledge and subject mastery were therefore not considered important as outcomes of education. Nor were they central to these teachers' professional identities. The in-service record of all three teachers was remarkably broad; not confined to, or dominated by, any single subject. Educational dilettantes rather than narrow specialists, this small group of developmental educators attached little importance to the academic subject, to the thing which is so central to the identity of many of their secondary colleagues. As Miss Gough put it 'I'm basically just a general teacher in that I can cover a lot of things in very little depth: you know, I'm not really a specialist in anything.'

Alongside this disregard for bodies of subject knowledge in particular ran a measure of disenchantment with 'academic' matters as a whole. Thus, Mrs Fletcher drew attention to excessive academic pressures she felt many high-aspiring middle class parents placed on her pupils, pressures which made it difficult for her to cater for other aspects of their educational development too.[2] One of the major problems she faced, 'in this kind of neighbourhood', she said, was

> ... persuading children to accept the right kind of balance of something which is going to help them to enjoy life and to make the most of life and to function successfully as an adult.... Because many of the parents in this kind of neighbourhood are very ambitious for the children to get on; they must be successful. And there's a lot of comparison. And they compare ... what the children are doing at school with what they did as children at school and they feel their children should be doing precisely what they did.... And they don't always realize that we're living a couple of decades later and that we're perhaps educating as much for leisure as just for a job.

As Mrs Fletcher pointed out earlier in the interview, such academic pressures created difficulties for her when pupils were given a measure of choice in what activities or projects they could undertake, since some pupils — the most academic — would often shy away from creative and expressive activities, not regarding them as 'real work' at all:

> I've got a group of very academic girls in my class and they seem to think that anything other than writing and reading and studying is taboo and I have to say to them, 'Look, it's quite alright to come and do some drama; it's quite alright to come and do some art, because this is part of life and when you leave school you're not just going to be earning your living, you're going to have leisure time and you're going to be really bored if you don't know how to use your leisure time and to enjoy painting and doing these other things. Come and enjoy it — you used to!'

Pedagogy

For these developmental teachers, if the curriculum was concerned with the process of knowing rather than possession of the known, this also demanded a particular kind of pedagogy; one involving teachers and pupils working in close collaboration. Mrs Raines, for instance, felt distinctly uncomfortable as 'a performer' and avoided addressing the whole class wherever possible. Miss Gough likewise attributed little importance to whole-class performance, choosing instead to emphasize her skills as 'an organizer', as someone who could keep several classroom activities moving efficiently at the same time. And Mrs Fletcher was much the same; identifying resourcefulness as one of her greatest strengths — 'I can exploit a situation to the childrens' interests and my own' — and particularly enjoyed 'being able to help children discover what's going on around them ... helping them to develop any creative ability'.

Certainly, the use of whole-class teaching among these teachers was a rare occurrence, confined in the main to brief stimulus sessions and class stories (a fact which made samples of tape-recorded classroom interaction among this group extremely difficult to obtain).

Guides, questioners, helpmates; these teachers saw themselves not as transmitters of facts, but as organisers of resources, manipulators of situations, exploiters of circumstantial opportunity. And at the heart of their pedagogical interest in aiding discovery and enhancing creativity — two of the most salient aspects of the 'Plowden approach' — lay the individual child. For whatever else mattered to these teachers, it was the quality of their relationship with individual pupils that counted most of all, that suffused and gave unity to all aspects of curriculum, pedagogy and discipline in which they were involved. Like many of the American elementary teachers interviewed by Jackson (1968) and Lortie (1975) and the English primary teachers interviewed by Nias (1981), the talk of these developmental teachers was saturated with a love of children and their company, with the individual 'psychic rewards', as Lortie calls them, that come from close and sustained contact with particular pupils. Miss Gough counted 'understanding the children' among her greatest strengths, for instance, and Mrs Raines most enjoyed simply 'being with children; just enjoying experiences with the children.'

Discipline or Relationships?

The immense importance these teachers attached to teacher-pupil relationships had implications not only for their pedagogical approach in the wider sense, but for their attitude to particular matters of discipline too. Unlike their ex-secondary modern colleagues, the developmental teachers showed no interest, still less any pride in disciplinary achievements. Maintaining and imposing discipline, dealing with naughtiness and misbehaviour, was not something that they enjoyed, nor even something whose difficult demands they took pride in conquering but a painful duty they despatched with reluctance, an irksome and distasteful chore; one of the unfortunate costs of teaching.

According to Mrs Raines, discipline was one of her greatest weaknesses: 'I don't react as a teacher yet. I much more react as a mother to the children and I haven't quite got the teacher aura about me yet'. Miss Gough similarly found difficulty dealing with 'the naughty ones'. But Mrs Fletcher had the most elaborate explanation for her unease with disciplinary matters;

> I most dislike regimentation, I think. Sometimes I feel that formal school is not in the best interests of boys in particular. In big classes and big groups, I think it's not possible to give children enough time to follow up the things that they're interested in and sometimes ... I think very often when we get a number of children who are uncooperative, it's because of this. And sometimes you feel that you've got no alternative because of the numbers

and the fact that you say 'You are all to come to school and you will all wear school uniform.' I think this upsets me: the lack of choice to be an individual that we put on children in school.'

There were powerful strains of what Hammersley (1977) calls 'radical non-interventionism' and D. Hargreaves (1972) calls 'new romanticism' in Mrs Fletcher's perspective here: echoes of the views of the deschoolers that school is, in Mrs Fletcher's words, 'a very unnatural place', an institutional imposition on individual children, enforced by the laws of compulsory attendance and prejudicial to personal development.[3] The enforcement of discipline was an unpleasant aspect of Mrs Fletcher's work. It upset her. It struck a wedge between the institutional demands of her role as a teacher and the beliefs of her personal self in creativity, discovery and personal growth.[4] In her case, as in the case of her developmental colleagues, it was an intrusion upon and threat to those close interpersonal relationships that played such a central part in her approach to classroom pedagogy.

Summary

To sum up: where the academic-elementary teachers in the upper years of the middle school were subject-centred, tough on disciplinary matters (sometimes enthusiastically so), and disposed to adopting formal, transmission pedagogies, the developmental teachers in the lower years put more store on creativity and discovery, tried to play down the disciplinary aspects of their role, and favoured pedagogies of a rather more informal, child-centred kind.[5]

Developmental Biographies and Careers

The differences between these two sets of orientations — academic-elementary and developmental — at the different ends of the middle school, may have been brought about by a number of things; by the pressures and constraints faced by the staff in different year groups or the personalities of the teachers involved, for instance. But in part, they also followed from the professional and personal biographies of the teachers concerned in each case.

School Experience

The academic-elementary teachers, we saw earlier, had a previous career record of teaching either secondary modern pupils or pupils in the upper years of primary school close to the point of secondary school transfer: and it was this that helped foster the subject-centredness and discipline consciousness that later dominated their educational perspectives in the middle school environment.

By contrast, the training and careers of the developmental teachers were almost entirely confined to the infant and lower primary age ranges. Mrs Raines was infant trained, Miss Gough's previous experience was with 7–8 year olds, and

Mrs Fletcher had spent most of her earlier career teaching infant and lower junior groups.

Blyth (1965, p. 43) has pointed out that the developmental tradition has always been at its strongest in infant departments which were well cushioned from the restrictive effects of the Revised Code and later the 11 +; and indeed, it seems that this very protection enjoyed by teachers of infant and 'lower primary' children has had a significant effect on the educational perspectives of the three 'developmental' teachers at Riverdale and Moorhead, too.

A sample of three teachers is, of course, an extremely precarious basis on which to advance generalizations about middle schools as a whole. But if the experience of this case study is at all generalizable, it could well be that many middle schools have been recruiting ex-primary teachers to their lower years not so much from the pool of academic-elementary 'scholarship' teachers at the top of the primary age range, but by siphoning 'developmental educators' up from the infant and lower junior years, or more likely in recent years, by recruiting such teachers from primary schools in already non-selective systems elsewhere, where the constraints of the 11 + are no longer present.

Such patterns of recruitment, I want to argue, would, if widely adopted, have highly significant implications for the status of teachers in the lower years of the middle school, and for that school's struggle to establish a unique identity for itself. In this respect, three of the most important factors which affected the status and influence of developmental teachers in this case study, and their impact on the middle school as a whole were their age, their sex, and the weakness of their academic subject attachments.

Age and Inexperience

All three developmental teachers were relatively young. Their mean age was considerably less than that of their academic-elementary counterparts (29.7 years as against 43.5 years), as was the mean length of their teaching career (5 as against 17.4 years). Such youth is a mixed blessing. On the one hand, it brings a high degree of that enthusiasm, industry and idealism which commonly accompanies the early years of a teaching career (Hanson and Herrington, 1976; Sikes, 1985). Yet it also engenders a preoccupation with the day-to-day business of sheer classroom survival among the most inexperienced (Nias, 1984; Sikes, 1985) which precludes whole-hearted involvement in wider school affairs.[6] As Mrs Raines, the probationary teacher put it, 'I have not got past the problems that are on a day-to-day level, to see greater problems behind'.

Youth is therefore associated with a not unrelated lack of influence on planning, coordination and decision-making within the middle school as a whole. Only the more experienced Mrs Fletcher had reached a position of substantial responsibility in teaching, but even her influence, as first and second year leader, was confined to the first and second year teams and to associated liaison with the first school. There was no evidence of her having a significant influence on her colleagues higher up the school.

Of course, the young can exert their influence in other ways. Blyth and Derricott (1977) for instance, talk of the existence of *professional status inversion* where 'members of an organization who occupy the lower status positions possess more of the currently valued professional skills than are to be found among their superiors' (p. 56). Such inversion, they argue, appears in middle schools where 'junior staff are more attuned to innovation than their seniors and are more likely, through sheer force of circumstance, to be at least permitted and probably encouraged to exercise their innovatory enthusiasm' (p. 184).

There is some evidence that status inversion of this kind sometimes operated *within* the first and second year teams at Riverdale with young, recently trained staff, acquainted with current educational trends, exerting an 'upward' influence on their more experienced colleagues (as with Mrs Raines, who impressed her colleagues with the 'fun' approach to things that her recent infant training had given her). However, there is *no* evidence that such inversion operated beyond the confines of the insulated year team. In this sense, it seems that at best, younger developmental teachers may simply be influencing their older, 'already converted' developmental colleagues. If that is so, then Blyth and Derricott's claims regarding the impact of status inversion on the middle school as a whole are probably exaggerated. The successful diffusion of such 'inverted' patterns of influence, it seems, will probably have to await some weakening of year group insulation within the middle school.

Sex

If age lowered the status and restricted the influence of these developmental teachers within the middle school, so too did their sex, albeit less directly. All three developmental teachers in the sample were women, as indeed were all but two of the entire group of lower middle school teachers at Riverdale and Moorhead. The National Union of Teachers (1980, p. 7) points to middle-deemed secondary schools as the only type of schools that 'have a sex balance in the staff which approximates to that in the world for which the children are being educated'. Yet if the Riverdale/Moorhead experience is anything to go by, this appearance of overall balance may simply disguise very substantial *imbalances* between male and female staff *within* the middle school on either side of the 11 + divide, with women teachers being most heavily concentrated in the earlier, 'primary' years. Such concentrations of primary experienced women within the lower years of the middle school restricts their influence and that of the developmental perspective they often espouse upon the school as a whole in at least three ways.

First, the teaching of young children is commonly associated with childcare rather than with 'rigorous' academic enquiry and firm discipline and therefore with the whole sphere of womens' domestic labour, one which enjoys little status in western industrial society. (Seifert, 1974; Lee, 1973; Oakley, 1974; Myrdal and Klein, 1956)

Mere 'mothering', Mr Stones called it, and this was not for the likes of him, an ex-secondary male P.E. teacher! Mr Button, previously an 11–16 comprehensive teacher and a teacher of third and fourth year pupils at Riverdale, but now 'on loan' to the otherwise all-female first and second year team, was more expansive. One of the major problems he faced in school, he said, was that

> There's too many women in a school this size ... There should be more incentives for men in middle schools. I think kids of this age need male influence. I try not to be a chauvinistic pig but I think women tend to be more sympathetic and can get on better with younger children than they can children up to 13 ... Thirteen-year-old boys are not interested in how pretty the teacher looks. They're more interested in whether what they say goes and if it doesn't what they can do about it.

Thus, not only was Mr Button in conflict with his first and second year female colleagues due to differences of educational perspective (as we saw in the previous chapter), but also because of the gender associations he attached to their perspective, ones which were in turn linked to his disvaluing of the professional contribution and influence of women teachers as a whole. With attitudes such as this among some of the male staff, ones which uncompromisingly dismissed the contribution that 'sympathetic' women teachers could make to the allegedly tough, rigorous world of teaching older pupils, it is easy to see why the views of these developmental female teachers should receive lesser prominence within the middle school as a whole.[7]

A second reason for the restricted influence of these teachers within the middle school is their own career orientation. Whether it be due to socially induced low aspirations, or to immediate domestic pressures and responsibilities, the promotion orientation of women in teaching, particularly those with young families, is often (though by no means always) lower than that of men (Lyons, 1981; Hilsum and Start, 1974). There was some evidence of this among the developmental women teachers at Riverdale. Mrs Raines, for instance, did not hope for major administrative responsibility in the future.

> My greatest ambition is to be a really good teacher, that's all ... I feel my responsibilities are to myself, you know. It doesn't worry me that I'm not in a post of responsibility ... if I can be satisfied in my own mind that what I'm doing is a good job. And that's all I think I'll aspire to. I perhaps am in the fortunate position that I can aspire to much more social ambitions than material ones; because it's a privileged position being a married woman, I think.

While this sort of aspiration may well have been as much due to Mrs Raines' professional inexperience as to her sex, domestic pressures were more starkly apparent in the case of Mrs Fletcher. While Mrs Fletcher also confessed to having 'never been ambitious at all' she had nonetheless attained a position of some responsibility as first and second year leader. Yet despite (or perhaps because of) that very responsibility, the pressures of her dual role in both a paid career and domestic labour (Myrdal and Klein, 1956) apparently became too much for her and at the end of the research she left teaching altogether to return full-time to her family 'duties'. Talking about her impending exit from teaching, she explained

It's a sort of personal thing really — a personal, family thing more than anything else. I'm interested to have my foot in the door and interested to do a little bit, but I'm not interested in teaching full-time, not being committed full-time, because I find it takes up too much of my time, that it creates all sorts of family problems which I've had one way or another which are best solved by my giving up full-time teaching.

Thus, while it may be the case, as Lortie (1975, p. 87) suggests, that many women see teaching as an 'in-and-out engagement', interspersed with full-time parenthood (also Purvis, 1973), Mrs Fletcher's case shows that the press of domestic responsibilities, falling as they customarily do upon the shoulders of married women; the immense difficulty that married women with family responsibilities have in managing what Clarricoates (1980, p. 80) calls their 'double workload', may have a much more direct effect in restriciting the commitment of many female teachers to promotion even where their wider vocational commitment (Acker, 1983) to childcare, classroom excellence and the value of education more generally is (as it undoubtedly was with Mrs Fletcher) exceptionally strong. Where the promotion orientation of many women teachers continues to be so restricted, be this due to socially induced 'choice' or immediate pressure, it is unlikely that enough women teachers with developmental views in the lower years of middle schooling will attain positions of sufficiently major responsibility to exert a strong influence on the character of the middle school as a whole.

The Specialist Career Ladder

The influence of women 'developmental' teachers in the middle school is not, however, restricted simply by their own promotion orientation and their associations with low status childcare. The objective career structure of middle schools systematically works to the disadvantage of female 'developmental' teachers too; presenting them with few clearly marked avenues for promotion and advancement.

For most people, career advancement in the middle school hinges on the possession of specialist expertise in at least one school subject. According to Taylor and Garson's survey (1982, p. 125), almost 90 per cent of scale posts in 9–13 middle schools have at least some measure of subject specialist responsibility attached to them. Yet, to the recent consternation of the Department of Education and Science (1983) and Her Majesty's Inspectorate,[8] primary teachers (the majority of whom — around 77 per cent — are women)[9] often lack expertise in any particular subject specialism. Their training has not prepared them for this; they have become generalists, not specialists. This places many ex-primary teachers at an immediate career disadvantage in the middle school setting and perhaps helps explain HMIs finding that only 20 per cent of scale posts in middle schools with a subject designation had been awarded to people with an exclusively primary background (HMI, 1983a, p. 141). The figures for headships and deputy headships were even lower than this, ex-primary people attaining 6 per cent and 15 per cent of such positions respectively. Little wonder, then, that Miss Gough, the most ambitious of the developmental teachers in the sense that she ultimately aspired to a headship, should seek this *outside* the middle school in infant education where her generalist skills and qualifications would be a more obvious asset (and where, we should note, the statistical chances of success would, given her sex, also be much higher).

Summary

This chapter has dealt with a small group of phase matched primary teachers in the lower years of the middle school; teachers with a developmental perspective on curriculum, pedagogy and discipline. Different from their academic-elementary counterparts in the upper years of the middle school, these teachers were generalists, not specialists; interested in relationships, not 'discipline'; enjoyed being *with* children not talking *to* them. Though a significant influence on the character of the middle school in their own year groups, their influence on the rest of the middle school *outside* those year groups was not great, not least because of their sex. Young and relatively inexperienced, depressed in professional status, lacking specialist expertise and with no long-term career ambitions for major responsibility in the middle school, these teachers were ill-placed to impress their developmental perspective upon the character of the middle school as a whole. In more senses than one, they were very much junior partners in the middle school enterprise.

Discussion: The Middle School's Dual Inheritance

In this chapter, and the one before it, I have examined the professional biographies and educational perspectives of sixteen teachers at Riverdale and Moorhead middle schools. This analysis suggested that there were two different, segregated and mutually opposed cultures of teaching within the schools; two distinct groups, each with their own socially approved ways of thinking, feeling, acting and believing in relation to educational matters.

The first of these consisted of teachers who held an academic-elementary perspective. Fugitives from the secondary modern schools, exiles from the scholarship year of primary schools, pursuers of promotion in an atmosphere where graduate competition would not be strong; seekers of 'horizontal' career moves to schools with more responsive age groups and in more congenial surroundings; or simply casualties of reorganization, left behind in the middle school for want of clear career alternatives elsewhere in the system; these thirteen teachers — half the interview sample — dominated the character and orientation of the upper years of the middle school, particularly at reorganized Moorhead. Advocates of specialism and setting, guardians of disciplinary firmness, and defenders of 'transmission' pedagogies, they brought to the middle school the assumptions and routines of the 'academic' and 'old elementary' traditions — traditions which had come together and thrived in the secondary modern schools from which so many of this group came. Even at purpose-built Riverdale, where the academic-elementary teachers were not nearly so numerous, this occupational culture still provided a major source of disruption and resistance to the Head's plans for curricular integration and relaxed pedagogies. Mr Stones formalized his own timetable within the blocked arrangement preferred by the Head; Mr Driver persisted in delivering periodic science lectures to his pupils, even though he knew this ran directly counter to the Head's wishes; and Mr Button became the focus of colleaguial friction in the first and second year team. All impeded Mr Kitchen's vision of the middle school as an extension of the best of primary practice.

The second group was the developmental teachers. Smaller in number, these teachers were concentrated in the lower years of the middle school. Recruited from infant education or the lower years of junior schools where the remoteness of formal educational selection had often eased restrictions on pedagogical and curricular innovation, these teachers were keen to organize their curriculum around projects and centres of interest rather than formal subjects as such; they emphasized the importance of relationships' *with* their children as against disciplining of them; and they preferred individual or group-based pedagogies rather than ones resting on whole-class teaching. For various interrelated reasons to do with their inexperience and their youth, the socially induced and culturally imposed handicaps of their sex and the low status commonly attributed to the age groups for which they were responsible, these developmental teachers had little impact on the character and direction of the middle school as a whole; their influence being confined to its 'lower' years (in both age and status terms) only.

In many respects, then, while proponents of the middle school have striven to establish a coherent and cohesive identity for it, in practice, the experience of Riverdale and Moorhead has pointed to the ways in which patterns of staff recruitment and deployment can strike an organizational wedge through the very centre of the middle school, giving it a split identity, one which in many respects reproduces that educational division at 11 which the middle school has struggled in vain to supersede.

Divided by the insulated year system, and kept apart by the architectural design of the school plant, while middle school teachers have not, as we saw earlier, established a strong degree of *phase match* between their past and present responsibilities, these two middle schools have nonetheless established, in the case of sixteen (i.e. 61.5 per cent) of the interview sample, a strong degree of *cultural match* between teachers' previous biographies, perspectives and educational allegiances and their present obligations and commitments. As a result, if these two cases are at all representative, it may well be that middle schools have become dominated by an academic-elementary culture in their upper years and by a developmental one in their lower ones. Experiments with cross-fertilization of staff between these two groups at Riverdale and Moorhead have been tried but, as Mr Button's case illustrates, these have rarely proved successful. For at the end of the day, the heads themselves have conceded that 'staff . . . can teach most efficiently when they are teaching the way with which they themselves are most familiar' (Mr Butcher), and that 'you have to match people up in terms of compatibility rather than complementary expertise' (Mr Kitchen).

Mere institutional reorganizations do not in this sense wipe away those long-standing and deep-rooted cultural inheritances which teachers have built up through the socialization of their training and the accumulated loyalties and commitments of their previous professional biographies. In this respect, middle schools and comprehensive schools more generally are much the same: in each case, inherited cultures of teaching have presented a major constraint to headteachers' strategies for change. But there is at least one important matter of substance which does distinguish them. While the non-graduate secondary modern teachers were very much the *victims* of 'conventional' comprehensive reorganization (i.e. with transfer at 11), the ones most likely to miss out on promotion and suffer loss of status; it seems that ironically, where systems with transfer at 9/10 and 13 have been adopted, these have been the very people to prosper within and dominate the character and direction of the new middle schools. Casualties of a change dominated by meritocratic assumptions in the first case, they have become the principal bearers of these assumptions in the second, anchoring middle schools to an academic-elementary position in their higher, more prestigious years, even despite frequent wishes of their heads to the contrary.

Much of the reason for the hiatus within the middle school and for the dominance within its upper years of academic-elementary interests connected with setting, subject specialization and so on, can therefore probably be attributed to the two different occupational cultures of teaching which that school has inherited. In this sense, the cultures and careers of middle school teachers are an important link between the political and administrative history of the middle school and its present patterns of organization; between policy and practice. In part, this is because when reorganization took place, the vagaries of *administrative convenience* (chapter 2) forced middle schools to draw *pragmatically* on local pools of staff labour with their different cultures and commitments. And in the absence of appropriate and suitably specific forms of in-service training to fit this generation of would-be middle school teachers for their new educational destiny, those cultural habits and loyalties tended to prevail, setting the pattern for middle school development in years to come.

One result of this administratively induced pattern of redeployment was that middle schools did not evolve to suit the special needs of children in 'the middle years' but were held back by forces of *historical lag*, by teachers' continuing identification with and commitment to educational traditions of a previous age. And foremost among these was the academic or meritocratic tradition with its emphasis on able pupils, subject specialization and conventional academic success in the high status subjects of the grammar school curriculum. It was to this tradition that the academic-elementary teachers at Riverdale and Moorhead retained a strong attachment, coupling it with their 'old elementary' interest in basic skills and firm discipline. The middle school's pursuit of unity was in that sense undermined by its inheritance of staff divisions. And its quest, in places, for greater egalitarianism and openness (Lynch 1975, Nias 1980) was restricted in the upper years by the commitment of many of its staff to the academic-elementary principles and meritocratic purposes of the secondary modern schools and scholarship classes from which they had been drawn.

The fate of middle schools has in this sense been heavily influenced by administrative expediency and occupational tradition; matters which lie far outside these schools' immediate compass. However, while the middle school's dual cultural inheritance goes a long way towards explaining its current dilemmas and difficulties, it is important that we do not overlook that substantial minority of staff who have been specifically trained for or had relevant experience with children spanning the primary/secondary divide — with groups of children in 'the middle years', that is. It is possible that such teachers might have had a very different, counterbalancing effect on the middle school's emerging identity; for in many ways, their training and experience would seem best suited of all to the middle school's needs and purposes. What contribution have these 'middle years' teachers made to the middle school's development?

Notes

1 These teachers were included in the phase match data but are excluded here since only the sketchiest details of their professional background were known.

2 In this sense, her remarks anticipated doubts that have emerged more recently at the level of public policy about the undue emphasis given to 'propositional' knowledge of an intellectual–cognitive kind within the school curriculum (CCOSS, 1984).

3 Such views in the writings of the deschoolers can be found in ILLICH (1972), GOODMAN (1971) and REIMER (1971), for example.

4 Perhaps it was as much due to this strain between institutional role and substantial self, as to reasons which will be discussed later, that MRS FLETCHER resigned her post at the end of the research period. In this respect, she appeared to experience the same personal dilemmas as one of the 'idealistic' teachers discussed by WOODS (1981) who also resolved this conflict between role and self by 'leaving the field'

5 Of course, these teachers' 'paradigms' or perspectives were, like those of most other teachers, not always at one with their actual practice (HAMMERSLEY, 1977; KEDDIE, 1971). But although there was a good deal of individual monitoring (GALTON, SIMON and CROLL, 1980), guiding and directing of pupils' own work and of their educational choices, as indeed there is in 'progressive' education generally (BERNSTEIN, 1975; HARGREAVES, A. 1977; KING, 1978; BERLAK and BERLAK, 1981; SHARP and GREEN, 1975), there were nonetheless many moments of genuine spontaneity and individual pupil initiative in these two year groups of a kind I rarely witnessed among the older children. The series of lessons which took off on the topic of bird's feet after a visit to a local aviary, and the spontaneous growth of a virtual cottage industry in soft toy kangaroos after one of the children had brought in his own for the others to see, illustrate the kind of developments made possible by the space for pupil initiative here.

6 See RICHARDSON (1981) for evidence on the diffidence with which probationary teachers approach matters to do with schoolwide innovation.

7 In some cases, the definition of lower middle school teaching as low status work was less directly linked with the sex of the teacher. Thus, for MR HOME, the specialist craft teacher,

it was simply a matter of the primary trained generalist being less able to make a 'really valuable' contribution to the middle school than the secondary trained specialist.

> Obviously being secondary trained helps a lot in the middle school situation because I can offer children a lot more than someone who's coming out of a primary situation ... I've probably got a greater depth to dig into and offer them in that respect.

While the link was less direct, though, the implications for the status of female, lower-middle, developmental views, remain just as strong.

8 See the report of an address given by the Senior Chief Inspector, ERIC BOLTON, to an audience of primary teachers, in the *Times Educational Supplement*, 18 May 1984.

9 According to Department of Education and Science (1981) *Statistics in Education*, Vol. II *Teachers*, London, HMSO, p. 6

Chapter 10

The Middle Years Teachers

Name	School	Age	Teaching experience (in years)	Responsibility	Year group	Background
Mrs Close	Moorhead	36–40	3	Formal English	4	Middle trained
Miss Curie	Moorhead	21–25	4	French	3	Middle experienced
Mrs Erikson	Moorhead	26–30	4	—	2	Middle trained
Mrs Handyman	Moorhead	41–45	14	—	2	Mixed age and preparatory
Mrs Speaker	Riverdale	36–40	4	—	3	Middle trained
Miss Rogers	Riverdale	26–30	2	—	4	Middle trained
Mrs Weaver	Riverdale	41–45	15	Music/Acting Deputy Head	4	3–13 hospital school
Mrs Home	Riverdale	21–25	2	—	2	Middle trained[1]

'The difficulty of obtaining and of retaining the right type of teacher for the middle school cannot be minimized', writes Reese Edwards (1972, p. 55) in *The Middle School Experiment*. Who might this 'right type of teacher' be? The evidence of the previous chapters suggests that neither teachers with a wholly primary training and experience, nor those whose training and experience is wholly secondary, are particularly well-equipped to carry the middle school forward in its quest for a unique identity. Nor, as we saw in chapter 9, does a junior/secondary training appear to prepare people adequately for the specific demands of the middle school environment either. The National Union of Teachers (1979, p. 18) has remarked that 'a junior/secondary course can no longer be regarded as a suitable substitute for a properly structured middle school course' and John Burrows, drawing on his long experience as a member of HMI, has pointed out that junior/secondary courses 'were not ... middle school courses: they studied children in the middle years, and curricular matters for the same age range, but they did not examine middle school potentialities, structures and problems.' (1978, p. 184; see also Barnett, 1972)

In view of these shortcomings, it would not be unreasonable to think that the teachers who would be best suited to the distinct purposes of the middle school would therefore be those who have received a specifically middle school training. Nationally, around 17 per cent of all middle school teachers (Taylor and Garson,

183

1978, p. 125) and 12 per cent of middle school teachers with posts of responsibility (HMI, 1983a, p. 141) fall into this category. By themselves, however, these figures do not convey a great deal. Just how far courses of initial training with a 'middle school' designation are in fact geared to specifically middle school needs is a moot point. Blyth and Derricott (1977, p. 155), for instance, point out that the redesignation of some courses as 'middle school' ones 'may be simply relabelling exercises accompanied by few fundamental changes in approach'.

Until we have evidence on the exact character of that training, conclusions about its suitability would be premature. In this chapter, therefore, I want to look at a small number of teachers with middle school training or experience or something closely akin to it, to see if their perspectives or orientations are at all similar, if there is any shared professional inheritance which uniquely fits them for the demands and purposes of the middle school system.

In the Riverdale and Moorhead sample, there were four teachers who had been trained on middle school courses, one whose junior/secondary training had included teaching practice in a middle school, one with experience of middle school teaching in her previous post, and two with experience of teaching mixed age groups across the conventional 11 + boundary (the first in a hospital school, and the second in a rural all-age school followed by a 9–12 preparatory school). In total, then, eight of the teachers in the sample (some 31 per cent) had direct experience of, or had in some way been specifically prepared for, age ranges which cut across the usual primary/secondary divide.[2] What had their training and other professional experience written upon this sizeable group of teachers? What form did their educational perspectives and orientations take? What kind of middle school teachers had they become? And what contribution did they see themselves making to the middle school in the future?

Age Range Preferences

In several respects, these middle years teachers were most unlike their academic-elementary and developmental counterparts. Their commitment to a clear set of educational precepts of whatever kind was not nearly so well-defined as it was among their colleagues. These teachers were, to say the least, catholic in the breadth of their educational tastes, particularly with regard to the age ranges they preferred to teach. In what were, on the whole, as yet only brief careers (just two of the group had spent five or more years in the profession), these teachers had either already acquired an impressive variety of experience across the age-range, or wished to do so.

Mrs Weaver was glad she had taught 'in various set ups', both 'formal' and not so formal, and was now seeking 'to marry the two' as a fourth year middle school teacher. She particularly revelled in the rich variety of experience she had managed to accumulate during her career to date

I've taught now anything from three year olds through to these 14s. I've had every age group, you know. And it doesn't really matter to me. Give me a room and thirty kids and sort of say 'Well. There you are!' and my days are made. I don't really want much more.

Mrs Home, in just her second year of teaching, recognized that the depth of her professional experience was not so great, but she did value the breadth of experience she gained teaching in a range of school types — from play schools to upper schools — on teaching practice. Miss Curie, a teacher with previous middle school experience, counted 'the variety which you get with this age group' as one of her two greatest sources of enjoyment within teaching. And Mrs Close too, while predominantly a fourth-year teacher, enjoyed renewing that contact with younger, second year pupils, if only for a few periods a week, that she had found such a rewarding feature of her teaching practice during initial training.

Undoubtedly, this variety of professional experience across the age-range was much valued, and it provided a source of stimulation and challenge to many of these middle years teachers. There were no reservations among them about merely 'mothering' younger pupils, nor were there any qualms about meeting the intellectual standards required for teaching older ones. In this sense, the flexibility of these teachers in responding to and indeed seeking out a variety of professional experiences across and sometimes even beyond the middle school age range was impressive.

Specialists or Generalists?

Alongside this flexibility and adapatability on the matter of age-ranges, there was also a measure of breadth in these teachers' curricular commitments too. In chapter 7, the tension between specialism and generalism was identified as one of the central 'dilemmas' or 'agonies' of the middle school curriculum. In subsequent chapters, we have seen how the perspectives of academic–elementary teachers in the upper years of the middle school were drawn towards the specialist end of this dilemma and how the developmental teachers' perspectives in turn clustered towards the generalist end. The middle years recruits, as might perhaps be expected, were positioned somewhere between these two points. But their perspective was not just a straight compromise between or simple mixture of generalist and specialist orientations. These teachers were more than merely in the middle. Four appeared, in fact, to be powerfully attracted to *both* poles of the generalism/specialism dilemma, *at the same time*.

This is how Mrs Close, a fourth year teacher with responsibility for 'formal English' at Moorhead put it:

> We've got, in a sense, the best of both worlds here because you've got what might be termed some specialized teaching which I have to confess I enjoy because I'm still interested in English as a subject. I still think it's important for one to be aware of the disciplines even though you do draw the connections for the children; encourage them to see the connections

between them as an aid to their understanding. So I do enjoy the specialism of that, but at the same time, I think I would be very bored if I was just teaching that all the time, and I enjoy the freedom to be able to link English to other areas of the curriculum ... especially with history.

Mrs Speaker, another teacher with broad curricular interests, also shared this special love of English. She too liked 'all the subject range', but she particularly enjoyed 'anything to do with words: English, poetry, drama, music, history'. 'Strongly English based things I enjoy doing most', she said, and counted this, the main subject of her training, among her greatest strengths. *Mrs Home*, a second year generalist teacher at Riverdale, also retained a strong interest in the main subject of her professional training — in her case PE and games — and felt it likely she would be awarded a scale 2 with responsibility for girls' games in the near future. And *Miss Curie*, in charge of French at Moorhead, particularly enjoyed 'both the fact that I'm a specialist and not a specialist' since this gave her 'contact with the children in the different subjects where you get completely different aspects of them showing and their reaction to different subjects even though it's the same person taking them'.

The remaining four middle years recruits, though all could claim an interest in some specialist area of the curriculum, appeared in the main to be drawn rather more strongly towards a generalist orientation within the middle school. Thus, *Mrs Erikson*, who had specialized in social studies at college and who continued to teach sociology 'O' level for evening classes 'because I do miss the academic side of things', nonetheless saw her role in school as a second year teacher very much as that of a generalist (I've no specialisms: I don't teach any specialisms'). Nor did she see her career developing through the pursuit of any particular specialism either. As might befit a teacher trained in social studies, pastoral care was the route along which she wished her future career to develop; the sphere of social relationships, 'the failures, in a way'.

Mrs Handyman was equally keen to extend her interests beyond her own particular specialism. A general subjects teacher in the second year at Moorhead, she had originally trained on a 'junior' age-range course where her main specialism had been art. Currently, though, she defined her curriculum interests much more broadly than this. The aspects of teaching she enjoyed the most, she said, extended to creative work in general; art, creative writing, poetry and drama — 'all creative things, particularly to do with speech and movement'. And her strengths, she felt, lay in giving pupils

> confidence in their creative abilities. I think I'm reasonably good at stimulating them at creative writing and for the other arts. I can pass on my enthusiasm for poetry and books ... generally for artistic things, creative things and painting, collage, modelling and drama — all these things, because I enjoy these very much myself. It's very much a part of me so I feel that I pass this on to the children.

Thus, Mrs Handyman's enthusiasm for one of the creative and expressive arts extended to the field of creative and expressive arts in general, an interest which was reflected in her choice of in-service courses, these falling mainly in the art and drama area.

Miss Rogers, a PGCE trained drama enthusiast was in a slightly different position. On the one hand, she possessed a strong interest in her subject and felt rather peeved that it did not receive wider recognition within the Riverdale curriculum ('drama's not on a very good footing really, at all'). On the other hand, she had no wish to become 'a sort of drama specialist', to be someone who would take over the 'drama bits' of the curriculum during identifiable parts of the timetable. Rather, for her, drama suffused her whole approach to teaching and learning right across the curriculum. When Miss Rogers spoke of subject matters, she spoke not of specialisms, favoured or unfavoured, but of *topics*, topics which generated or failed to generate her own enthusiasm and which therefore made her effective or less effective as a classroom teacher:

> Like the Scottish one we did last term. I started working on Culloden and I
> got really interested in it and was beginning to develop ideas of my own
> and they were beginning to develop actually in the classroom.

At moments like this, Miss Rogers felt, teachers and pupils *together* became involved in a genuine process of collaborative enquiry. The teacher's enthusiasm was sincere ('I mean, it's the self educative thing . . . you're really learning yourself about something'), not pedagogically contrived ('I'm not very good at artificially creating an interest in something that doesn't really interest me. It becomes run of the mill and it becomes run of the mill for the kids too, I think').

This is where Miss Rogers' drama background set her apart from her colleagues. For it had equipped her not with the 'essential' teacher arts of dramatic role performance (Goffmann, 1959), with the artifice of simulated enthusiasm and discovery, the ability to stage convincing 'mock ups' of real learning (Atkinson and Delamont, 1977); but with a particular mode of relating to children, one characterized by sharing and mutual personal growth and understanding. This, she argued, was difficult to attain in a conventional school setting, but her experience of small group work 'in out-of-school situations' in theatre workshops and the like, had led her to appreciate that more collaborative relationships *were* possible. And although like many fellow 'new romantics' (Hargreaves, 1972), she was generally pessimistic about the possibility of achieving such educational ends within the compulsory school system, she still felt that there were moments — when the topic was right and the teacher's own interests in self-education could be stimulated — when collaborative learning *could* take place.

> As I say, I'd like to see more of that going on as a sort of sharing thing
> between both myself and the kids; and with certain topics it can happen.

For Miss Rogers, then, drama was not a source of intellectual excitement about subject matter but a base for her whole pedagogy. And given that pedagogy, virtually any subject matter would do, on condition only that it could stimulate genuine educational enthusiasm on her part, as well as the child's.

Mrs Weaver, a year team colleague of Miss Rogers', also had her professional roots in the creative and expressive arts — in her case, as a music specialist — but again like Miss Rogers, she too felt drawn most strongly towards the generalist aspects of her work. When asked about the in-service courses she had attended, she replied,

> A great variety, really. Because when you're doing a job like this, you've got to look at all aspects. It's no good just, sort of only going on art courses or only going on music courses. You've to try to keep apace with everything you're expected to have a hand in. So I haven't sort of specialized at all.

This generalist orientation was also reflected in her impending career move to be Head of Second Year in a nearby 11–18 comprehensive where she would belong to the English department, though also continuing to teach some music. As a contained specialism, then, music added but one (albeit important) string to Mrs Weaver's broader professional bow. But in the main, this was not how it exerted its greatest influence on her teaching. Music did not dominate her timetable, her formal responsibilities or her career aspirations. Its influence was much more diffuse than that. Just as in Miss Rogers' drama teaching, what Mrs Weaver's involvement with specialist music education had done was to lay the foundations of her whole pedagogical orientation, right across the middle school curriculum. This is how she explained it in interview. Music, she said,

> is one of these areas, as art is, where your communion with children is very close. And it's an emotional subject as English is and as art can be. You've got to *talk* your ideas and you've got to *talk* your feelings and I think this is where the communication comes in because as soon as you're communicating that way with a child, they start immediately giving back and this carries on to when they're doing other things. Sort of rapport is still there because it carries on from that area. I think anybody who teaches in the creative arts has this with the kids because it's emotionally based ... whereas if you're dealing with a factual subject, a scientific subject, you're dealing more with things and objects and reactions. Actually how you *feel* about SO_2 coming out of a bottle doesn't come into it, you know.

What Mrs Weaver revealed here is the way her contact with and experience of her subject (one which often stressed the importance of communication, personal relationships and emotional development) underpinned her approach to and perceptions of her whole *pedagogy*, along with the overall range of her curricular interests. Paradoxically, her very commitment to generalism seemed to grow from her experience of and commitment to a particular kind of specialism; one located in the creative and expressive arts.

This position, as I shall go on to show, was shared by many of her middle years colleagues. Their perspectives too were more than just a simple mixture of specialism and generalism, but ones where these two elements existed in a situation of close interdependence; where the generalist orientation flowed out of a commitment to and an experience of *particular types* of specialism. What did all this mean for these middle years recruits? Were they specialists, generalists, semi-specialists, or what?

Semi-Specialists or Quasi-Generalists?

It has often been suggested that the emergence of middle schools would bring with them a new kind of teacher: the semi-specialist (Edwards 1972, pp. 54–5). For Alec Ross and the Schools Council (1975, p. 230), this effectively meant 'generalists with several semi-specialist strings to their teaching bow'. More recently, Williamson (1982, p. 19) has asserted that middle schools 'use effectively a group of teachers — the so-called general specialists, who have been under-valued and certainly misused elsewhere'. The implication here is that middle school trained teachers would, like their primary colleagues, have a grasp of and competence in the whole curriculum, but in addition to this, would also possess particular expertise in more than one specialist subject to a level where they could perceive 'the relationship of the work being done at the age of 8, at 10 and at 12, to the subject as it is presented at age 14, at 16 and at 18' (Schools Council, 1975, p. 231). By this definition of semi-specialism, middle school trained teachers would be basically generalists on the one hand and *extended specialists* (i.e. specialists in more than one area of the curriculum), on the other.

This definition of semi-specialism does not seem to apply to the middle years recruits at Riverdale and Moorhead. These teachers were not so much generalists with an extra degree of *extended specialism* but specialists (in art, drama, music etc.) who had broadened their interests into a *restricted kind of generalism*. In other words, they professed strength and interest only in those areas of the curriculum which were perceived and experienced as being closely connected to their own particular specialism. Their interest in adopting a generalist role in addition to their own specialism by no means extended to all areas of the curriculum. The Riverdale and Moorhead middle years recruits, that is, were not so much *extended specialists* as *restricted or quasi-generalists*. While their particular subjects may have varied between them, all but one were nevertheless located within the arts rather than the sciences, and all but two belonged to English and the creative/expressive arts. It was to these curricular areas that the middle years recruits restricted their generalist interests.

At the same time, these teachers showed a great deal of diffidence about extending their work into the scientific and mathematical areas of the curriculum. Only one teacher, Mrs Handyman, proclaimed a definite enthusiasm for mathematics, and many displayed a great deal of unease about the scientific and mathematical aspects of their work. *Mrs Handyman*, a primary trained teacher, confessed that 'the thing I shun away from, I suppose, is science mainly because I haven't taught it before. I must say, I'm rather apprehensive about doing that.' *Mrs Close* also disliked science:

> I have to teach science topic. Now this time we've taken it from television broadcasts which has helped, but I'm still conscious of the fact that I don't

really feel that I've got sufficient background knowledge to be able to stretch the children, to help them as much as I feel I ought to be able to.

This diffidence was related to the fact that she had never been interested in or successful at science right from her schooldays

I was never particularly interested in science at school. I did it. I passed the subjects in it at School Certificate level but I can't say I'm really interested in it . . . I always have a conscience about this. I always feel that I should in some way try to become more interested, try to become more competent at science but the thing is I just don't want to!

Miss Rogers was less tied than Mrs Close to a timetabled science commitment, but when the topics with which she was involved in integrated studies had a strong scientific cast to them, she admitted losing that enthusiasm she regarded as so essential to her effectiveness as a teacher.

The project we're doing at the moment is a more scientific-based one and I've only got a fairly hazy idea of what I really want to do with it . . . I've been struggling a bit with it because . . . I'm vaguely interested but it doesn't really turn me on like the Scotland one did so . . . I'm just not working as well on it as ones that really interest me.

With *Mrs Speaker*, the major problem area was mathematics. This, she felt, was her major weakness.

I'm a reasonable mathematician but I would like to be better. I would like to have that quickness of mind, that logical mind, that is such a help in maths but I haven't got it so I have to make do with hard graft.

These teachers were ill at ease with science and mathematics and much more at home in the general field of humanities and creative/expressive arts. This was not just because of the subject matter, but, as should now be apparent, also because of the pedagogical approaches these subjects implied. These teachers' subject identities seemed to carry with them certain kinds of pedagogical identity too.[3] Their subjects and the broad field of humanities and creative/expressive arts with which these teachers saw them being associated, gave them the opportunity to concentrate on communication, creative expression, personal relationships, emotional development and so on. As *Mrs Weaver* put it when she recalled her strengths as a teacher; 'Subjects, relationships, discipline — of course, they're all tied together aren't they!'. For her (as indeed for her colleagues too), science was just not part of that personalized relationship-centred educational bond — 'how you feel about SO_2 coming out of a bottle doesn't really enter into it!'.[4]

The Bases and Consequences of Quasi-Generalism

Why these middle years teachers should turn out to be restricted, quasi-generalists within the English and creative/expressive arts domain is a matter about which, at this stage, one can only speculate. Perhaps it has something to do with the fact that all but one of these teachers (Miss Rogers) were college, not university trained. As Grace (1978, p. 200) notes 'the strongest advocates of curriculum integration tend to be teachers from colleges of education rather than university departments of education'. And this, Grace argues, may arise from the weaker subject identity of college trained teachers compared with their university counterparts. This would certainly help explain the positive interest that the middle years teachers displayed in broadening their professional experience beyond their own particular specialisms. But it would not account for their tendency to fall within and confine their enthusiasms to the humanities and creative/expressive arts areas of the curriculum in particular.

This more specific restriction might presumably be explained by the content of these teachers' initial training: it may be that their courses overemphasized the humanities and social sciences and creative/expressive arts at the expense of scientific and mathematical areas of the curriculum. Equally, the extent to which these teachers were inclined toward the humanities and creative/expressive arts, and away from the sciences may be explained, in large part, by their sex. *All* these middle years' recruits were women; and in general, they exemplified that gender-based pattern of girls preferring to study and women preferring to teach arts rather than sciences (particularly physical sciences), which has been consistently documented as a major source of inequality between the sexes. (Kelly, 1981; DES, 1975; Deem, 1978)

I have no data on the detailed content of these teachers' initial training, still less on the content of middle school courses in general. Nor does there appear to be any evidence available on the sex balance of the intake to middle school courses, or on the extent to which male and female students opt for or are channelled into arts or science related specialisms respectively within those courses.

What the case study data suggest though, is a possible connection between three characteristics of middle years teachers — that they are more likely to be college-trained than university graduates, to specialize in and be strong on arts rather than sciences, and to be women rather than men. If these patterns were to be repeated on a national scale; if most middle years teachers did indeed turn out to be college trained, female and arts-biased, the integrity of the middle school curriculum and middle school identity as a whole could well be placed in serious jeopardy. Clearly, these issues warrant further research.

Whatever the reasons for middle years teachers being weak in certain areas of the curriculum, a strong subject advisory system where subject/curriculum co-ordination played an influential role, might have compensated for this. As we saw in chapter 7, though, this did not happen at either Riverdale or Moorhead. Lateral continuity was stronger than vertical continuity; communication within the year groups better than with the subject coordinators. Only Mrs Close, one of several middle years teachers to express unease about science teaching, felt that help was available in this area.

> Its useful to know that I can say to Mr Greek sometimes, you know, mention things to him, and it's useful to know that if you need the help . . . you've got somebody to go to.

Unlike the systematic organization of the year groups, though, where colleagues were always in close proximity, this subject support was, in the main, available only on an *ad hoc* basis. Contact had to be made and advice solicited *despite* rather than *because* of the prevailing systems of colleaguial support — with their lateral rather than vertical pattern of formal and informal organization. As Mrs Close herself put it

> The coordination only takes place when it's imperative and I don't think that that's quite satisfactory enough. I think that there could be more meetings ... the machinery should be there if it's needed.

The middle years teachers at Riverdale and Moorhead, then, were not so much extended specialists as restricted, *quasi-generalists*. In effect, they were enthusiastic teachers of integrated humanities and creative/expressive arts who, by and large, felt ill at ease with subjects outside that domain, and with science and mathematics in particular. Their age range preferences were broad; but their curricular ones, less so. Nor were these curricular shortfalls compensated for by the middle school's much vaunted subject advisory system. The practical impact of such vertical support at Riverdale and Moorhead was weak; occluded by the dominance of the year group system. These middle years teachers' background and training, then, appeared to restrict the scope of their influence on the middle school curriculum as a whole, leaving certain, important parts of that curriculum, like science and mathematics, poorly covered with their own groups and also subject to control by their academic-elementary, specialist orientated colleagues in the school as a whole. Did this mean that their influence on the middle school in general was limited; that their distinctive contribution to the middle school identity was weak? What kind of commitment did these teachers have to middle schools and middle schooling, and how far were they able to follow that commitment through?

Commitment

The concept of commitment, as Nias (1981, p. 181) reminds us, is not only a subject for sociological discussion but is used widely by teachers themselves too. In the community of teachers, 'commitment' is commonly (though by no means always) associated with the investment of time and energy, the giving of loyalty to one's school or to teaching and education in general (Nias, 1981). This is closely akin to the notion of commitment defined by Kanter (1974, p. 126); as 'willingness ... to give ... energy and loyalty to social systems'. As Nias and others have pointed out, though, this loyalty may take different forms; it may be given for different reasons, revealing different *kinds* of commitment. (Nias, 1981; Lacey, 1977; Woods, 1983)

One kind of commitment that Nias and others point to is vocational commitment, commitment to broad ideals of education, to missions or vocations of learning, caring, enhancing personal growth or engineering social change (Woods, 1983, pp. 155–6; Acker, 1983). This kind of commitment was particularly strong among the developmental teachers at Riverdale and Moorhead. It figured strongly in the educational perspectives of the middle years teachers too. It is hard to convey, through a few snapshot quotations, the depth, the intensity of these teachers' commitments to their work, for their enthusiasm, their love of learning (not least their own learning) and of being with children, suffused their whole perspective. They spoke a great deal about the joys of 'being with' children (Mrs Erikson), of involving themselves in their pupils' emotional development (Mrs Weaver), of having a 'special relationship as a class teacher with their pupils' (Mrs Close). Miss Rogers felt she had 'got a concern for the children which is very genuine, particularly for the children who I feel are sort of getting a raw deal', and linked this to her educational idealism in general:

> I'm much more interested in the kind of social and general educative aspects. Education for life rather than just education for exams or work or bits of paper or what have you.

Mrs Speaker simply liked the job: 'I suppose the biggest advantage is liking the job, liking children and liking teaching. Being happy in what I'm doing is a great advantage and a great help.'

These middle years teachers, then, had a powerful vocational commitment to children, teaching and education in general. They were enthusiastic. They cared. Staff with this kind of educational orientation would be an enviable asset to any school, no matter what its age range. But did these commitments have any implications for the middle school in particular? Did they offer it any special assistance in its search for a unique identity?

The middle years teachers may have had broad vocational commitments to education in general but in interview, they displayed little specific commitment to the middle school or the idea of middle schools as such. Unlike their heads, they advanced no views about the purpose and character of middle schools as a whole, and they made even less reference to such matters than did their other middle school colleagues. Nor did these teachers display any awareness that their initial training had alerted them to the distinctive purposes of middle schooling, or to the special role that they might play within it. In the main, the four members of this group who had undertaken specifically middle school courses were not enamoured of their training. Miss Rogers was the most caustic: 'it was a terrible, appalling course and, well, absolutely abysmal'. 'It talked a lot', she said 'It didn't *do* at all'. The ideas, she said, were 'incredibly out of date'. The only value she felt she gained from it was in her own subject, drama, where the inspirational, charismatic leadership of her tutor had excited her about the teaching of that subject. But there was no mention of that course's contribution to middle school purposes and needs in particular: it was only a 'supposedly' middle school course as far as she was concerned.

The other three middle school trained teachers had all been educated at the same college where the course, according to Mrs Speaker, had been 'particularly aimed at middle school'. Mature students every one, these women had had time to consider their careers with some care and one at least, Mrs Close, had been positively attracted to the course 'because this was the range I was particularly interested in'. Yet, while both she and Mrs Erikson praised their course much more than

Miss Rogers did hers, it appeared to be the general aspects that most appealed to them; the lectures in psychology, philosophy and history (in addition, that is, to the ubiquitously acknowledged merits of practical classroom experience on teaching practice). Even Mrs Speaker, who claimed to have been influenced by her teacher training 'not at all', nonetheless identified these things as the most useful aspects of her professional preparation. No mention was made by any of these four teachers of what implications these aspects of their training had for their particular role as *middle school* teachers. The inputs to which they referred — the study of the growth of education as a whole, the psychology of individual differences, the difficulties of mixed ability teaching and so on—were ones that would have been pertinent to almost any age range, any educational institution. Judging by the reaction of these teachers it would seem that their professional training did little to identify or clarify the special character and destiny of the middle school, still less to edify them about their own distinctive contribution to it.

From the point of view of middle school proponents, this account of the perspectives and commitments of the middle years teachers perhaps paints a rather depressing picture of the middle school and its search for a unique identity. Variety may well be the spice of life, but in teaching, its celebration always carries with it the danger that teachers will lose sight of more specific educational purposes, that they will fail to recognize and appreciate the particular educational structures and arrangements, the particular kinds of educational institution which might best help them realize their general ideals and commitments. The broad vocational commitment of these teachers was admirable. Their flexibility in coping with and in fact positively welcoming the experience of teaching a variety of age ranges was impressive. And their willingness to take on curricular challenges outside their own specialism, if less extensive than it first seemed, was still encouraging. But such was the breadth of their vocational commitment and the extent of their flexibility, that many of these teachers were not really attracted to any particular institutional definition of education at all, least of all a middle school one. This was most clearly illustrated by the nature of their career expectations and aspirations.

These middle years recruits not only possessed a set of powerful commitments to education in the round, but to promotion and career advancement too; to *career continuance*, as Woods (1983, p. 155) calls it. What is interesting about these career commitments, though, is that in three cases, they were seen as being pursued *outside* the middle school. *Mrs Weaver* was about to move to a post as Head of Second Year in a local comprehensive. *Mrs Erikson* said she 'would like to teach older children' and ultimately aspired to a post with responsibility for pastoral care, which, she felt, would probably take her out of the middle school system. *Mrs Home*, having only recently begun her teaching career admitted 'it's difficult when you're in your probationary year to be able to think of your career ahead', but felt, at present, that she would eventually like to be Head of Games in a secondary school. Indeed, she had 'already thought about moving into an upper school to teach PE and games'.[5]

In a fourth case, Miss Rogers made it plain that she had virtually no interest in career continuance within the school system at all. Her commitment was one of almost pure vocationalism — to the idea of education as a whole — but this, too, took her away from the middle school:

> I don't want to stay in (teaching) as a continued career pattern. I can quite
> forsee that I may eventually come back to teaching later. I mean, sort of my
> broader interests are in education but as I say not necessarily within the
> schools because on the whole, I don't tend to like the school set-up. You
> know, there are factors about the school set-up itself which hinder
> education, which I've found very frustrating.

One year later she had found her escape: a post in educational broadcasting.

Loyalty to the vocation of education these teachers certainly had. And their
commitment to personal career advancement was more than negligible too. But
their commitment to the middle school in particular seemed rather weak. In
retrospect, this should be a source of no great surprise. As I argued in the
introduction, at the time these teachers were being trained and commencing their
middle school careers, the ideology of the middle school had little to offer in the way
of guidance as to what shape these schools should take, other than appeals to vague
notions of identity and transition. There was therefore no clearly defined middle
school vision these middle years recruits could commit themselves *to*.

Nor were these teachers committed *by* much either. Three had domestic
commitments which tied them to the locality or placed self-conscious limits on
promotional aspirations. But, unlike their developmental and academic-elementary
colleagues, none had built up long-established careers in particular sectors or cultures
of teaching elsewhere. They had, in Howard Becker's (1960) terms, laid down no
'side-bets', made no investments in particular approaches to teaching of a kind that
might be difficult to give up later. Educationally speaking, in most respects, they
were very much 'free agents'. Neither committed *by* any well trodden past, nor
committed *to* any clearly waymarked future, these teachers carried with them
neither the certainties of biographical habit nor the reforming confidence of some
particular educational vision. They were surrounded by uncertain hopes and
expectations, their middle school roles swathed in ambiguity (Grace, 1972). What
were the implications of this for their practice?

Situational Vulnerability

Howard Becker (1964) has noted that all of us are both creatures of commitment, to
ends and ideals that transcend the vicissitudes of the moment; and of situational
adjustment too, adjustment to the pressures, constraints and expectations of the
immediate situation. The relationship between these two aspects of our being are, of
course, immensely complex; today's commitments in many respects being the
outcome of yesterday's repeated adjustments. But while all of us are in part creatures
of *both* commitment *and* adjustment, some of us — those whose commitments are,
for whatever reason, somewhat ill defined or uncertain — are more adaptable than
others. So it was with the middle years teachers. Miss Rogers put it this way:

> I moved into a set-up that was already set up, if you know what I mean.
> The fourth year pattern was already established as a way of teaching before
> I joined the group so that I kind of adapted to that rather than necessarily

being able to have a very big influence on it myself. As I say, I felt we taught very differently in the second year, mainly because there was more interaction between us as teachers ... So the present style of teaching is very much affected by the set up rather than by how I would necessarily like to do it ideally.

This unusually high degree of adaptability, of course, did not just arise from uncertainties surrounding the purpose and direction of middle schooling. Inexperience played its part too. The fact that middle schools had not been in existence for very long before the research was conducted, automatically meant that any middle school trained teachers in the sample would have limited professional experience. Hanson and Herrington (1976) have noted that teachers are especially adaptable in their first years of teaching and the fledgling middle years teachers seemed in part to exemplify this pattern. As Mrs Close put it 'I think in a sense to begin with, you're feeling your way anyway and then you tend to adapt'.

Together, the professional inexperience of these teachers along with their uncertain institutional commitments, tended to lead them to take on the characteristics of the year teams in which they found themselves. Thus, while Miss Rogers, Mrs Speaker and Mrs Weaver – all third and fourth year teachers at Riverdale — varied a great deal in their educational *perspectives*, their classroom *practice* was remarkably similar. Miss Rogers, as we have seen, inclined towards a new romanticism; Mrs Speaker spoke in favour of education contributing to the conservation of the existing social order ('it's part of our job to see that a child is as socially acceptable as possible. It is part of our job so see that they can be assimilated into a community'); and Mrs Weaver fell somewhere between. But despite these differences in perspectives, these teachers were less easily distinguishable at the level of practice: all spending a good deal of time during the operation of the block timetable, circulating, reminding pupils of deadlines, taking maths sets aside for more structured transmission-types of input and so forth.

The same applied to the two third and fourth year middle years recruits at Moorhead, Mrs Close and Miss Curie. Their pedagogies were closely akin to the transmission-based, recitation-type ones of their academic-elementary colleagues who dominated the third and fourth year teams. Mrs Close, for instance, may have been less of a 'a tartar' than Mr Bird, say; she may not have reduced the pupils to tears as he sometimes did. 'Firm but approachable' was how she liked to be regarded. But, despite these differences of emphasis and degree, the general patterns of interaction that prevailed in her classroom were not significantly different from those that could be found in his — whole-class presentation, teacher-led question and answer sessions, individual seatwork with the teacher circulating round the class etc.

In the lower years of the middle school, the adaptability of the middle years teachers was no less strong. Both Mrs Home and Mrs Erikson shied away from the transmission-like approaches of their third and fourth year colleagues. Mrs Home wrote options, agendas of work on the board and moved around to help children complete them and to ensure that they did so on time. And Mrs Erikson, even though 'isolated' in a terrapin classroom, devoted a great deal of her time to individualized patterns of working, to allowing children to study, draw and write about their own chosen specimens they had collected during a vist to a local pond, for instance.

Wherever these teachers were placed, then — be it in Riverdale or Moorhead, or in the upper or lower parts of the middle school — their uncertain institutional commitments and professional inexperience led them to adjust to the pressures and demands of the particular school and year groups in which they found themselves. There were certainly few signs of active resistance among them to the immediate pressures of their environment; no disapproved-of instances of university-style lecturing after the fashion of Mr Driver, for instance, nor expressions of truculent opposition to change in the manner of Mrs Priestley. Though adaptability has its merits, teachers who are adaptable to *this* extent scarcely seem the right ones to staff a school searching for a new identity. For this kind of adaptability does not reveal a shrewd capacity to adjust one's commitments to the constraints and opportunities of the immediate situation in order to increase the likelihood of their successful realisation. Rather, in the absence of well-formed and suitably specific educational commitments, it amounts to a kind of *situational vulnerability*, an incapacity or unwillingness to resist the pressures of one's immediate surroundings.

It is possible, of course, that this pattern of situational vulnerability may not persist among middle years teachers for long. Many of the first generation of middle years teachers, having now reached mid-career, might now be better placed to give greater coherence to the emerging character of middle schooling. Equally, more recent patterns of middle school training might have been more successful in communicating a clearer picture of the actual and possible nature of the institutions for which their students were being prepared. Much of that training has been discontinued though. Only further research will provide reasonably dependable answers to these important questions. But the evidence of this study suggests that there is no *necessary* reason why teachers with a middle school training should make a distinctive contribution to the middle school's future. They may be teachers *of* the middle years by training, but this by no means guarantees they will also be *for* the middle school in the shaping of its future.

Conclusion

Although some writers have claimed that the balance of staff in middle schools by sex, age and experience might be 'an immediate and unique advantage and potentially a source of strength',[6] the evidence of the past three chapters — albeit based on two case studies — suggests this optimism may be misplaced. Overall impressions of balance may disguise serious internal imbalances in the distribution of staff. At Riverdale and Moorhead, the upper years were dominated by teachers with their roots in secondary modern schools or the scholarship classes of primary schools who bequeathed to the middle school an academic-elementary inheritance of subject specialism, setting by ability, basic skills and disciplinary firmness. By contrast, in the lower years, teachers who were experienced in or had been trained for infant or lower junior teaching brought to the middle school the very different perspectives and orientations of the developmental tradition with its emphasis on generalism not specialism; relationships not discipline.

These two cultural inheritances tended to create an organizational hiatus, not a smooth transition within the middle school; to reproduce that split at 11 which has customarily separated primary from secondary education. Nor, it seems, were these gaps and divisions alleviated by the influx of a first generation of teachers specifically trained for or with experience in 'the middle years'. Though lovers of variety and possessors of great vocations enthusiasm and commitment, these teachers had no clearly articulated commitment to the middle school in particular. They were not able to infuse it with any special character of their own. Through their *situational vulnerability*, they yielded the middle schools' destiny to the academic-elementary and developmental traditions respectively. The two cultures of teaching persisted. The proposed new culture of the middle years was not sufficiently powerful to take their place.

Notes

1 Mrs HOME is counted as 'middle trained' here on the grounds that while her course was a junior/secondary one, she experienced a substantial period of teaching practice in a middle school.

2 The three categories of teachers — academic-elementary, developmental and middle years — have therefore taken account of all teachers in the interview sample except two. One, Mr HOME, has already been discussed (chapter 8, note 1). The other was Mr MOOR who also cannot be neatly included in any of the three analytical cells already identified.

   Mr MOOR was junior-secondary trained, was a primary teacher in his first post (8–9 year-olds) and had taught in the lower end of the middle school with 10–11 year-olds for his first three years at Moorhead. Phase-matched up to this point, he then took responsibility for teaching third year pupils, and thus became one of the very few 'mismatched' teachers in the sample.

   His perspective was a mixture of developmental and academic-elementary elements. A generalist in orientation (his specialism — games — was distinctively non-academic in character), he gained his rewards, he said, from being with children and working with them individually. On the other hand, his approach to discipline bore a distinctly academic-elementary tone: he could be bad-tempered, he said, and this was not altogether a weakness, and though disciplining was unpleasant, he went on, 'it's one of those things that you have to do in order to keep a civilized society throughout the school'.

   His approach to pedagogy was equally ambivalent. Though having, for timetabling reasons, 'to do a fair amount of formal teaching — in other words, teaching the whole class a particular thing at a particular time,' he preferred to work with individual pupils wherever possible.

   The ambivalence of Mr MOOR's position is interesting and may have important implications for possibilities concerning future middle school staffing arrangements. But there are insufficient data to take the analysis any further here.

3 A number of writers have pointed to this link between subject and pedagogical

perspectives. See ESLAND, 1971; BALL, 1981; BARNES and SHEMILT, 1974; BARNES, 1976; REID *et al*, 1981; and EVANS, 1985.

4   In this respect, the pedagogical perspectives of these teachers had strong affinities with their colleagues in similar subjects elsewhere in the school system — for instance in art (BENNETT, 1985) and certain versions of English. (ST JOHN BROOKES, 1983; BALL, 1982; BALL and LACEY, 1980; BARNES and SHEMILT, 1974)

5   However, there were indications that this route may already have been in the process of being closed down, for Mrs HOME was hoping to be offered a scale post at Riverdale in the following year for girls' games, and was showing early signs of accommodating to the career implications of this: 'it could help me, this PE background, to further my career, even if I do stay in a middle school'.

6   The quote is from two middle school heads (GANNON and WHALLEY, 1975, p. 8).

Part IV:
Conclusion

'I will live in the Past, Present and
Future. The Spirits of all Three shall
strive within me. I will not shut out
the lessons that they teach'.

(Ebenezer Scrooge, in Charles Dickens, *A Christmas Carol*)

Chapter 11

Middle Schools past; Middle Schools present; Middle Schools yet to come

Introduction

Much of what goes on in schools is a result of the historical context in which they develop and the pressures and expectations they have to meet. It is the complex interplay of these factors — historical and situational — and the ways in which they are managed that in many respects makes schools what they are. In this book, I have tried to examine some of these interrelationships. I have looked at past and present, policy and practice, history and ethnography, in order to identify some of the dominant traditions, priorities and assumptions that are at work in the English educational system. And I have illustrated some of the ways in which these things make themselves felt in the day-to-day business of schooling.

These purposes, traditions and assumptions are diverse in nature. In practice, though, they receive nothing like equal weight in the formulation and implementation of educational policy and practice. So, while English education has been suffused with talk about children's educational needs, their personal growth and development; it has also consistently been presented as needing to serve social ends, particularly ones concerned with the creation of wealth and economic stability. It is important to know which of these 'needs' — personal or social, child-centred or economic has been dominant in practice. Similarly, it is important to know whether English education has systematically pursued the goals of equality and social fairness for all pupils, or whether these have been overshadowed by the requirements of academic and social selection at 16 plus, and by patterns of differentiation (setting) and high status specialisation before it.

My case for examining these sorts of questions has been the English middle school — especially the 9/10–13 variety. Here we have a school poised precariously between the exploratory but essential first years of primary education on the one hand, and the urgent demands and necessities of examination, selection and 'the world of work' (or non-work) on the other. What better place could there be to assess the relative importance of different cultures and traditions of educational thought and practice in English schooling — primary and secondary; academic, elementary and developmental? Where else could we find a truer measure of the system's biases and priorities in general than this point where they come most directly into competition?

When we look at the middle school's past and present, then, there are clearly not only messages for these schools in particular, but for the system as a whole too. And as we try to learn from the lessons of past and present, questions about the middle school's future must also inevitably raise major questions of purpose and priority for state education as a whole as we approach the next millenium. In this respect, the linking of the middle school's past, present and future demands of us a depth of educational questioning and a breadth of educational vision that is fundamental and far-reaching in its implications. Let us now commence this daunting task, by drawing together our understanding of middle schools past.

Middle Schools Past

When a pupil moves from primary to secondary school, it usually involves quite a substantial shift in experience: from having close contact with one class teacher who knows that pupil well as an individual across all areas of the curriculum, to encountering a vast, bureaucratically complex assortment of different teachers and subjects where individual pupil needs are all too easily neglected or overlooked. It is little wonder that the transition from primary to secondary school is so often such a traumatic experience for young people.

For some years now, many people have rightly thought that things should and could be otherwise. In recent years, attempts of various kinds have been made to smooth the transition between primary and secondary school. Closer liaison has been established between the two sectors, more and better records have been transferred, link schemes experimented with, induction programmes set up, teachers exchanged, and so forth (Thomas 1984). Building adequate bridges between two quite separate sectors which, in the main, have very different approaches to curriculum and teaching style, has not been an easy task, though; and the difficulties have often seemed insuperable. Because of these problems, many influential administrators and school heads have felt that only a separate institution with its own special character and purpose could meet the need for improved and smoother transition.

In England and the United States alike, these were the kinds of hopes and sentiments that surrounded the early development of middle schools in many districts; hopes for schools with their own special purpose or destiny, schools that would meet the special educational needs of children 'in the middle years', ease the transition from primary to secondary education, and extend the best of primary practice to older children. This was an optimistic vision of middle schooling, in harmony with broader social democratic values advocating the virtues of balance and unity, and attuned to the context of relative economic expansion which characterized the 1960s.

But if the middle school vision united, it also disguised. It overlooked or underemphasized the administrative, political and economic circumstances surrounding and occasioning the middle school's development. For whatever rhetorics of educational purpose accompanied the establishment of middle schools — be these to do with primary school extension or the special needs of the middle years — it was the political and economic problems encountered in educational policy and state management more generally in the 1960s that were at the root of their emergence. The impulsion of educational policy and state management towards intervention and reform on comprehensive lines as a way of 'buying' social loyalty and enhancing economic growth; along with the economic limits to the scale of that intervention — this contradictory combination of expansion and constraint explained the development of middle schools as an administratively convenient form of comprehensive reorganization 'on the cheap'. But more than this, middle schools were often preferred to other, equally expedient alternatives because, by preserving viable school communities and retaining an adequate three-year run up to 16+ examinations, they did not threaten the socially and politically important purposes of meritocracy and social unity that were central to the comprehensive movement. Middle schools were economically expedient and fundamentally meritocratic in nature. That was their essential political justification.

Even so, the state — that assemblage of agencies and departments claiming authority for the coordination and control of the population (McLennan, Held and Hall, 1984, p. 3) — did not engineer the introduction of comprehensive education in general or middle schools in particular in a uniform way. The British educational system in the 1960s and early seventies was a structurally loose one, decentralized in its administration, and allowing for wide variations in policy and practice. This allowed different social and educational ends to be pursued and argued about in different localities through a process of multisided negotiation. The egalitarianism of the Mexborough councillors, the meritocratic preoccupations in Ecclesfield and the enduring concern with social unity in all the deliberations of the West Riding Education Committee — illustrate the range of purposes that were pursued in relation to comprehensive reorganization here (see chapter 3).

Equally, differences arose between the two major levels of the state — local and national — as well as within the local state itself. This led, for instance, to principled disagreements about the desirability of junior high schools, and sometimes just to breakdowns in communication or to problems of synchronization as different parts of the system (different West Riding divisions, for instance) unknowingly pursued different and contradictory policies simultaneously. The resistance of Keighley to Clegg's middle school scheme, and its vigorous promotion of its own junior high school alternative provides a good example of this process.

But if the structurally loose character of British education at this time sometimes created difficulties in synchronizing policy, in many instances it did quite the opposite. It created a kind of *functional autonomy*, where centrally induced initiatives could be adjusted to the peculiar circumstances, the specific inheritance of buildings and so on, within each locality. The strategic intervention of just a few key educational administrators like Sir Alec Clegg in securing this kind of adjustment and in pressing for a change in the laws regarding the age of transfer was absolutely vital here for the early development of middle schools. Such people were the creative architects of that adjustment and indeed of the 'bottom–up' pressure to secure the necessary legal changes and political encouragement that would make the middle school pattern of adjustment possible on a wider scale.

However, while this strategic intervention on occasion revealed local-national differences over the technical means, the administrative forms of policy implementation (especially in regard to decisions concerning appropriate ages of transfer), there were few visible differences between local and national policy makers regarding their most fundamental educational and social assumptions — the contribution of education to the preservation and expansion of the existing economic system, the overriding importance attached to meritocratic educational ends, and so on. It was these shared assumptions and purposes that gave local and national educational policy at the time an overriding unity, despite technical and administrative differences of interpretation and implementation, and despite other more liberal, child-centred ambitions for the middle school that policy makers like Clegg also held to be dear. It was the middle school's apparent compatability with these hegemonic goals and assumptions which, together with its economic benefits, made its development possible. It did not threaten the hegemonic and economic limits to educational policy; and within those limits, it provided a negotiable solution to local pressures, difficulties and interests in many areas.

The middle school's emergence in this context of meritocratic purpose and administrative constraint had important implications for its practice. Both national surveys and case studies indicate that in many respects, 9/10–13 middle schools came to be characterized by sharp divisions, not gentle transition or unity; and by the downward permeation of conventional secondary school practices and patterns more than the upward percolation of 'progressive' primary ones. Arranged into a series of well insulated horizontal units of year-based organization, and marked by a sharp increase in secondary-like patterns of setting and subject specialization at age 11, the reality of middle school practice appeared in most instances to be far removed from those ideological images of uniqueness and transition which accompanied their early development.

In large part, the character of middle schools as organizationally divided institutions dominated by secondary-like practices in their upper years was attributable to the conditions of administrative expediency which surrounded their establishment. The constraints of administrative convenience entailed the redeployment of local teaching labour to schools with unfamiliar age ranges and a set of educational purposes whose distinctiveness and novelty was not at all clear or specific. These redeployed teachers who, in many cases, had no definite commitment to the idea of middle schools as such, brought to their new posts the educational assumptions and orientations of the occupational cultures of teaching to which they had already become attached in their previous careers. Two such cultures of teaching were prominent, though only one was dominant, within the middle school.

The first was the culture of the academic-elementary tradition. Judging by the case study evidence, it seems that the teachers who came to dominate the upper years of the middle school had their career roots in secondary modern schools or the scholarship streams of primary schools. Tied by their domestic commitments to the locality, fearful of having to compete with grammar school colleagues for positions of prestige in the new upper schools, or seekers of an 'easier life' with younger, less truculent pupils in a more desirable suburban environment; these teachers were, by and large, not middle school zealots, but people simply taking refuge from secondary modern 'dirty work' or attempting to repair their 'spoilt careers'. The academic-elementary inheritance of these teachers showed in their educational preferences and practices. They preferred teaching older pupils rather than merely 'mothering' younger ones; they were orientated to high academic standards, teaching able pupils and the importance of their subject; they favoured setting and a high degree of subject specialist teaching; they attached great importance to the maintenance of firm discipline; and they tended to adopt rather formal, transmission-type pedagogies in the classroom. Even at open-plan Riverdale, with its Head's aspirations towards implementing a primary extension model, the academic-elementary staff succeeded in sabotaging his curricular intentions in the upper years by presenting university-style lectures or tightening up the timetable within their own class bases. Paradoxically, then, the very occupational culture which, given its associations with secondary modern teaching, frequently became devalued or disvalued within mainstream comprehensive reorganization, gained prominence within and came to dominate the character of the new middle schools, at least in their upper years.

The teachers within the lower years of the middle school, the developmental teachers, exerted much less influence than their academic-elementary counterparts on the school's overall development. Though the evidence here is fragmentary, and therefore highly provisional, it points to the possibility that these teachers became consigned to positions of lower status and influence within the middle school for several interrelated reasons: the inexperience of their youth, the culturally imposed handicaps of their sex, the low status attached to and dearth of career opportunities arising from their preferred pattern of generalist teaching, and the association conventionally made between teaching lower age groups and the low-status childcare of womens' domestic labour. With their career roots in the lower primary years, these (mainly female) teachers with their preference for generalism rather than specialism, and relationships rather than discipline, therefore seemed poorly placed to influence the overall character and direction of the middle school in any substantial way.

In the face of such cultural divisions among middle school teachers, much hope has been invested in the recruitment of people with training and experience specifically geared to the middle school sector. Yet, in the absence of any clear and distinctive philosophical basis for the middle school, these teachers have been given few guides or clues as to the unique educational contribution they might make compared with their ex-primary and ex-secondary colleagues. As a result, while their approach to teaching seemed to display an admirable breadth and flexibility of age-range and curricular preferences, in practice this flexibility extended to a kind of situational vulnerability, a hyper-adaptability to the situational demands and pressures of the immediate year group. Moreover, their status as restricted generalists rather than extended specialists, with shortfalls of expertise in mathematics and science in particular, meant that they were not in a strong position to influence, still less to control, what are taken to be some of the major areas of the middle school curriculum.

The consequence of the middle school's staff inheritance, then, was the domination within it of the academic–elementary tradition and, therefore, in the absence of any clear alternative educational and social justification for the middle school, that school's capitulation by default to the academic, socially selective and discipline-focussed assumptions of meritocratically orientated schooling.

These cultural tendencies, legacies of staff redeployment and administrative convenience, were compounded by architectural constraints (*also* a consequence of administrative convenience). The architectural division between upper and lower school segments in new and old schools alike reproduced that split at 11+ which middle schools were supposed to overcome. The housing of many 9/10–13 middle schools like Moorhead in old secondary modern premises left them an egg-crate structure of compartmentalized classrooms in their higher years which tended to reinforce specialization and differentiation. While open-plan premises like Riverdale's perhaps mitigated these tendencies to some extent, the shortage of specialist practical facilities in both types of school led to the necessity for a large number of fixed timetable points which had widespread curricular consequences. Where the school, given its meritocratic orientation, was already committed to fixed timetabling and setting in the high status subjects and where, as in most cases, there was limited staff provision for specialist subjects like science and French; the combination of architectural constraint, specialist staffing restrictions and meritocratic purpose reverberated throughout the whole timetable: subjects had to be offered alongside other subjects, setting in the first leading, by default, to 'residual' setting in the second. In this way, both setting and specialization extended far beyond the levels first thought necessary or desirable in curricular policy. Along with the demands voiced by the meritocratically orientated, examination-dominated upper schools for setting and specialization in the 'important' high status subjects, such pressures on the middle school tended to reinforce the academic–elementary inclinations already embedded in their administrative origins and cultural inheritance.

In summary, the combination of teachers' cultures, careers, strategies and perspectives which followed from the meritocratic orientation of and administrative constraints upon the middle school meant that in its upper years, this school directed itself towards realizing the assumptions and goals of a secondary inspired meritocratic vision for which it was never properly equipped. In many cases, then, in their upper years, middle schools like Moorhead operated like diluted secondary moderns, seeking to fulfil conventional secondary goals with a degree of difficulty that followed almost inexorably from their organizational handicaps of buildings and staffing. While some middle school heads struggled hard to implement an alternative extended primary interpretation of the middle school, as we saw at Riverdale, although this certainly weakened some of the more overtly secondary aspects of the middle school's organizational pattern, the combination of architectural constraint, upper school expectations and the inheritance of a number of staff with academic-elementary allegiances, together produced a system which retained a high degree of setting, segregated treatment for the high status specialisms, and elsewhere, the maintenance of high status subject priorities, even within the more open, apparently integrated parts of the 11–13 curriculum.

If, like Ebenezer Scrooge, we could be escorted by the ghost of Middle Schools Past into years gone by, we would see a middle school system shaped by the constraints and limitations of financial stringency while also being directed towards the diligent and wealth creating ends of meritocratic purpose. Creative and influential administrators like Sir Alec Clegg, of course, passionately supported the middle school for other ends as well as these more narrowly utilitarian ones — to extend the best of primary practice, to protect young adolescents from the cramping effects of examinations etc. But notwithstanding these more child-centred potentials, it is unlikely that middle schools would ever have got off the ground without their economic and meritocratic benefits. The ghost of Middle Schools Past would also have shown us a system which, in the details of its practice, was heavily influenced by the presence of and relationship between the two dominant cultures of teaching on which it drew; a relationship in which the academic-elementary tradition of secondary modern and scholarship teaching prevailed. The details of these patterns of interrelationship are summarized in figure 4.

But if economic stringency, meritocratic purpose and the assumptions and habits of the academic-elementary tradition make up the middle school's past, what does the ghost of Middle Schools Present have to show us? Does it have different characteristics to reveal? Does it hold out any greater hope or optimism?

Middle Schools Present

Certainly, many of the more recent images of the middle school are similar to those revealed to us by the ghost of Middle Schools Past. The continuing fragmentation of the year system, the persisting interest in setting and the unabating pressure for subject specialism — these are, in one way and another, abiding features of the middle school identity. But through the mists of time, some of those images have changed their appearance a little, and altogether new ones have appeared on the middle school scene too. Most important of all, perhaps, is the change in the scale of austerity, of economic hardship that middle schools have had to endure. To understand the nature and importance of this shift and all its implications for the middle school's development, we need to know something of the changing economic and political scene between the mid 1970s and 1980s, so we can be clearer about the context in which middle schools now operate and the demands that context makes upon them.

Figure 4: *THE DETERMINANTS OF MIDDLE SCHOOLING* — *a summary model*

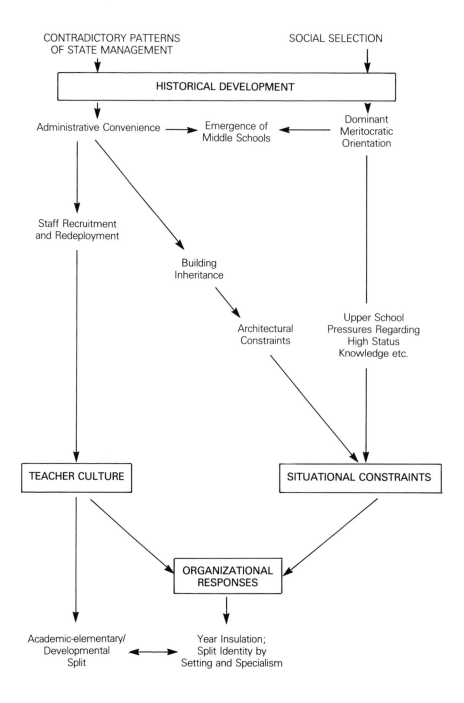

The Context

Until the early to mid-1970s, major educational problems were predominantly tackled by administrative means, by institutional reorganizations which sought to open and equalize pupils' access to educational goods. Administrative intervention in education and other spheres was perceived as one of the dominant ways of achieving state regulation of social and economic progress. Access to desired educational goods was the point at issue: the worth, the nature, the legitimacy of those goods, the content of the school curriculum, was not seriously questioned. This pattern of administrative intervention with all the financial contradictions of state funding that it entailed, may have generated certain irrationalities in educational provision, but as long as the British economy continued to expand and living standards improved then they could be tolerated by government and public alike. (Held, 1984)

With the waning of growth and the onset and deepening of economic recession in the early to mid-1970s, however, the 'irrationalities' quickly became more noticeable and overt. Education, like many other state institutions, suddenly became subject to what Kogan (1978) called the 'onset of doubt' and found itself in the midst of a 'crisis of rationality' — a crisis in which the administrative system (of which education is a part) was patently failing to fulfil economic imperatives (Habermas, 1976, p. 46). This was swiftly followed and compounded by a further crisis — one of belief in the very worth and legitimacy of social institutions as they seemed not to meet those ideals and aspirations of openness, opportunity and improvement with which they had become associated during the post-war period of economic expansion and social reconstruction. What schooling and other institutions had to offer, the processes that went on within them and the promises they contained were subject to questioning and redefinition. In the mid-1970s, state education was therefore at the centre of two overlapping social crises — a crisis of rationality and a crisis of legitimation and belief (Habermas, 1976) — which together began to reshape its orientation. This double crisis contained two interrelated elements — one economic, the other ideological.

Economically, while Britain had attained a position of relative prosperity during two decades or so of post-war reconstruction, the base of this expansion had always looked less than secure, as witnessed by a series of inflation and balance of payments problems (Jessop, 1980). Though Britain's economy was expanding, it was expanding much more slowly than many of its advanced industrial competitors, and when world economic recession was precipitated by the oil crisis of 1973, Britain was therefore hit especially hard. Balance of payments deficits, increases in overseas borrowing and a sterling crisis in 1976 all led to Dennis Healey, the Labour government's Chancellor of the Exchequer, having to take a loan of almost £4 million from the International Monetary Fund, one condition of which was that Britain restricted the expansion of domestic credit. This in turn placed limits on government borrowing for public expenditure. Suddenly the Labour government and its Chancellor found themselves in the unenviably ironic position of presiding over a containment of state spending (Thompson, 1984).

This had powerful implications for expenditure on education. While Labour's initial position was, perhaps, one of reluctant compliance with economic imperatives deriving from Britain's unfavoured place in the world economy; by 1977 a commitment to and rationale for cutbacks in educational spending had been clearly outlined in *Education in Schools* (The 'Green Paper'), produced by the Department of Education and Science (DES, 1977). Financial constraints on state expenditure were presented as evidence of 'our' incapacity to live within 'our' means in the context of current market forces. Schools therefore had to take their share of 'the cuts' like anyone else and become more 'cost effective' at the same time. (Donald, 1979; Wallace, Miller and Ginsburg, 1983). The era of optimism and expansion had ended; schooling was in decline. (Bernbaum, 1979)

Between 1974/75 and 1978/79, capital spending on schools fell sharply (Lynch, 1980, p. 109), but one of the major areas of saving was that made in teachers' salaries (the major consumer of educational expenditure) through a reduction in the teacher workforce. This was made possible by a 'fortunately' coincidental fall in the pupil population, resulting from a 35 per cent decline in the number of live births between 1964 and 1977 (DES, 1978, p. 13). As schools shrank, many teachers were redeployed or encouraged to take early retirement (Ball, 1984). Staffing of schools often became stretched in trying to maintain adequate curriculum coverage (Briault and Smith, 1980). And when these problems seemed too great, schools were closed or amalgamated where convenient. In some areas, this numbers game led to fresh juggling with the age of transfer to find more economically expedient ways of distributing this declining pupil population among existing buildings. Within less than a decade, then, some LEAs had begun to consider changing the age of transfer all over again! (Hargreaves and Tickle, 1981; Fiske, 1979)[1]

All these trends were accelerated by the Conservative government of 1979. If Labour had reluctantly taken on the businessman's mantle of value-for-money, cost-effectiveness and belt-tightening in its defence of educational retrenchment, the Conservatives, led by Mrs Thatcher, made of these things the very highest virtue. In their pledge to 'roll back the state', the Conservatives not only promised the prudence of good shopkeeping, but also celebrated the anticipated release of individual freedom from the grip of meddling bureaucracy.

In practice, this rolling back of the state proved to be somewhat selective. The amount of public expenditure as a percentage of overall Gross National Product did not change substantially; not least because of the increased burden of unemployment benefit, and the decline in economic output (Thompson, 1984). Yet if cuts in state expenditure were selective, the axe fell particularly harshly on education. Through a complex set of legislative controls over the Rate Support Grant, the Conservative government significantly reduced the flexibility of local authorities in allocating their resources (Hunter, 1983 and 1984), with severe consequences for school plant, staffing, curriculum coverage etc — as a series of annual HMI reports have, to the parliamentary government's consternation, attested.[2] These continuing and escalating financial constraints have made the issues concerning economically expedient forms of administrative provision and cost-effective ways of maintaining adequate staffing levels all that more pressing.

Ideologically, this process of economic retrenchment in education has been accompanied by a shift of public and political purpose and expectation. What this has meant is that alongside falling rolls and budgets, people in the education service have also had to cope with a set of rising expectations for improved standards of provision too. It is scarcely surprising, then, that some of those involved in the task of educational administration have been worried about 'the management of declining total resources of finance and manpower at a time of rising expectations among parents and teachers'. (Jaggar, 1979, p. 59)

This contradictory juxtaposition of rising expectations and falling rolls and budgets was not altogether coincidental, for the changing ideological pressures were themselves born out of the conditions of severe economic decline. By the mid 1970s, a mounting crisis of legitimation, of belief in society's existing institutions, was beginning to make itself felt in education in the form of a crisis of curriculum (Reid, 1978); a basic lack of confidence in education's capacity to deliver the much-needed economic goods. Publicly, debate was sparked off by the writings of a group of right wing educationalists who, amongst other things, accused education (and educational progressivism in particular) of being responsible for Britain's inability to maintain industrial competitiveness with overseas rivals (Cox and Boyson, 1975). Although these views had been expounded for some time in a series of ominously titled *Black Papers* on education (for example, Cox and Dyson 1969, 1970a and 1970b), they had initially been regarded as little more than eccentric extremism. By 1975, however, they occupied the heart of educational debate. Fuelled by sociological reports of the relationship between education and social mobility which attributed most of the explanations for pupils' progress not to their schooling, but to 'luck' or 'chance' (Jencks *et al*, 1972), and by well-publicized critiques of the damaging effects of primary school progressivism on pupils' attainment (Bennett, 1976); and fanned by the dramatic media attention given to the ostensibly outrageous activities of a group of 'left-wing', 'trendy' teachers at the William Tyndale Junior School in Islington, London (Gretton and Jackson, 1976),[3] public imagination and fury was quickly roused to the level of a moral panic about education's 'demonstrable' failure to secure and sustain economic growth and political stability.

In the face of this mounting educational critique, the Labour government stole the Right's thunder by issuing the first major Prime Ministerial statement on education for more than two decades (CCCS, 1981).[4] In it, James Callaghan set in motion a major governmental shift in approach to educational policy, and began a process of (albeit stage-managed) debate — The (so-called) Great Debate — through which the very terms according to which education was analyzed and evaluated came to be redefined.

Two components of this ideological redefinition of educational purpose are important for the present discussion. First, there was a turning to some of the assumed virtues of the old elementary tradition — to a more narrow vocationalism in the 14–19 age-range, to closer and more harmonious links between schools and industry, and to the merits of children having a thorough grounding in 'basic skills'. Prime Minister Callaghan's demands for a skilled and literate work-force were presented as a necessary guard against the creation of 'socially well adjusted members of society who are unemployed because they do not have the skills'.

This 'back-to-basics' movement placed a lot of indirect pressure upon schools. Ashton (1981) has produced some evidence that between 1971 and 1979, primary school teachers, for instance, had, on balance, shifted their views away from the 'progressive' end of the educational continuum. By 1979, Ashton comments, '"basic skills" were substantially more important' (p. 30). 'A primary school child in the early 1980s,' she concludes, 'is more likely to meet teachers concerned to equip him with skills and attitudes which they judge society to require. Probably more attention will be given to his mathematic and formal language competence.'

Secondly, alongside this neo-elementary emphasis on work-relevant skills, Callaghan's speech, and the spate of DES and HMI papers which followed it, also began to open up the whole 'secret garden' of the school curriculum to governmental scrutiny. The attempt, through these papers, to establish an agreed and common core curriculum for the secondary sector was an unprecedented and ambitious one. But despite fears that the DES 'mandarins' might turn the anxieties of economic recession to their own advantage by increasing centralized curricular control (Lawton, 1980; Salter and Tapper, 1981), the first efforts at curricular redefinition proved to be something of a damp squib. In an attempt to avoid the controversial value questions which normally surround proposals for a common curriculum (see, for instance, Williams, 1961; Hargreaves D., 1982; Boyson, 1975), HMI defined the curriculum in terms of eight very broad areas of educational experience to which all pupils had an entitlement, areas which overlapped with (and were certainly not presented as threatening to or replacements for)existing specialist subject divisions. In seeking an educational consensus, HMI produced categories which were exceedingly broad. Moreover, the values they were supposed to fulfil were unhelpfully vague (the price paid for consensus): contentious choices between specific subject contents were avoided, allocations of timetable priority not established, and implications for the status and importance of existing subjects not spelt out (Halpin, 1980). Unsurprisingly, when HMI themselves worked with teachers in five LEAs as part of an exercise designed to reappraise the whole curriculum using the broad areas of experience as a guide, they found that the maintenance of existing subject divisions and examination commitments among secondary teachers seriously undermined successful implementation. (HMI, 1983b)

And so, in curricular terms, in the 1980s, the 'mandarins' set about doing the easier thing. If they could not weaken the vipers' nests of vested inerests that constituted the subject departmental divisions of secondary schooling, then they would strengthen them still further. The way they proposed to do this was through the improvement of what the authors of an influential White Paper on *Teaching Quality* called 'the match between the teacher's training and his (sic) work' (DES, 1983, p. 8). In their secondary school survey, HMI had already pointed to 'evidence of insufficient match in many schools between the qualifications and experience of teachers and the work they are undertaking' (HMI, 1979, p. 51) and in a survey of nearly 300 probationary teachers, they had also expressed the worry that among the secondary school teachers they observed, one in ten 'revealed insecurity in the subject they were teaching.' (HMI, 1982a, p. 81). In *Teaching Quality*, the DES proposed measures to set about rectifying this 'mismatch' between teachers and their subjects. With that ring of self-arrogated authority which has come to characterize the emerging political tone of the 1980s, it was robustly asserted that 'The government ·attach high priority to improving the fit between teachers' qualifications and their tasks as one means of improving the quality of education' (DES, 1983, p. 9). While it was conceded that improvement might not be easy to achieve, the DES nonetheless insisted that 'progress can and should be made' (p. 12) — and a periodic review of secondary schools was proposed to ensure that this would be so.

The overall ideological climate of 1980s new-conservatism was a propitious one for the establishment of such 'robust' initiatives to tighten up the organization of subject specialist teaching. The application of monetarist, market economy principles to educational provision and practice both sanctioned and sanctified the commitment to competitiveness (as in the increasing emphasis given to public examinations at 16 +)[5] and the resurgent respectability of educational differentiation. On this second matter, as the Secretary of State for Education and Science, Sir Keith Joseph, himself remarked 'If . . . selection between schools is largely out, then I emphasize that *there must be differentiation within schools*' (quoted in Simon, 1984, p. 21). A key feature of that emerging strategy of differentiation, it appears, has come to be a central (in both senses of that term) commitment within the 14–16 curriculum to preserving a predominantly subject-specialist, examination-dominated intellectual-cognitive curriculum of the grammar-school type for the socially and educationally favoured on the one hand, alongside a broadly basic- and vocational-skills centred neo-elementary curriculum (with 'community' and 'life-skills' additives) for the euphemistically labelled 'low attainers' on the other.

Together, these escalating and centrally monitored commitments to higher standards of subject specialist and basic skills teaching have therefore contributed not only to a climate of rising educational expectations, but to rising expectations of a particular kind (neo-elementary and still more academic) for secondary, primary and middle schools alike. Quality, of a narrow and elitist kind, has replaced equality as one of the central, organizing principles of educational reform.

Yet, as we have seen, these mounting expectations, part of that intensifying crisis of legitimation running through Britain's state institutions as a whole, have been accompanied by growing deficits of finance and funding, deficits which have eroded the capacity of schools to do what is increasingly expected of them. The pressures on schooling are therefore contradictory, reflecting and reinforcing wider contradictions in the modern British state and its strategies of economic management as a whole. What implications do these current contradictions of rising expectations and falling budgets; intensifying ideological pressure and declining material support have for the English middle school?

The Consequences

Middle schools started to be influenced by the mounting pressure of rising expectations marginally before falling rolls made their full impact upon them. In the wake of the Great Debate, they began to increase their emphasis on neo-elementary 'basic skills'. As Ginsburg and his colleagues (1978) found in their study of teachers in five middle schools, 'many teachers ... see the instructional aims of the middle schools as being very much concerned with the acquisition of basic skills; the theme of accountability and standards in the 'Great Debate' is seen by heads, at least, as being important and relevant' (p. 17). This concentration on basic skills in the 'important' subjects was in turn linked to a growing preference for even more widespread adoption of setting by ability than existed already. Thus, commenting on a study of sixty middle school teachers, Wallace and Tickle (1983, p. 235) note that before 1980 'none of the teachers ... actually quarrelled with the idea that ability sets could improve 'standards' in the 'important' subjects and many had indeed *extended* setting to include even the first year, 9-year-old pupils. Between 1976 and about 1980, then, it appears that ideological pressure was pushing middle schools still further in the conventional secondary direction of academic-elementary concerns to which they were already predisposed, both culturally and historically.

The fortunes of middle schools were about to change again, however, as education cuts and falling rolls began to bite with increasing severity during the early 1980s. In some respects, the consequences of these pressures for middle schools were little different than for other school-types. In ability-grouping practice, for instance, Wallace and Tickle (1983) found that the necessity of having to adjust the numbers of pupils in different sets year by year because of falling rolls, of then being faced with difficult decisions concerning the promotion and demotion of pupils between sets as a result of these administrative pressures, and of having to engage in all the time-consuming procedures which these adjustments involved, led a number of middle schools towards unscrambling their sets in favour of mixed ability grouping.

According to Wallace and Tickle (1983), this easement of setting did not carry with it a declining emphasis on basic skills and differentiation between pupils, however. Rather, drawing on the increasing technical armoury of educational testing, teachers turned to processes which entailed 'increasing atomization of pupil differences based on individual progress through exercises graded by skill level'. (p. 234)

Such patterns of change in processes of ability grouping and differentiation were evident not just in middle schools but elsewhere in the system too (Reid *et al*, 1981). In other respects, though, demographic and economic constraints seemed to 'weigh more heavily and urgently upon the middle school than any other' (National Union of Teachers, 1979, p. 17). The reason for this has to do with middle schools' commitment to and capacity to offer patterns of subject specialist teaching of the conventional secondary school kind. In earlier chapters, we have already seen from national and case study evidence, how the inclination towards organizing its teaching along subject specialist lines in the 11–13 age range, especially for the 'important' high status subjects, was for a long time a dominant feature of the middle school's meritocratic commitment. Because of pressure from the receiving upper schools and because of the ingrained cultural assumptions of the academic-elementary tradition, subject specialist teaching was actually the preferred curricular pattern for many teachers in the top two years of middle schooling.

With the onset of falling rolls and economic cuts, this pattern began to change. It is commonly understood that when pupil numbers in 9–13 middle schools fall below 300–400 or so, then, assuming an unchanged teacher-pupil ratio, those schools no longer have sufficient numbers of staff to offer specialist teaching expertise in all the major subject areas (NUT, 1979; HMI, 1983a). Ironically, then, despite their own cultural inheritance and despite increasing pressure from upper schools and elsewhere to maintain subject specialist teaching, in the late 1970's, middle schools found themselves drawn, for good or ill, into more and more generalist patterns of curriculum provision. Generalist qualities — ability and willingness to offer skills in more than one area — became a major criterion in making staff appointments (Shaw 1978, p. 43). As one headteacher interviewed by Hunter (1980) put it

> Certainly, in interviewing, I am looking for someone who openly says they are willing to have a go at various areas — and although they knew nothing about a certain area, they would be willing to teach it, be willing to try it.

Whatever one's views about the desirability of such a shift away from a more specialist orientation, the important point to recognise is that materially impelled as it was to adopt this 'generalist' curricular strategy as a response to demographic and economic constraints, the middle school was, and still is, *at the very same time* being placed under growing ideological pressure to *increase* its commitment to subject specialist teaching. Most directly, this pressure has derived from the earlier-mentioned advocacy by HMI and the DES alike of the need for more attention to be given to subject specialist skills and competencies at all levels of the education system (itself an integral part of a strengthening ideological climate of competitiveness and differentiation within modern Conservative education and state policy). In the case of middle schools, the exertion of that pressure has been made most forcefully and most influentially through HMI's 9–13 survey. (HMI 1983a)

In paragraph 2.23 of that survey, HMI summarize their analysis of 'associations between particular modes of staff deployment and overall standards'. Two criteria were adopted to assess the influence of subject specialist teaching on educational standards — 'the proportion of teachers (in a school) who spent over half their week teaching one specific subject' and 'the proportion of the teaching in the schools which was undertaken by teachers who had studied the subjects they taught as main subjects in initial training' (the subject match criterion). 'In both cases', HMI conclude, 'there was a statistically significant association between a greater degree of subject teaching and better standards of work'.

HMI's analysis, it should be said, is shot through with methodological and interpretative errors, as the National Union of Teachers (1984) has ably demonstrated in a critique of the survey. What counts as 'standards', for instance, is left to HMI's own imprecise subjective judgment, the nature and basis of which they do not share with their readers. Similarly, while there is, in their view, a correlation between the fashionable target of subject specialist teaching and overall standards, their results also show, though their discussion makes very little of, *much stronger* correlations between standards on the one hand and the politically less tractable issues of resource levels and strength of heads' influence on the other.

However, HMI do not appear to have allowed their evidence to cloud their judgment. Aware of the economic and demographic pressures which were beginning to press middle schools in a more generalist direction at the time the survey was conducted in 1979–80, and with an eye on the likely need for administratively expedient reorganizations of educational provision in the near future, HMI spell out the ominous implications of their (rather specious) subject match argument, their subjection of middle schools to the yardstick of the grammar school curriculum, in their final two paragraphs.

These paragraphs begin by emphasizing the pressures of administrative expediency in the harsh economic climate of the 1980s:

> At a time of falling rolls and financial constraint, the difficulties inherent in being 'in the middle' are exacerbated. For example, in 9–13 middle schools of less than four-form entry, as in small schools generally, if they are not disproportionately staffed, the quality of the education offered will suffer. If they are so staffed, the costs per pupil offered may be higher than those of providing equivalent education for the 9–13 age range in separate primary and secondary schools. (paragraph 8.21)

Having thus outlined the middle school's contemporary economic and *administrative* shortcomings, HMI then advance their academic, meritocratically slanted indictment of the middle school curriculum.

> The subject sections of this report reveal deficiencies in specialist accommodation and facilities, uncertainty that even for the oldest pupils all subjects can or will be covered by subject specialists and too much teaching that is aimed at the average level of ability. (paragraph 8.21)

These deficiencies, they argue are related to 'the relatively high cost of meeting the need both for the generalist teachers that may be required for the primary phase and for specialist teachers which are required for the secondary phase'. (paragraph 8.21)

Once again, it seems, the fate of middle schools is here hanging in the balance between the economically induced pressures of *administrative convenience* (pressures of even greater severity than at any point hitherto), and the ever-tightening influence of a more and more grammar school-like version of *meritocratic purpose*; one which is further exacerbated by the even greater prominence given to conventional examination success, following the 1980 Education Act's requirement that schools publish their results to provide a basis for parental choice. While these two forms of pressure and constraint were broadly responsible for the middle school's creation in the 1960s, the irony is that now, in times of far greater economic stringency and more robust ideological pressure, they are the very factors responsible for hastening its decline. The final sentences of HMI's main text, in bringing together these concerns of economic constraint and meritocratic purpose as they affect the middle school in the 1980s, would serve well as a political epitaph for those middle schools and middle school systems which, as we saw in chapter 1, have already been closed down or are about to do so.

If 9–13 middle schools are to continue to provide a transition from primary to secondary modes ... and to perform, age for age, as well as primary and secondary schools *are expected to perform* (a clever and deceptive phrase! — full of implication but devoid of any specific content — A.H.), given the present and likely trend of falling rolls, they will become increasingly expensive ... Some of the practical difficulties of 9–13 middle schools have been revealed in this survey and, in the present economic circumstances, carrying the relatively higher costs of middle schools sharply decreasing in size will have consequences elsewhere in the system'. (paragraph 8.22)

This summary statement is about as close as HMI will probably ever come to serving its own closure notice upon a whole system of educational provision.

We have witnessed then the scene of Middle Schools Present — and a ghastly picture it is too: of middle schools struggling desperately to survive as they are assailed by mounting academic-elementary expectations and weakened by a diminishing material capacity to meet them. The Dickensian tones of this chapter are not accidental; for in many ways we live in Dickensian times. But though present times are depressing, it is not enough merely to hope, like Mr Micawber that' something will turn up'. We should, for instance, ask ourselves whether present expectations for middle schools the best or most appropriate ones? Is it right that middle schools and their teachers and heads should in fact try to meet expectations which seem to be rooted more in definitions of conventional secondary school practice than in anything else? Should middle schools operate as watered down secondary modern schools? Should they be primarily geared to meeting meritocratic ends of a rather narrowly defined sort? Or is there another destiny, another set of purposes for which middle schools might be better fitted? Even given limited resources? It is these important questions and choices that must be put to the ghost of Middle Schools Yet To Come.

Middle Schools Yet to Come

'Spirit', said Scrooge ... 'tell me if Tiny Tim will live'. 'I see a vacant seat', replied the ghost, 'in the poor chimney-corner, and a crutch without an owner, carefully preserved. If these shadows remain unaltered by the Future, the child will die'. (Charles Dickens, *A Christmas Carol*, 1970, p. 78)

One story foretold by the ghost of Middle Schools Yet To Come is a depressing one; a story of a weakening school, starved of resources and struggling to survive in a 'robust' world of tough expectations and uncompromising demands — demands for higher quality in subject specialist attainment and the acquisition of basic skills. Here, we can envision middle schools, in their eagerness to please and anxious wish to survive, continuing to react, reflex-like, to the crises and pressures of the moment. We can see middle schools reacting to change, never shaping it; responding to other peoples' purposes and agendas, never their own. In my view, and, I believe, in the view of a large number of people working in middle schools too, the great pity of this is that such purposes and agendas are wholly inappropriate to the middle school experience — they are rooted more in the academic conventions and priorities of selection at 16+ than in the educational needs of children on the threshold of adolescence. In this bleak vista for the middle school, at worst we can expect more and more instances of LEA closures; a piecemeal reversion to safer, alternative ages of transfer at 11 or 12 (much the less controversial of the two middle school options — and cheaper too).[6] Death by a thousand cuts! At best, we can anticipate only a more diffuse and debilitating withering of purpose, morale and hope among middle school teachers, as secondary-like pressures persist, and middle schools strive in vain to meet them. And yet, as Ebenezer Scrooge himself said as he looked upon a vision of his own barren future:

> 'Men's courses will foreshadow certain ends to which, if persevered in, they must lead . . . But if the courses be departed from, the ends will change'. (*A Christmas Carol*, p. 117)

There is, I believe, an alternative, more hopeful, positive and dynamic future for the middle school than the one I have just outlined. To stand any chance of being effective, that vision must of course be more distinctive, more definite than those early rhetorical appeals to the notion of a middle school identity that were advanced when such schools were first developed. It will also need to do more than merely fend off criticism. In this sense, while the National Union of Teachers (1984, paragraph 38, 44, 45 and 49), for instance, effectively criticizes HMI for attacking 9–13 middle schools on the basis of inappropriate criteria — as if they were secondary schools — that Union only really succeeds in demonstrating what middle schools are *not* (especially *not* secondary schools). It gives very little indication as to what middle schools distinctively *are* or might be. The nature of the 'goals or achievements' of middle schools, of 'the education that many aim to provide' is never clearly spelt out. Apart from a not unexpected plea for more resources, the Union has disappointingly little to say about the positive and distinctive contribution that 9–13 middle schools might make to the English educational system.

A constructive vision of the middle school, then, should be specific, not general; and positive, not negative. As a starting point for discussion among people who work in middle schools, I want to outline what I see as the beginnings of one such alternative vision — one which lists a number of interconnected areas of middle school practice where substantial changes of direction might usefully be considered. The vision is drawn from three sources of influence and inspiration. First, it rests in part on my own personal value judgments of educational purpose, the nature of which, if they are not by this time already clear, will increasingly become so as this chapter proceeds. Second, the vision draws extensively on the earlier findings of this book, to identify those aspects of middle school practice which would require alteration if the middle school is to be unhinged from its present ill-fated preoccupation with a narrowly defined set of academic-elementary goals it is not resourced to meet. Third, the alternative is also informed by visits I have made to many middle schools where I have seen fragments of the kinds of suggested practice outlined below at work. There is, in this sense, little that is wholly new about the recommendations that are to follow. It is only their bringing together that gives them an air of distinctiveness.

1 Extended Generalism

Contrary to the current fashions of educational preference among the DES and the Inspectorate, there is a case for arguing that the middle school might well benefit from a strong commitment to a broader generalist orientation within its curriculum, for possibly 60 per cent or so of the timetable. The HMI survey, with its assertion that subject teaching was often weak where it was not taught by trained specialists, would seem to suggest that such a generalist move would be inadvisable. However, at no point did HMI demonstrate that such weaknesses arose because specialist subjects were being taught by broad generalists: this interpretation was simply left implicit. Interestingly, there is evidence that subject insecurity among middle school teachers might arise for rather different reasons — when secondary-trained specialists are required to teach specialisms other than their own. As two teachers interviewed by Hunter and Heighway (1980) remarked

> I am English trained and I don't always feel safe in class subjects in the same way that I do in English.

> I am English trained and I don't like having to teach maths. God, some days I'm only just in front of the twelve-year olds — that makes me feel bad.

In addition to this, my own evidence on teachers specifically trained for and experienced in the middle years suggests that they often feel diffident in subjects like mathematics and science. In their case, the reason is that they are neither true generalists nor even extended specialists. Rather, they tend to be generalists of a restricted kind; trained, skilled and confident only in the broad area of humanities teaching.

If these latter trends are in fact more common than the ones implied by HMI, then the policy implications run directly counter to the subject-centred ones that HMI have proposed: towards *less* rather *more* specialism. For when teachers are trained and develop experience in particular subjects, they do more than merely master appropriate content and gather bodies of relevant technical expertise (though the DES and HMI write as if that really is all there is to the matter). Induction into a subject is also induction into a subject culture or community — into a set of shared assumptions about how children learn, how they are best taught, how one should relate to them, and so on (Bernstein 1971, Goodson 1983). Induction also brings with it the development of commitment and loyalty to the subject (and, by implication, weakened commitment and loyalty to others). In these circumstances, where subject commitment is exceptionally strong, to step into another subject is not merely to step into an area of difficult and perhaps unfamiliar content. In many respects it is also a giant step into a completely different world, an entirely different way of perceiving the business of education. And this world will, almost by definition, be one to which the teacher has a considerably smaller commitment.

Higher up the secondary sector, these difficulties may be an unfortunate but unavoidable price we have to pay for a curriculum geared to the subject specialist interests and priorities of public examinations at 16+. With younger age groups, though, at least up to 13, it seems much less sensible or justifiable to tighten up teachers' own subject specialist commitments in the way that HMI recommend. For the likely consequence of that is that when teachers are required by falling rolls, the demands of changing technology or whatever to step out of their own subject loyalties and related teaching styles into other, less familiar, specialisms, they will then lose their sense of professional competence in the way that the teachers interviewed by Hunter and Heighway (1980) described.

A more generalist orientation, involving committed, enthusiastic and adaptable teachers able to rise to almost any curricular challenge as part of their own professional development would seem a more educationally appropriate and organizationally practical route for the middle school to follow. In line with that move, the similarities between subjects need to be stressed more, not the differences. Science, for instance, will need to be located less in the intimidating territorial domain of the laboratory with the gas jars, bunsen burners and conical flasks, and more in the classroom with the teacher's familiar armoury of glue, scissors and felt tipped pen. Such non-specialist trends will increase broad teacher competence, not diminish it, by reducing anxiety and strangeness, and placing emphasis on common skills and processes. If this were to be the chosen organizational pattern (and HMI present no *prima facie* evidence that it should *not* be), then this would carry strong implications for the initial training of middle school teachers too — away from the greater emphasis on subject studies currently being advocated by HMI and their colleagues at the DES in their criteria for the accreditation of initial teacher training courses,[7] and towards a more generalist pattern of a genuinely comprehensive kind.

2 A Strong Curricular Advisory System

This advocacy of a more generalist middle school curriculum does not, I should stress, carry with it a recommendation for the abolition of subject specialism. What I am proposing, rather, is a substantial reduction in the amount of specialist subjects which are taught by 'appropriately' qualified subject specialists. The role of the middle school specialist is, as the early middle school documents suggested, properly one of adviser to and coordinator of his/her colleagues. Without the availability of such expertise, the different curricular components of and possibilities within generalist teaching could easily be overlooked and, as many HMI reports (not just ones on middle schools) have recorded, 'topic' or 'project' work could then rapidly degenerate into tedious and unimaginative copying from books and filling out of worksheets.

While the importance of such subject advisors/curriculum coordinators has long been recognized in the middle school literature, the research evidence of this book and of the HMI survey suggests that in many cases, the role has in practice not been deployed effectively; advice has been lacking and vertical coordination has been disappointingly weak. Middle schools and their staffs might therefore do well to consider how the advisory influence of such subject coordinators might be strengthened — by appointing more subject coordinators and not just heads of year to senior management teams for instance.[8] And they will need to press their LEAs even harder for the extra resources to make this possible. But this would not just be one more Union-like plea for resources as such. Rather, it would be a demand for resources to support particular and clearly thought out policy needs.

3 Weakening Year Insulation

This book and HMI's survey have both indicated that one of the major reasons for the weakness of vertical subject coordination throughout the middle school is the dominance within it of the lateral year system and its heads. Strengthening of subject coordination would therefore seem to require some weakening of the year system and the managerial dominance of year heads witin the middle school's organizational pattern. This would loosen staff relationships and cultures to such a point where new alliances could be formed, broader networks of support established and alternative sources of curricular advice made easily available. There are many ways in which this may be done — rotating year group leaders between one year and the next, encouraging staff to vary their year group attachments over the course of their careers, ensuring that staff teach for around 30 per cent of their time outside their own year group, and so on. Whatever strategy is adopted, though, some easement of year group attachments would seem to be a necessary prerequisite for strengthening the much-needed forms of vertical curricular support. The year system is one of the middle school's great strengths — a model of curricular and pastoral integration worthy of emulation elsewhere in the school system. But this strength must not inhibit other important developments too. That is the difficult balance which middle schools must strike.

4 Reduced Setting

It is the wish of the current Secretary of State to increase the amount of explicit educational differentiation between pupils in schools. The language of differentiation is indeed now a commonplace in the vocabulary of HMI reports. Yet it is not all that long ago that a rather different official view prevailed. In 1972, for instance, the Schools Council argued that differentiation should be kept to a minimum in the middle school curriculum (Schools Council 1972, p. 9; Gannon and Whalley 1975, p. 73). In line with this earlier vision and contrary to more recent trends, then, I want to suggest there would be some advantage in either significantly reducing the amount and range of differentiation-by-setting in middle schools or abolishing it altogether. This is not because of any direct effects that setting might have on pupil attainment and motivation. Rather, it is, as this book has indicated, because in small schools, setting has a reverberative effect throughout the curriculum, creating further 'residual' setting, the proliferation of specialisms, timetabling difficulties in redeploying staff, and so on. If setting were retained in any substantial way in middle schools, therefore, it would place timetable restrictions on the expansion of generalism and make the deployment of staff between different years difficult, thereby knocking away two of the cornerstones of this alternative middle school strategy.

5 Diversification of Purpose

Of course, it is possible that readers of this book may find such a strategy — with its advocacy of a more generalist curriculum, strengthened forms of specialist advice, a weakened year system and the abolition or significant reduction of setting — educationally unsuitable or inappropriate; at odds with their own values and commitments. That is, of course, properly a matter for their choice. But I would want to warn that without the adoption of this or some similar alternative, and without serious questioning of the middle school's academic-elementary, subject specialist, meritocratic orientation which such a shift would necessarily entail, it seems to me that the 9–13 middle school may not only be doomed to decline, but that it would not be unreasonable to attribute some of the blame for that decline to the meritocratic intransigence of its own practitioners, and their deference to the subject-centred, academic values of their administative and upper school 'superiors'. There *is*, I believe, an alternative for the middle school, but its successful implementation will demand not just technical adjustments and managerial ingenuity on the part of those who work within them, but the collective will and confidence to assert an alternative and broader system of educational values to those which currently hold the political stage.

In this respect, middle schools might do well to consider how they can give equal recognition and reward to a variety of educational achievements among their pupils — not just the meritocratically valued ones that fall in the 'academic', intellectual-cognitive domain. How can middle schools put greater emphasis on practical, personal and social achievements for *all* pupils, as well as academic ones, for instance? How can they offer a balanced and broad curriculum across a wide range of educational experiences — aesthetic and creative, human and social, moral, technological etc? How far, in other words, are they prepared to break clear from and move beyond the high status priorities of the academic, grammar school curriculum?

These questions are not, of course, the exclusive preserve of middle schools. They have been a prominent feature of curricular debate in the secondary sector too over recent years. But the persistence of subject specialist priorities, the continuing influence on the curriculum of public examinations at 16 +, and the active and wilful strengthening of both these things through government policy have served as a strong deterrent at school level to anyone pursuing curricular breadth for *all* pupils with seriousness. This much, HMI have already demonstrated to us, in their telling analysis of the difficulties of undertaking whole school curricular appraisal where examination commitments and subject loyalties continue to be regarded as inviolate.[9] It is true that with certain, selected categories of pupils, success in giving them access to a broader range of educational achievements and experiences has in recent years been considerable — as the government-sponsored Technical and Vocational Education Initiative, and its Low Achieving Pupils Project have shown. But the widening of educational experiences and achievements for *all* pupils — even or perhaps especially the most academically able — within the later years of compulsory schooling, remains an elusive goal (and not surprisingly, given the academically and socially selective nature of current Government policy).

By comparison, middle school teachers, freed from the immediate grip of examinations, in principle have an enviable degree of space and opportunity to strive for greater curriculum and experiential breadth in a way that their secondary colleagues do not. Of course, Sir Alec Clegg and other advocates of the middle school recognized this potential many years ago, when middle schools were first being considered. But the findings of this study concerning the middle school's emphasis on setting and specialization within a surrounding culture of academic-elementary teaching in its upper years suggest that this exploratory potential has been exploited much less well than it might. Reflecting on these findings and considering the broad purposes of comprehensive education that I have just outlined, it is my view that middle schools should now make full use of that curricular flexibility, that freedom from direct exam pressures, to demonstrate to schools elsewhere in the system what a genuinely comprehensive education can really achieve. A stronger commitment to mixed ability grouping through out the middle school; more sustained efforts at curriculum integration (with the added and indispensable benefits of vertical specialist support); and a set of more imaginative scale post appointments in areas of educational experience rather than in subjects as such (a policy which, in the short term, will also benefit the influence and promotion prospects of women teachers and teachers in the lower half of the middle school)[10] — these things, together, would be useful steps in the direction I have been indicating.

6 Collective Commitment

This is not an impossible challenge for the middle school, but it is undoubtedly a tough one. It would certainly be a brave headteacher who would act alone in pursuing it. I know, for instance, a number of heads who are in broad sympathy with many of the aims outlined here, and much of what I write owes a good deal to conversations with them and visits to their schools. Yet these very same heads confess to me that in practice they are fearful of appearing too adventurous lest at a time of falling rolls parents should place their schools in jeopardy by sending their children to safer, more conventional neighbourhood institutions instead.

At the time of writing, this spectre of falling rolls is just beginning to lift from middle schools. Yet the subjection of middle (and other) schools to the principles of what HMI (1983b) have interestingly called the 'market force of parental choice' continues to steer heads towards running their schools as if they were competitive individual enterprises. Not surprisingly, therefore, many of them are and will remain anxious of appearing too innovative, too far removed from parents' experience and retrospective valuing of their own education. In a study of setting in a 9–13 middle school, for instance, Troman (1986) describes the school's head who 'feels that the well-informed and articulate parents ... may "shop around" and choose an alternative if any radical change were made'. Presenting his staff with the 'veiled threat' of having to teach '100 per cent estate children' if such parents went elsewhere, and of the likelihood of 'redeployment and loss of points' if rolls fell as a result, this head successfully blocked experimentation and innovation. It is in such fear that many middle schools now live. And it is a fear that feeds upon the anxieties of (state-sponsored) inter-school competition.

Because of these difficulties, it seems to me that a worthwhile and distinctive educational purpose for the middle school of the future will be a realistic possibility only if middle school heads and teachers work not in isolation, but collaborate closely together, on a local basis (of 3 or 4 schools, or so) — to forge common policies and assert agreed purposes and directions for the middle school in years to come. Although that would be a bold step — for the individualistic tradition of headteacher management remains strong within British education — it is, in my view, probably essential to the achievement of any substantial, internally generated shift in middle school policy. For many years now, heads have advocated the virtues of cooperation among their pupils and their staff. Perhaps it is now time that they also took in hand the important business of collaboration among themselves. That may provide the best defence of all of professional educational values against the intrusion and imposition of shifting and capricious party political wishes. I would like to think that this study and the recommendations arising from it might serve as a useful starting point for such collective deliberations about the middle school's future — ones which would at least enable it to transcend the two cultures that history has bequeathed it and politics has sustained.

Conclusion

Throughout this book, I have tried to foster an appreciation of the middle school's past, a grasp of its present, and a glimpse of its future. With middle schools, as with Ebenezer Scrooge, it is my belief that the need for change, the possibilities of change, and the most appropriate directions for change can be seen at their clearest when Past, Present and Future and all their interrelationships are clearly understood. It is my hope that in clarifying some of those relationships, I may in some small way help those concerned with and concerned for the middle school to find for it its proper destiny.

Notes

1   On this matter, the LEAs received direct governmental encouragement through the issuing of Circular 5/77, which asked LEAs to

> make the most realistic assessment possible of future school population trends in their own areas and then ... to examine systematically the educational opportunities offered to children in their schools and to consider how the premises, both buildings and sites, might best be used, either for primary or secondary education (including nursery education) or for some other educational purpose. (paragraph 3)

2   See, for example, HMI (1982), *On the Effects on the Education Service in England and Wales of Local Authority Expenditure Policies — Financial Year 1980–81*, London, HMSO.

3   The labels, 'left-wing', 'trendy' etc., were attributed by the popular press.

4   At Ruskin College, Oxford, in October 1976.

5   As exemplified in the passing of the 1980 Education Act with its insistence that schools publish their examination results.

6   In this connection, where middle school systems transferring at 12 appear to have strong economic attractions compared to their 9–13 counterparts, the lesser criticism and greater blandness to be found in the HMI *8–12 Middle School Survey* is of particular interest.

7   See Circular 3/84 (DES, 1984).

8   See CAMPBELL (1985) for a case study review of how this kind of consideration can be exercised in 8–12 middle schools.

9   In HMI (1983b).

10   Especially by making available and giving high status to posts of responsibility in areas like aesthetic education, personal and social development, and so on (there are, in fact middle schools which already have such posts).

Teacher Interview Schedule

Section 1: Basic Data

1 NAME
2 CLASSES and SUBJECTS TAUGHT

Section 2: Career Pattern (past) — factual information

1	TEACHER TRAINING	(a)	dates;
		(b)	length of course, for example, 2, 3 or 4 years;
		(c)	type of institution, for example, teacher training college, university dept., polytechnic, etc;
		(d)	type of course, for example, primary, middle, secondary, subject specialisms, etc.
2	PRE-TRAINING	(a)	Higher education before teacher training — (type of institution, course, etc,);
		(b)	employment (including 'year off' but not vacation work);
		(c)	National Service.
3	POST-TRAINING		Career *between* training and teaching — including parenthood.
4	GAPS		Has teaching been continuous employment? Nature of any intervening work.
5	PREVIOUS POSTS		Full history including type of school, main year levels and subject areas, scale posts and associated responsibilities (including intra-school promotion) and teaching style required (integrated/class-based).
6	PRESENT POST		Scale, responsibilities, duties, etc.

7   IN-SERVICE TRAINING   (Current, past or projected)
    Long courses   (a)   Academic — diploma, degree, Open
                                     University,
                               (b)   Retraining — Dip. Ed., Remedial, etc,
                               (c)   Vocational — Managerial, Admin, etc,
    Short courses   (d)   Skill area — reading, env. studs. etc.

Section 3: Curriculum

1   Could you tell me which aspects of teaching you most dislike, if any?
2   Which aspects of teaching do you enjoy the most?
3   What would you say are your strengths as a teacher?
4   What would you say are your weaknesses?
5   Do you think that there are certain things which children ought to know by the
    time they leave this school?
    What? (If answer was Yes)
6   To what extent do you plan out long range work-schemes in advance?
    Probe: (a)   *length* of notice;
           (b)   *amount* of planning;
           (c)   degree of *flexibility*, for example, resources or teacher-based;
           (d)   *scope* and *variation* of schemes;
           (e)   *decision making* process.
7   Do you plan specific lessons in advance?
8   (If yes): How do you do this? — allow for variation.

Section 4: Pedagogy

1   How far do you allow children to work under their own steam? i.e. to choose
    what to do, when to do it, etc.
2   How do you see your role here in terms of the amount and kind of help which
    you offer?
    Note – obtain information regarding childrens' decisions about *what* to study,
            when tasks are selected, when topic or learning areas are switched; and
            teacher's general principles of guidance.
3   Are there any children to whom you offer more help than others?
4   What are your reasons for offering help to them in particular?
5   When do you feel most dissatisfied with a child's performance in school?
6   When do you feel most satisfied with a child's performance?
7   Why do you think some children get along better than others in school?
8   Could you say where you have got these beliefs/ideas from?
9   As a teacher, what do you feel are the major types of problems with which you
    are confronted?
10 Do you mark work at all?

11 How?
12 What are your reasons for marking in this way?
13 Do you ever give tests of any kind?
14 Could you specify what kinds of test these are?
15 What are your reasons for using those tests in particular?
16 Why, generally speaking, do you use tests at all?
17 Do you think that the age of children affects the way they learn? How?
18 Do you gear your teaching to this criterion at all? (variation)
19 Could you say where you have got these beliefs/ideas from?

Section 5: Career Perspective

1 Are you at all interested in gaining a higher scale post in the future?
2 How strongly are you committed to this?
3 Do you look for jobs fairly regularly?
4 Do you have any idea of what you are aiming to be at the peak of your career?
5 (For promotion seekers only) In your present job, how best do you think you can maximise your chances of promotion?

Section 6: Sources of Influence

1 Given your whole teaching career, what factors would you say have influenced your present teaching style more than any other?
2 Would you say that your teacher training affected your teaching style?
3 What aspects of your training did you find most useful?
4 What aspects of your training did you find least useful?
5 Did your early days of teaching have any marked effect upon your present style?
6 Have any of your in-service training spells been of any value to you?
7 Would you say that the Headmaster affects the way you teach?
8 Would you say that other staff affect the way you teach?
9 Are you happy about the amount of control which you have in deciding what the children learn?
10 Do you ever read articles on educational theory in books, journals, newspapers, official reports, etc? (specify)

Appendix 2:

Headteachers' Interview Schedule

1 CAREER PATTERN — past, since entering teaching.
2 Reasons for choosing this particular post.
3 What should a middle school *be*, as far as you are concerned?
4 In pursuing your aims or even in setting up those aims in the first place, do you feel there are any factors, human or material which restrict you in any way?
5 What do you do regarding the *separation* or *integration* of different areas of *knowledge/learning* throughout the school?
6 How do you view the *role of the teacher* in this school:
   (i)   Child help?
   (ii) Variation?
7 How far do you wish to allow children to *choose what* to do, *when* to do it, and *how quickly* they can do it?
8 What are your views regarding the *marking/evaluation* of children's work?
9 Are there certain things which you feel children ought to know by the time they leave this school?
10 What, as you see it, is your LEA's policy regarding middle schools?
11 Does this differ from your own personal viewpoint?
12 Are there any aspects of school policy concerning curriculum, methods of teaching, organization of staff etc., which you have needed to negotiate with the LEA? Could you offer examples?
13 Do you see any disadvantages in the way the school is organized at present?
14 You have discussed your aims and objectives. How do you try to ensure that these are taken up or carried out by your staff?
15 Without naming any names, are there any sections of the staff, or types of teacher who attempt as far as possible to carry on in their own way regardless? Examples?
16 How do you deal with this particular difficulty?
17 Do your objectives, methods etc., differ at all according to:
   (a) Age ⎫
   (b) Ability ⎬ ... Reasons?
   (c) Subject ⎭

233

18 *Recruitment* of staff. Factors guiding choice.
    Check for: (a) subject;
               (b) age level;
               (c) responsibility required;
               (d) experience/attitude.
19 Could you explain briefly the nature of *ability grouping* in this school and your particular reasons for this?
20 Could you tell me how and why the school *uniform* came to be established here? Check for degree of enforcement.
21 What is your policy as regards homework? Reasons?
22 Do you consider yourself at the peak of your career or would you like to progress further? Details?
23 How, as far as you are aware, does the other middle school differ in terms of the way the school is organized, compared to yourself?
24 Do you see any advantages/disadvantages of one system compared to the other?

Bibliography

ACKER, S. (1983) 'Women and teaching: A Semi-detached sociology of a semi-profession', in WALKER, S. and BARTON, L., *Gender, Class and Education*, Lewes, Falmer Press.

ADAMS, P. (1978) 'Social control or social wage: On the political economy of the 'Welfare State', *Journal of Sociology and Social Welfare*.

ALDAM, J.H. (1978) 'Secondary reorganization within an area — Hampshire' in Department of Education and Science, *Comprehensive Education*, London, HMSO.

ALEXANDER, W.M. *et al* (1968) *The Emerging Middle School*, New York, Holt, Rinehart and Winston.

ALEXANDER, W.M and GEORGE, P.S. (1981) *The Exemplary Middle School*, New York, Holt, Rinehart and Winston.

ANYON, J. (1981) 'Social class and school knowledge' *Curriculum Inquiry*, 11, 1.

APPLE, M. (1979) *Ideology and Curriculum*, London, Routledge and Kegan Paul.

APPLE, M. (1982) *Education and Power*, London, Routledge and Kegan Paul.

ARCHER, M. (1979) *Social Origins of Educational Systems*, London, Sage.

ASHTON, P. (1981) 'Primary teachers' approaches to personal and social behaviour' in SIMON, B. and WILLCOCKS, J., *Research and Practice in the Primary Classroom*, London, Routledge and Kegan Paul.

ASSISTANT MASTERS' ASSOCIATION (1976) *The Middle School System: A.M.A. survey*, London, A.M.A.

ATKINSON, P.A. and DELAMONT, S. (1977) 'Mock ups and cock ups: The stage management of guided discovery instruction' in WOODS, P. and HAMMERSLEY, M., *School Experience*, London, Croom Helm.

BALDWIN, J. and WELLS, H. (1979) *Active Tutorial Work*, Oxford, Basil Blackwell.

BALL, S. (1981) *Beachside Comprehensive*, London, Cambridge University Press.

BALL, S. (1982) 'Competition and conflict in the teaching of English: a socio-historical analysis' *Journal of Curriculum Studies*, 14, 1.

BALL, S. (1984) 'Becoming a comprehensive — Facing up to falling rolls?', in *Comprehensive Schooling: A reader*, Lewes, Falmer Press.

BALL, S. and LACEY, C. (1980) 'Subject disciplines as the opportunity for group action: A measured critique of subject subcultures' in WOODS, P. (Ed), *Teacher Strategies*, London, Croom Helm.

BANKS, O. (1955) *Parity and Prestige in English Secondary Education*, London, Routledge and Kegan Paul.

BARKER, R. (1972) *Educational Politics 1900–51: A Study of the Labour Party*, Oxford, Oxford University Press.

BARNES, D. and SHEMILT, D. (1974) 'Transmission and interpretation' *Educational Review*, 26, 3.

BARNETT, J.V. (1972) 'Training teachers for middle schools' *Trends in Education*, 25, January.

BATLEY, R.; O'BRIEN, O. and PARRIS, H. (1970) *Going Comprehensive*, London, Routledge and Kegan Paul.

BECKER, H. (1952) 'The career of the Chicago public school-teacher' *American Journal of Sociology*, 57, *March*.

BECKER, H. (1960) 'Notes on the concept of commitment', *American Journal of Sociology*, 66, July.

BECKER, H. (1964) 'Personal change in adult life', *Sociometry*. 66, July.

BECKER, H.S., GEER, R., HUGHES, E.C. and STRAUSS, A.L. (1961) *Boys in White*, Chicago, University of Chicago Press.

BELLABY, P. (1977) *The Sociology of Comprehensive Schooling*, London, Methuen.

BENN, C. (1973a) 'The experiment of middle schools' *New Society*, 24, 553.

BENN, C. (1973b) 'Middle school planning surveyed', *Forum*, 15, 3.

BENN, C. and SIMON, B. (1970) *Half Way There*, Harmondsworth, Penguin.

BENNETT, C. (1985) 'Paints, pots or promotion: Art teachers' attitudes towards their careers', in BALL, S. and GOODSON, I. (Eds.) *Teachers' Lives and Careers*, Lewes, Falmer Press.

BENNETT, N. (1976) *Teaching Styles and Pupil Progress*, London, Open Books.

BERLAK, A. and BERLAK, H. (1981) *The Dilemmas of Schooling*, London, Methuen.

BERNBAUM, G. (1979) *Schooling in Decline*, London, Macmillan.

BERNSTEIN, B. (1971) 'On the classification and framing of educational knowledge' in YOUNG, M.F.D. (Ed.), *Knowledge and Control*, London, Collier-Macmillan.

BERNSTEIN, B. (1975) 'Class and pedagogies: visible and invisible', in BERNSTEIN, B. *Class, Codes and Control Vol. 3: Towards a Theory of Educational Transmissions*, London, Routledge and Kegan Paul.

BEST, R. JARVIS, C. and RIBBINS, P. (1980) *Perspectives in Pastoral Care*, London, Heinemann.

BIDWELL, C. (1965) 'The school as a formal organization' in MARCH, J.G., *Handbook of Organizations*, Chicago, Rand-McNally.

BLENKIN, G.M. and KELLY, A.V. (1981) *The Primary Curriculum*, London, Harper and Row.

BLYTH, W.A.L. (1965) *English Primary Education: A Sociological Description — Vol. II: Background*, London, Routledge and Kegan Paul.

BLYTH, W.A.L. and DERRICOTT, R. (1977) *The Social Significance of Middle Schools*, London, Batsford.

BOLTON, E. (1984) Address to an audience of primary teachers, quoted in *Times Educational Supplement*, 18 May.

BORGHI, L. (1980) 'Lower secondary education in Italy with particular reference to the curriculum' *Compare*, 10, 2.

BORNETT, C.R. (1976) 'The social relations of the middle school curriculum: some preliminary observations', M. Ed dissertation, School of Education, University of Bath.

BORNETT, C.R. (1980) 'Staffing and middle schools: The routes and roots of hierarchy' in HARGREAVES, A. and TICKLE, L. *Middle Schools: Origins, Ideology and Practice*, London, Harper and Row.

BOYSON, R. (1975) 'Maps, chaps and your hundred best books', *Times Educational Supplement*, 17 October.

BRIAULT, E. and SMITH, F. (1980) *Falling Rolls in Secondary Schools*, Windsor, NFER.

BRIGHTON EDUCATION COMMITTEE (1973) *Middle Schools: Report of a Working Party of Teachers*, Brighton, Brighton Education Committee.

BROOKES, J.E. (1980) *Timetable Planning*, London, Heinemann.

BRYAN, K.A. (1980) 'Middle schools: A sociological interpretation of their development and practice' Ph.D. thesis, School of Education, Open University, Milton Keynes.

BRYAN, K.A. and HARDCASTLE, K.W. (1977) 'The growth of middle schools: Educational rhetoric and economic reality', *British Journal of Educational Administration and History*, January.

BRYAN, K.A. and HARDCASTLE, K.W. (1978) 'Middle years and middle schools: An analysis of national policy' *Education 3–13*, 6, 1.

BURGESS, R. (1983) *Experiencing Comprehensive Education*, London, Methuen.

BURROWS, J. (1978) *Middle Schools: High Road or Dead End?* London, Woburn Press.

BYRNE, E. (1974) *Planning and Educational Inequality: A Study of the Rationale of Resource Allocation*, Slough, NFER.

CAMPBELL, R.J. (1982) 'Unproductive pessimism', *Education 3–13*, 10, 2.

CAMPBELL, R.J. (1985) *Developing the Primary Curriculum*, London, Holt, Rinehart and Winston.

CENTRAL ADVISORY COUNCIL for EDUCATION (England) (1959) *Central Advisory Council for Education 15–18* (Crowther Report), London, HMSO.

CENTRAL ADVISORY COUNCIL FOR EDUCATION (England) (1963) *Half our Future* (Newsom Report), London, HMSO.

CENTRAL ADVISORY COUNCIL FOR EDUCATION (England) (1967) *Children and their Primary Schools*, London, HMSO.

CENTRE FOR CONTEMPORARY CULTURAL STUDIES (CCCS) (1981) *Unpopular Education*, London, Hutchinson.

CLARRICOATES, K. (1980) 'All in a day's work' in SPENDER, D. and SARAH, E. (Eds.), *Learning to Lose: Sexism and Education*, London, The Women's Press.

COLLINS, R. (1979) *The Credential Society*, New York, Academic Press.

COMMITTEE ON THE CURRICULUM AND ORGANIZATION OF SECONDARY SCHOOLS (CCOSS) (1984) *Improving Secondary Schools*, London, ILEA.

COMMITTEE ON HIGHER EDUCATION (1963) *Higher Education* (Robbins Report), London, HMSO.

CONSULTATIVE COMMITTEE TO THE BOARD OF EDUCATION (1939) *Secondary Education with Special Reference to Grammar Schools and Technical High Schools* (The Spens Report), London, HMSO.

COOPER, I. (1983) 'The maintenance of order and use of space in primary school buildings', *British Journal of Sociology of Education*, 3.

COX, C.B. and BOYSON, R. (1975) *Black Paper, 1975*, London, J.M. Dent and Sons.

COX, C.B. and DYSON, R. (1969) *Fight for Education: A Black Paper*, London, Critical Quarterly Society.

COX, C.B. and DYSON, R. (1970a) *Black Paper 2: The Crisis in Education* London, Critical Quarterly Society.

COX, C.B. and DYSON, A.E. (1970b) *Black Paper 3: Goodbye Mr Short*, London, Critical Quarterly Society.

CROSLAND, C.A.R. (1964) *The Future of Socialism*, London, Jonathan Cape.

CROUCH, C. (1977) 'The state, capital and liberal democracy', in CROUCH, C. (Ed.), *State and Economy in Contemporary Capitalism*, London, Croom Helm.

CULLING, G. (1973) *Teaching in the Middle School*, London, Pitman.

CUTLER, A. *et al.* (1977) *Marx's Capital and Capitalism Today, Vol. I*, London, Routledge and Kegan Paul.

DALE, R. (1981) 'The state and education: Some theoretical approaches', in *Society, Education and the State*, Unit 3, Open Univeristy Course E353, Milton Keynes, Open University.

DALE, R. (1982) 'Education and the capitalist state: Contributions and contradictions', in APPLE, M. (Ed.), *Cultural and Economic Reproduction in Education*, London, Routledge and Kegan Paul.

DAUNT, P.E. (1975) *Comprehensive Values*, London, Heinemann.

DAVID, M. (1977) *Reform, Reaction and Resources*, Windsor, NFER.

DAVIES, E.R. (1973) 'Nine to thirteen middle schools', *Forum*, 15, 3.

DEEM, R. (1978) *Women and Schooling*, London, Routlege and Kegan Paul.

DELAMONT, S. (1983) 'The ethnography of transfer' in GALTON, M. and WILLCOCKS, J., *Moving From the Primary Classroom*, London, Routledge and Kegan Paul.

DENSCOMBE, M. (1980) 'Keeping 'em quiet: The significance of noise for the practical activity of teaching', in WOODS, P. (Ed.), *Teacher Strategies*, London, Croom Helm.

DEPARTMENT OF EDUCATION AND SCIENCE (1965) *The Organisation of Secondary Education (Circular 10/65)*, London, HMSO.

DEPARTMENT OF EDUCATION AND SCIENCE (1966a) *Schools Buildings Bulletin No. 35: New Problems in Middle School Design*, London, HMSO.

DEPARTMENT OF EDUCATION AND SCIENCE (1966b) *School Building Programmes (Circular 13/66)*, London, HMSO.

DEPARTMENT OF EDUCATION AND SCIENCE (1970a) *Launching Middle Schools*, (Education Survey, 8), London, HMSO.

DEPARTMENT OF EDUCATION AND SCIENCE (1970b) *Towards the Middle School*, (Education Pamphlet No. 57), London, HMSO.

DEPARTMENT OF EDUCATION AND SCIENCE (1975) *Curricular Differences for Boys and Girls*, (Education Survey 21), London, HMSO.

DEPARTMENT OF EDUCATION AND SCIENCE (1977) *Education in Schools: a consultative document*, (Cmnd 6869), London, HMSO.

DEPARTMENT OF EDUCATION AND SCIENCE (1978) *Progress in Education: A Report on Recent Initiatives*, London, HMSO.

DEPARTMENT OF EDUCATION AND SCIENCE (1980) *The Secondary School Staffing Survey*, Statistical Bulletin 6/80, July.

DEPARTMENT OF EDUCATION AND SCIENCE (1983) *Teaching Quality*, London HMSO.

DEPARTMENT OF EDUCATION AND SCIENCE (1984) *Initial Teacher Training: Approval of Courses*, (Circular 3/84), London, HMSO.

DICKENS, C. (1970) *A Christmas Carol*, London, Minerva Press.

DOE, B. (1976) 'The end of the middle', *Times Educational Supplement*, 26 November.

DOE, B. (1981) 'Empty seats could lead to closure for 200 middle schools', *Times Educational Supplement*, 6 November.

DONALD, J. (1979) 'Green Paper: Noise of crisis', *Screen Education*, Vol. 30.

DROITWICH WORKING PARTY (1969) *Report of the Droitwich Working Party on Middle Schools*, Worcestershire Country Council Education Committee.

EDWARDS, A.D. and FURLONG, V.I. (1978) *The Language of Teaching*, London, Heinemann.

EDWARDS, R. (1972) *The Middle School Experiment*, London, Routledge and Kegan Paul.

EGGLESTON, J. (1977) *The Ecology of the School*, London, Methuen.

EICHORN, D.H. (1966) *The Middle School*, New York, Centre for Applied Research in Education.

ELBAZ, F. (1983) *Teacher Thinking*, London, Croom Helm.

ESLAND, G. (1971) 'Teaching and Learning as the organization of knowledge' in YOUNG, M.F.D. (Ed), *Knowledge and Control*, London, Collier-MacMillan.

EVANS, J. (1985) *Teaching in Transition*, Milton Keynes, Open University Press.

FENWICK, I.G.K. (1976) *The Comprehensive School 1944–1970*, London, Methuen.

FINCH, J. (1984) *Education as Social Policy*, London, Longman.

FISKE, D. (1979) 'Falling numbers in secondary schools: Problems and possibilities', paper given to the North of England Education Conference, January.

FORD, J. (1969) *Social Class and the Comprehensive School*, London, Routledge and Kegan Paul.

FOWLER, G. (1983) 'The changing nature of educational politics in the 1970s', in BROADFOOT, P., BROCK, C. and TULASIEWICZ, W. *Politics and Educational Change*, London, Croom Helm.

FREELAND, J. (1973) 'Middle Schools in Southampton', *Forum*, 15, 3.

GALTON, M., SIMON, B. and CROLL, P. (1980) *Inside the Primary Classroom*, London, Routledge and Kegan Paul.

GALTON, M. and WILLCOCKS, J. (1983) *Moving from the Primary Classroom.*, London, Routledge and Kegan Paul.

GANNON, T. and WHALLEY, A. (1975) *Middle Schools*, London, Heinemann.

GEORGE, V. and WILDING, P. (1976) *Ideology and Social Welfare*, London, Routledge and Kegan Paul.

GILLESPIE, P. (1968) 'The middle school', *Educational Development*, 8, 2.

GINSBURG, M.B. and MEYENN, R.J. (1980) 'In the middle: First and upper school teachers' relations with middle school colleagues', in HARGREAVES, A. and TICKLE, L., *Middle Schools: Origins, Ideology and Practice*, London, Routledge and Kegan Paul.

GINSBURG, M.B., MEYENN, R.J., MILLER, H.D.R. and RANCEFORD-HADLEY, C. (1977) *The Role of the Middle School Teacher*, Aston Educational Monograph No. 7, Birmingham, University of Aston.

GINSBURG, M.B., MILLER, H. and WALLACE, G. (1983) 'Teachers' responses to education cuts' is AHIER, J. and FLUDE, M., *Contemporary Education Policy*, London, Croom Helm.

GLENNESTER, H. and PRYKE, R. (1973) 'The contribution of the public schools and Oxbridge' in URRY, J. and WAKEFORD, J., *Power In Britain*, London, Heinemann.

GOFFMAN, E. (1959) *The Presentation of Self in Everyday Life*, Garden City, Doubleday.

GOODMAN, P. (1972) *Compulsory Miseducation*, Harmondsworth, Penguin.

GOODSON, I. (1983) 'Subjects for study: Aspects of a social history of curriculum', *Journal of Curriculum Studies*, 15, 4.

GORWOOD, B. (1978) '9–13 middle schools: A local view', *Education 3–13*, 6, 1.

GORWOOD, B. (1981) 'Continuity — with particular reference to the effectiveness of the middle school experience upon upper school achievement in Kingston-upon-Hull', unpublished Ph.D. thesis, University of Hull.

GOSDEN, P.H.J.H. and SHARP, P.R. (1978) *The Development of an Education Service: The West Riding 1889–1974*, Oxford, Martin Robertson.

GOUGH, I. (1980) 'Thatcherism and the welfare state', *Marxism Today*, July.

GOULDNER, A. (1973) *For Sociology: Renewal and Critique in Sociology Today*, Harmondsworth, Penguin.

GRACE, G. (1972) *Role Conflict and the Teacher*, London, Routledge and Kegan Paul.

GRACE, G. (1978) *Teachers, Ideology and Control*, London, Routledge and Kegan Paul.

GRACEY, H. (1974) *Curriculum or Craftsmanship: Elementary Teachers in a Bureaucratic System*, Chicago, University of Chicago Press.

GRAMSCI, A. (1971) *Selections from the Prison Notebooks*, London, Lawrence and Wishart.

GRETTON, M. and JACKSON, R. (1976) *William Tyndale: Collapse of a School or a System*, London, Penguin.

GRIFFITHS, A. (1971) *Secondary School Reorganization in England and Wales*, London, Routledge and Kegan Paul.

GROOMS, M.A. (1967) *Perspectives on the Middle School*, Columbus, O.H., Charles E. Merrill.

HABERMAS, J. (1976) *Legitimation Crisis*, London, Heinemann.

HALPIN, D. (1980) 'Exploring the secret garden', *Curriculum*, 1, 2.

HALSALL, E. (1973) *The Comprehensive School: Guidelines for the Reorganization of Secondary Education*, Oxford, Pergamon Press.

HAMMERSLEY, M. (1977) 'Teacher perspectives', in *Schooling and Society*, Units 9 and 10, Course E202, Milton Keynes, Open University.

HANSON, D. and HERRINGTON, M. (1976) *From College to Classroom: The Probationary Year*, London, Routledge and Kegan Paul.

HARGREAVES, A. (1977) 'Progressivism and pupil autonomy', *Sociological Review*, 25, 3.

HARGREAVES, A. (1978) 'The significance of classroom coping strategies', in BARTON, L. and MEIGHAN, R., *Sociological Interpretations of Schooling and Classrooms: A Reappraisal*, Driffield, Nafferton Books.

HARGREAVES, A. (1980) 'The Ideology of the Middle School' in HARGREAVES, A. and TICKLE, L. (1980) *Middle Schools: Origins, Ideology and Practice*, London, Harper and Row.

HARGREAVES, A. (1981) 'Contrastive rhetoric and extremist talk: Teachers, hegemony and the educationist context', in BARTON, L. and WALKER, S., (Eds) *Schools, Teachers and Teaching*, Lewes, Falmer Press.

HARGREAVES, A. (1982) 'Resistance and relative autonomy theories: Problems of distortion and incoherence in recent Marxist sociology of education', *British Journal of Sociology of Education*, 13, 2.

HARGREAVES, A. (1983) Marxism and Relative Autonomy, Unit 23, E205 *Conflict and Change in Education*, Open University, Milton Keynes.

HARGREAVES, A. (1984) 'Experience counts, theory doesn't: How teachers talk about their work', *Sociology of Education*, 57, 4.

HARGREAVES, A. (1985) 'English middle schools: An historical and ethnographic study', unpublished Ph.D thesis, University of Leeds.

HARGREAVES, A. (1986a) 'Past, imperfect, tense: Reflections on an historical and ethnographic study of middle schools' in WALFORD, G. (Ed.) *Doing Sociology of Education*, Lewes, Falmer Press.

HARGREAVES, A. (1986b) 'Record breakers?' in BROADFOOT, P., *Profiles and Records of Achievement*, London, Holt, Rinehart and Winston.

HARGREAVES, A. (in process) *Social Theory and Education*, Oxford, Polity Press.

HARGREAVES, A. and TICKLE, L. (1980) *Middle Schools: Origins, Ideology and Practice*, London, Harper and Row.

HARGREAVES, A. and TICKLE, L. (1981) 'Middle school muddle', *Times Educational Supplement*, 13 November.

HARGREAVES, D.H. (1967) *Social Relations in a Secondary School*, London, Routledge and Kegan Paul.

HARGREAVES, D.H.H. (1967) *Social Relations in a Secondary School*, London, Routledge and Kegan Paul.

HARGREAVES, D.H.H. (1980) 'The occupational culture of teaching', in WOODS, P. (Ed.), *Teacher Strategies*, London, Croom Helm.

HARGREAVES, D.H.H. (1982) *The Challenge for the Comprehensive School*, London, Routledge and Kegan Paul.

HELD, D. (1984) 'Power and legitimacy in contemporary Britain', in McLENNAN, G., HELD, D. and HALL, S., *State and Society in Contemporary Britain*, Oxford, Polity Press.

HER MAJESTY'S INSPECTORATE (1978a) *Curriculum 11–16: Working Papers by H.M. Inspectorate*, London, HMSO.

HER MAJESTY'S INSPECTORATE (1978b) *Primary Education in England: A Survey by H.M.*

Inspectors of Schools, London, HMSO.

HER MAJESTY'S INSPECTORATE (1979) *Aspects of Secondary Education in England: A survey by H.M. Inspectors*, London, HMSO.

HER MAJESTY'S INSPECTORATE (1980) *Aspects of Secondary Education in England: Supplementary Information on Mathematics*, London, HMSO.

HER MAJESTY'S INSPECTORATE (1981) *Curriculum 11–16: A Review of Progress*, London, HMSO.

HER MAJESTY'S INSPECTORATE (1982a) *The New Teacher in School*, London, HMSO.

HER MAJESTY'S INSPECTORATE (1982b) *Report by Her Majesty's Inspectorate on the Effects of Local Authority Expenditure Policies on the Education Service in England, 1981*. London, HMSO.

HER MAJESTY'S INSPECTORATE (1983a) *9–13 Middle Schools: An Illustrative Survey*, London, HMSO.

HER MAJESTY'S INSPECTORATE (1983b) *Curriculum 11–16: Towards a Statement of Entitlement*, London, HMSO.

HER MAJESTY'S INSPECTORATE (1985a) *The Curriculum from 5 to 16*, London, HMSO.

HER MAJESTY'S INSPECTORATE (1985b) *Education 8 to 12 in Combined and Middle Schools*, London, HMSO.

HILL, M. (1972) *The Sociology of Public Administration* London, Wiedenfield and Nicholson.

HILL, M. (1980) *Understanding Social Policy*, Oxford, Basil Blackwell.

HILSUM, S. and START, K. (1974) *Promotion and Careers in Teaching*, Slough, NFER.

HOETKER, J. and AHLBRAND, W.P. (1969) 'The persistence of the recitation', *American Educational Research Journal*, 6.

HOLNESS, D. (1973) 'Policy and Expediency: The evolution of the middle school', MA (Ed.) Dissertation, Institute of Education, University of London.

HOWELL, D.A. and BROWN, R. (1983) *Educational Policy Making: An Analysis*, London, Heinemann.

HUGHES, E.C. (1937) 'Institutional office and the person', in HUGHES, E.C., *Men and Their Work*, New York, Free Press.

HUGHES, E.C. (1958) *Men and their Work*, Free Press.

HUNTER, C. (1980) 'Falling rolls and morale in middle schools: Some implications for career and management', paper delivered to the Middle Schools Research Group Conference, Maryland College, Woburn, April.

HUNTER, C. (1983) 'Education and local government in the light of central government policy', in AHIER, J. and FLUDE, M., *Contemporary Education Policy*, London, Croom Helm.

HUNTER, C. (1984) 'The political devaluation of comprehensives — What of the future?, in BALL, S. (Ed.), *Comprehensive Schooling: A Reader*, Lewes, Falmer Press.

HUNTER, C. and HEIGHWAY, P. (1980) 'Morale, motivation and management in middle schools', in BUSH, T.; GOODEY, J. and RICHES, C. (Eds), *Approaches to School Management*, London, Harper and Row.

ILLICH, I. (1971) *Deschooling Society*, London, Harper and Row.

JACKSON, P.W. (1968) *Life in Classrooms*, New York, Holt, Rinehart and Winston.

JAGGAR, T.F.B. (1979) 'Falling Rolls in the Secondary Schools', *Forum*, 21, 2.

JAMES, P.H. (1980) *The Reorganisation of Secondary Education*, Windsor, NFER.

JENCKS, C. *et al.* (1972) *Inequality: A Reassessment of the Effect of Family and Schooling in America*, New York, Basic Books.

JENNINGS, R.E. (1977) *Education and Politics: Policy Making in Local Education Authorities*, London, Batsford.

JESSOP, B. (1980) 'The transformation of the state in post-war Britain', in SCASE, R. (Ed.). *The*

State in Western Europe, London, Croom Helm.

JOHNSON, K. (1980) *Timetabling*, London, Hutchinson.

KANTER, R.M. (1974) 'Commitment and social organization' in FIELD, D. (Ed.), *Social Psychology for Sociologists*, London, Nelson.

KEDDIE, N. (1971) 'Classroom knowledge', in YOUNG, M.F.D. (Ed.), *Knowledge and Control*, London, Collier-Macmillan.

KELLY, A. (1981) *The Missing Half: Girls and Science Education*, Manchester, Manchester University Press.

KELLY, A.V. (1978) *Mixed Ability Grouping*, London, Harper and Row.

KINDRED, L.W., WOLOLTKIEWICZ, R.J., MICKELSON, J.M. and COPLEIN, L.E. (1976) *The Middle School Curriculum: A Practitioners Handbook*, Boston, MA, Allyn and Bacon.

KING, R. (1978) *All Things Bright and Beautiful?*, London, Wiley.

KING, R. (1980) 'Weberian perspectives and the study of education', *British Journal of Sociology of Education*, 1, 1.

KOGAN, M. (1978) *The Politics of Educational Change*, London, Fontana.

KOGAN, M. and VAN DER EYCKEN, W. (1974) *County Hall: The Role of the Chief Education Officer*, Harmondsworth, Penguin.

LACEY, C. (1970) *Hightown Grammar*, Manchester, Manchester University Press.

LACEY, C. (1977) *The Socialization of Teachers*, London, Methuen.

LAWTON, D. (1980) *The Politics of the School Curriculum*. London, Routledge and Kegan Paul.

LEE, P.C. (1973) 'Male and female teachers in elementary schools: An ecological analysis', *Teachers' College Record*, 75, 1.

LEEDS CITY COUNCIL EDUCATION COMMITTEE (1966) *The First Report of the Working Party on the Reorganisation of Secondary Education in Leeds*, Leeds, Leeds City Council.

LEEDS CITY COUNCIL EDUCATION COMMITTEE (1969) *The First Report of the Working Party on the Organization of Schools in Leeds*, Leeds, Leeds City Council.

LORTIE, D. (1975) *Schoolteacher*, Chicago, University of Chicago Press.

LYNCH, J. (1975) 'Legitimation of innovation: An English path to open education', *International Review of Education*, 1, 4.

LYNCH, J. (1980) 'Legitimation crisis for the English middle school', in HARGREAVES, A. and TICKLE, L., *Middle Schools: Origins, Ideology and Practice*, London, Harper and Row.

LYONS, G. (1981) *Teacher Careers and Career Perceptions*, Slough, NFER.

McLENNAN, G., HELD, D. and HALL, S. (1984) *State and Society in Contemporary Britain*, Oxford, Polity Press.

MacLURE, S. (1975) 'In search of the best of both worlds — Middle schools for the middle way', *Times Educational Supplement*, 18 June.

MACHURE, S. (1984) *Educational Development and School Building: Aspects of Public Policy 1945–73*, Harlow, Longman.

MARSDEN, D. (1971) 'Politicians, equality and comprehensives', *Fabian Tract 411*, London, Fabian Society.

MARSH, C. (1973) 'The emergence of the English middle school', *Dudley Education Journal*, 1, 3.

MARSH, C. (1980) 'The emergence of 9–13 middle schools in Worcestershire', in HARGREAVES, A, and TICKLE, L, *Middle Schools: Origins, Ideology and Practice*, London, Harper and Row.

MARX, K. and ENGELS, F. (1976) *Collected Works, Vol. 5*, London, Lawrence and Wishart.

MASON, S.C. (1964) *The Leicestershire Experiment and Plan: 3rd. edition, revised.* London, Councils and Education Press.

MEYENN, R.J. and TICKLE, L. (1980) 'The transition model of middle schools: Two case studies', in HARGREAVES, A. and TICKLE, L. *Middle Schools: Origins, Ideology and Practice*, London, Harper and Row.

MILLS, C.W. (1959) *The Sociological Imagination*, Harmondsworth, Penguin.

MOON, B. (1983) *Comprehensive Schools: Challenge and Change*, Windsor, NFER-Nelson.

MOULD, A.H.; WICKHAM, R.G. and WOODCOCK, H.E.P. (1973) *The Preparatory Years*, a report prepared for the Council of the Incorporated Association of Preparatory Schools.

MURPHY, J. (1967) *Middle Schools*, New York, Educational Facilities Laboratories.

MUSGROVE, F. (1979) *School and the Social Order*, London, Wiley.

MYRDAL, G. and KLEIN, V. (1956) *Women's Two Roles*, London, Rovtledge and Kegan Paul.

NATIONAL UNION OF TEACHERS (1964) *First Things First: A Memorandum of Evidence Submitted to the Central Advisory Committee for Education under the Chairmanship of Lady Plowden.*, London, NUT.

NATIONAL UNION OF TEACHERS (1969) *Plowden — the Union's Comments on Some of the Major Issues of the Plowden Report.* London, NUT.

NATIONAL UNION OF TEACHERS (1979) *Middle Schools: Deemed or Doomed?* London, NUT.

NATIONAL UNION OF TEACHERS (1980) *Promotion and the Woman Teacher*, London, NUT.

NATIONAL UNION OF TEACHERS (1984) *9–13 Middle Schools*, London, NUT.

NEEDHAM, G. and TROWN, A. (1980) *Reductions in part-time teaching: implications for schools and women teachers*, report of a research project funded by the Equal Opportunties Commission and the Assistant Masters' and Mistresses Association, EO/AMMA.

NIAS, J. (1980) 'The ideal middle school' in HARGREAVES, A. and TICKLE, L. (1980) *Middle Schools: Origins Ideology and Practice*, London, Harper and Row.

NIAS, J. (1981) 'Commitment and motivation in primary school teachers', *Educational Review*, 33, 3.

NIAS, J. (1984) 'The definition and maintenance of self in primary teaching', *British Journal of Sociology of Education*, 5, 3.

OAKLEY, A. (1974) *The Sociology of Housework*, London, Martin Robertson.

O'CONNOR, M. (1968) 'Middle schools take shape', *New Education*, 14, 4.

ORWELL, G. (1970) *Nineteen Eighty Four*, Harmondsworth, Penguin.

PARKINSON, M. (1970) *The Labour Party and the Organization of Secondary Education, 1918–1965*. London, Routledge and Kegan Paul.

PATTISON, M. (1983) 'Intergovernmental relations and the politics of comprehensive education' in *Decision Making in Britain*, Block 3, Part 6, Open University Course D208, Milton Keynes, Open University.

PESCHEK, D. and BRAND, D. (1966) 'Policies and politics in secondary education', *Greater London Papers No. 11*, London, London School of Economics.

PEDLEY, R. (1969) *The Comprehensive School*, Harmondsworth, Penguin.

POLLARD, A. (1984) 'Ethnography and social policy for classroom practice', in BARTON, L. and WALKER, S., *Social Crisis and Educational Research*, London, Croom Helm.

POLLARD, A. (1985) *The Social World of the Primary School*, London, Holt, Rinehart and Winston.

PRITCHARD, M. (1977) 'Which scheme? Oxford City Council's debate on comprehensive reorganization 1964–1967', *Oxford Review of Education*, 3, 3.

PURVIS, J. (1973) 'Schoolteaching as a professional career', *British Journal of Sociology*, March.

RAZZELL, A. (1978) 'Mixed ability teaching in the middle school: A personal view', *Forum*, 20, 2.

REID, M. *et al.* (1981) *Mixed Ability Teaching: Problems and Possibilities*, Windsor, NFER.

REID, W.A. (1978) *Thinking About the Curriculum*, London, Routledge and Kegan Paul.

REIMER, E. (1971) *School is Dead*, Harmondsworth, Penguin.

REYNOLDS, D. and SULLIVAN, M. (1979) 'Bringing schools back in', in BARTON, L. and MEIGHAN, R., *Schools, Pupils and Deviance*, Driffield, Nafferton Books.

REYNOLDS, D. and SULLIVAN, M. (1981) 'The Comprehensive Experience' in BARTON, L. and WALKER, S. (Eds), *Schools, Teachers and Teaching*, Lewes, Falmer Press.

RICHARDSON, E. (1973) *The Teacher, The School and the Task of Management*, London, Tavistock Press.

RICHARDSON, G.A. (1981) 'Personal variables in student-teacher attitudes towards teacher participation in school decision-making', *Durham and Newcastle Research Review*, IX, 47.

RISEBOROUGH, G. (1981) 'Teacher careers and comprehensive schooling: An empirical study', *Sociology*, 15, 3.

RUBINSTEIN, D. and SIMON, B. (1963) *The Evolution of the Comprehensive School 1918–1962*, London, Routledge and Kegan Paul.

RUTTER, M., MAUGHAN, B., MORTIMORE, P., OUSTON, J. and SMITH, A. (1979) *Fifteen Thousand Hours: Secondary Schools and Their Effects on Children*, London, Open Books.

ST JOHN BROOKS, C. (1983) 'English: A curriculum for personal development?', in HAMMERSLEY, M. and HARGREAVES, A., (Eds) *Curriculum Practice: Some Sociological Case Studies*, Lewes, Falmer Press.

SALTER, B. and TAPPER, T. (1981) *Education, Politics and the State*, London, Grant-McIntyre.

SARAN, R. (1973) *Policy Making in Secondary Education: A Case Study*, Oxford, Oxford University Press.

SCARTH, J. (1983) 'Teachers' school-based experiences of examining', in HAMMERSLEY, M. and HARGREAVES, A., (Eds) *Curriculum Practice: Some Sociological Case Studies*, Lewes, Falmer Press.

SCHOOLS COUNCIL (1969) *The Middle Years of Schooling from 8 to 13*, Working Paper No. 22, London, Evans/Methuen.

SCHOOLS COUNCIL (1972) *Education in the Middle Years*, Working Paper No. 42, London, Evans/Methuen.

SCHOOLS COUNCIL (1975) *The Curriculum for the Middle Years*, Working Paper No. 55, London, Evans/Methuen.

SCHUTZ, A. (1973) *Collected Papers I*, The Hague, Martinus Nijhoff.

SEABORNE, M. and LOWE, R. (1977) *The English School: Its Architecture and Organisation 1870–1970*, London, Routledge and Kegan Paul.

SECONDARY SCHOOLS EXAMINATION COUNCIL (1943) *Curriculum and Examination in Secondary Schools* (The Norwood Report), London, HMSO.

SEIFERT, K. (1974) 'Some problems of men in childcare centre work', in PLECK, J.H. and SAWYER, J. (Eds), *Men and Masculinity*, Engelwood Cliffs, N.J., Prentice-Hall.

SHARP, P.R. (1980) 'The origins of middle schools' in the West Riding of Yorkshire', in HARGREAVES, A. and TICKLE, L., *Middle Schools: Origins, Ideology and Practice*, London, Harper and Row.

SHARP, R. and GREEN, A. (1975) *Education and Social Control*, London, Routledge and Kegan Paul.

SHAW, B. (1983) *Comprehensive Schooling: The Impossible Dream?*, Oxford, Basil Blackwell.

SHAW, K. (1978) 'Managing the curriculum in contraction', in RICHARDS, C. (Ed.) *Power and the Curriculum*, Driffield, Nafferton Books.

SIKES, P. (1985) 'The life cycle of the teacher', in BALL, S. and GOODSON, I. (Eds) *Teachers' Lives and Careers*, Lewes, Falmer Press.

SIMON, B. (1974) *The Politics of Educational Reform 1920–1940*, London, Lawrence and Wishart.

SIMON, B. (1984) 'Breaking school rules', *Marxism Today*, September.

SIMPER, R. (1980) *A Practical Guide to Timetabling*, London, Ward Lock Educational.

SKIDELKY, R. (1969) *English Progressive Schools*, Harmondsworth, Penguin.

STILLMAN, A. and MAYCHELL, K. (1982) *'Transfer Procedures at 9 and 13: The Interim Report of the School Liaison and Transfer Procedure Project*, Slough, NFER.

STILLMAN, A. and MAYCHELL, K. (1984) *School to School*, Windsor, NFER-Nelson.

SZAMUELY, T. (1971) 'Russia and Britain: Comprehensive inequality' in COX, C.B. and DYSON, A.E. (Eds), *The Black Papers on Education*, London, Davis-Poynter.

TAPPER, T. and SALTER, B. (1978) *Education and the Political Order*, London, Macmillan.

TAYLOR, G. and SAYER, B. (1984) 'Middle school attitude survey' *British Educational Research Journal*, 10, 1.

TAYLOR, M. and GARSON, Y. (1982) *Schooling for the Middle Years*, Trentham, Trentham Books.

TAYLOR, W. (1963) *The Secondary Modern School*, London, Faber.

TYE, R.A. (1985) *The Junior High: Schools in Search of a Mission*, Lanham, University Press of America.

THOMAS, N. (1984) *Improving Primary Schools*, London, ILEA.

THOMPSON, G. (1984) 'Rolling back the state? Economic intervention 1975–82', in McLENNAN, G., HELD, D. and HALL, S. *State and Society in Contemporary Britain*, Oxford, Polity Press.

TICKLE, L. (1983) 'One spell of ten minutes or five spells of two...? — Teacher-pupil encounters in art and design education', in HAMMERSLEY, M. and HARGREAVES, A., (Eds) *Curriculum Practice: Some Sociological Case Studies*, Lewes, Falmer Press.

TROMAN, G. (1986) 'Processes of allocation and typification in a 9–13 middle school.' Thesis submitted for examination by B. Phil., Open University.

WALLACE, G. (1980) 'The constraints of architecture on aims and organization in five middle schools', in HARGREAVES, A. and TICKLE, L., *Middle Schools: Origins, Ideology and Practice*, London, Harper and Row.

WALLACE, G. (1985) 'Middle schools through the looking glass' in WALFORD, G. (Ed) *Schooling in Turmoil*, London, Croom Helm.

WALLACE, G., MILLER, H. and GINSBURG, M. (1983) 'Teachers' responses to the cuts', in AHIER, J. and FLUDE, M., *Contemporary Education Policy*, London, Croom Helm.

WALLACE, G. and TICKLE, L. (1983) 'Middle schools: The heart of schools in crisis', *British Journal of Sociology of Education*, 14, 3.

WALLER, W. (1932) *The Sociology of Teaching*, New York, Wiley.

WARWICK, D. (1974) 'Ideologies, integration and conflicts of meaning', in FLUDE, M. and AHIER, J., *Educability, Schools and Ideology*, London, Croom Helm.

WEBB, J. (1962) 'The sociology of a school', *British Journal of Sociology*, 13, 3.

WEBER, M. (1968) *Economy and Society: Vol. 2*, Berkeley, CA, University of California Press.

WESTBURY, I. (1973) 'Conventional classrooms, open classrooms, and the technology of teaching, *Journal of Curriculum Studies*, 5, 2.

WEST RIDING OF YORKSHIRE EDUCATION COMMITTEE REPORTS (WRYECR) (1963) *The Organization of Education in Certain Areas of the West Riding*, WRYECR.

WEST RIDING OF YORKSHIRE EDUCATION COMMITTEE REPORTS (WRYECR) (1965) *The Organization of Comprehensive Schools in Certain Areas of the West Riding*, WRYECR.

WEST RIDING OF YORKSHIRE EDUCATION COMMITTEE REPORTS (WRYECR) (1967) *The Middle School*, WRYECR.

WILLIAMS, R. (1961) *The Long Revolution*, London, Chatto and Windus.

WILLIAMSON, B. (1979) *Education, Social Structure and Development*, London, Macmillan.

WILLIAMSON, G. (1982) 'The future of middle schools', in *The Headteachers' Review*, winter.

WILLIAMSON, G. (1984) 'Too little, too late', *Times Educational Supplement*, 24 February.

WILLIS, P. (1977) *Learning to Labour*, Farnborough, Saxon House.

WOODS, P. (1979) *The Divided School*, London, Routledge and Kegan Paul.

WOODS, P. (1981) 'Strategies, commitment and identity: making and breaking the teacher role', in BARTON, L. and WALKER, S. (Eds) *Schools, Teachers and Teaching*, Lewes, Falmer Press.

WOODS, P. (1983) *Sociology and the School*, London, Routledge and Kegan Paul.

WRIGHT, E. (1979) *Class, Crisis and the State*, London, New Left Books.

YOUNG, M. and ARMSTRONG, M. (1964) *New Look at Comprehensive Schools*, Fabian Research Series No. 237, London, The Fabian Society.

YOUNG, M.F.D. (1971) *Knowledge and Control*, London, Collier-Macmillan.

INDEX